THE GREAT KAGYU MASTERS
The Golden Lineage Treasury

THE GREAT KAGYU MASTERS
The Golden Lineage Treasury

Translated by Khenpo Könchog Gyaltsen
Edited by Victoria Huckenpahler

Snow Lion
Boston & London

Snow Lion
An imprint of Shambhala Publications, Inc.
Horticultural Hall
300 Massachusetts Avenue
Boston, Massachusetts 02115
www.shambhala.com

Printed in the United States of America

♾ This edition is printed on acid-free paper that meets the American National Standards Institute Z39.48 Standard.
♻ Shambhala Publications makes every effort to print on recycled paper. For more information please visit www.shambhala.com.
Distributed in the United States by Random House, Inc., and in Canada by Random House of Canada Ltd

The Library of Congress catalogues the previous edition of this book as follows:

Great Kagyu masters: the golden lineage treasury / translated by Khenpo Könchog Gyaltsen; edited by Victoria Huckenpahler.
p. cm.
Translated from Tibetan.
ISBN 978-0-937938-88-1 (first edition)
ISBN 978-1-55939-244-0 (second edition, revised)
1. 'Bri'guṅ-pa lamas—China—Tibet—Biography. I. Gyaltsen, Khenpo Rinpochay Könchok, 1946- . II. Huckenpahler, Victoria, 1945- .
BQ7684.9.G74 1990
294.3'923'0922—dc20
[B] 90-42995
CIP

Contents

Acknowledgements

Our thanks go to Snow Lion Publications for making this book available to the public, and to Their Holinesses the Drikung Kyabgöns Chetsang Rinpoche and Chungtsang Rinpoche for their blessings on the project.

We are also grateful for the support of the members of the Drikung Centers throughout the United States.

Special thanks are offered to Lama Könchog Samten for his time and compassionate patience, which have created an auspicious environment in which this work could flourish. Also thanks to Faith Putorti for her line drawings of the masters.

A particular debt is owed to Rick Finney for his assistance in translating the three special invocations included in this volume: *The Supplication to the Kagyu Forefathers; Twenty Verses of Praise;* and *Meaningful to Behold.*

Finally, our gratitude goes to Rick Woodbury for his generous and compassionate act in donating his typesetting facilities and labor.

May this work open the door to liberation, establish harmony both in the inner and outer worlds, and end the root of suffering in this degenerate time.

Khenpo Könchog Gyaltsen
Victoria Huckenpahler
October 1989

Introduction

No one is insincere in his own regard, but ignorance and confusion cause most beings to create their own suffering. For this reason the Buddha, who began as an ordinary being, determined throughout three limitless kalpas to sacrifice his own comfort, and with great effort and loving motivation to accumulate merit and wisdom and purify all obscurations. In Bodh'gaya he completely annihilated the mountain of ego and fully developed pervading compassion and primordial wisdom; thereafter he turned the wheel of Dharma three times not out of the intention to establish a religion, but rather to free all beings. He taught for forty-five years.

By the strength of his boundless compassion, the Buddha's holy and precious teachings travelled generally throughout all of Asia, and particularly in Tibet, producing scholars and realized beings as numerous as stars in the sky. One way in which these teachings were perpetuated was through the system of lineages in which the instructions were transmitted from one lineage member to the next, from guru to disciple, in an unbroken succession. This method maintains the continuity of blessing and experiences.

The present text, compiled by Dorje Dze Öd of whom we will say more presently, recounts the lives of the great beings forming the Kagyu lineage, also known as the lineage of transmission. It is so designated because the Tibetan word

Ka signifies oral teachings, or the Buddha's own teachings, while *gyu* means lineage. This noble line has been likened to a golden rosary, for each of the individuals constituting it is as precious and perfect as the finest gold: Each is a repository of extraordinary realization, learning and attainment, and each confers upon the next the Deep Pointing Out instructions which cause the direct perception of the nature of the mind as Mahamudra. To meet these Lamas, even if only through the medium of the written word, is an event of such power that any person making that contact will not be reborn in the lower realms for many lifetimes. These life stories are therefore more than just history; they are an example which inspires one to follow the path. They become a cause for freeing us from samsara, enabling us to dispel mental obstacles and achieve enlightenment. Thus, the publication of such a text as *The Great Kagyu Masters: The Golden Lineage Treasury* represents a blessing indeed!

Our volume begins with a description of the all-pervasive and limitlessly beneficial qualities of Vajradhara (Tib: *Dorje Chang)* who is also known as the primordial Buddha. Vajradhara is not to be confused with the historical Buddha Shakyamuni, for while the latter was an emanation, the former represents the ultimate aspect of enlightenment. Alternatively, it could be said that while Shakyamuni is the nirmanakaya, or form body aspect of compassion, Vajradhara is the formless or dharmakaya body whose all-permeating qualities, while beyond ordinary conception, are yet inherently at the core of every living being. Again one may consider that while the historical Buddha represents the heat and light of the sun in terms of the way he is experienced by beings, Vajradhara is the sun itself, making its presence felt universally and without discrimination. In reality there is no separation between Shakyamuni and Vajradhara, for Shakyamuni's wisdom mind is dharmakaya, his speech is sambhogakaya, and his body nirmanakaya. But this truth is recognized according to the level of realization achieved by the different practitioners.

Vajradhara transmitted the sacred teachings directly to the Indian master Tilopa who, because of his extraordinarily high realizations, was able to see the sambhogakaya, or subtle form body manifestation of Vajradhara. In the process Tilopa became the first in the line known as Kagyu.

Tilopa was an emanation being, meaning that he was one who was born in an extraordinary way and continued to live outside the norm. Travelling throughout India, he received teachings from many different masters and extracted their essence, particularly the Buddha's Vajrayana with its emphasis on commitment until the end of samsara to the welfare of others.

Tilopa's heart-son was the scholar Naropa, who became a chancellor of Nalanda University, and whose repute was such that thousands of lesser panditas relied on his wisdom. But though Naropa was perfectly versed in the theoretical aspect of the Buddha's teachings, he realized that his own mind could not remain stable even for a moment. Thus, he determined to seek a great teacher who could point him toward the direct nature of the mind. Eventually, he met Tilopa and underwent twelve major and twelve lesser hardships in order to purify his karma and emotion-induced obscurations. When at last Naropa's ordeals had ended, his teacher Tilopa pointed toward the sky and said: "Kyeho! This is the primordial wisdom of Self-awareness which is beyond words and mental objects. I, Tilo, have nothing to show. Just realize by looking at Self-awareness." At that moment, through the great magnificent blessings of the Lama and his own complete purification, Naropa realized harmony of mind and attained the state of Vajradhara. He received the complete teachings and transmitted them to numberless disciples in many different places, especially Kashmir. To this day we can see the remains of a great monastery established by Naropa in that area. Both Tilopa and Naropa combined peerless scholarship and personal realization, and were among the eighty-four great Mahasiddhas.

It was the translator Marpa Lotsawa who, among Naropa's

star-like disciples, became his successor and lineage-holder in Tibet. Marpa was a manifestation of Dombi Heruka, and appeared in order to cause the Dharma teachings to flourish. Initially, he attended Drogmi Lotsawa from whom he received teachings and learned Sanskrit, but this alone did not satisfy him. After trading his personal possessions for gold to offer to the guru, he made repeated journeys to India and Nepal. Generally, he attended one hundred eight masters, particularly thirteen great Lamas, but among them the most crucial to his path were Naropa and Maitripa. Like Naropa, he underwent great hardships, even risking his life for the Dharma. By day he received teachings and by night he practiced, in this way mastering both the theory and realization aspects.

It was because of Marpa's mastery that Naropa appointed him as his successor in Tibet and prophesied that his lineage would continue indefinitely like a flowing stream. Although Marpa had a wife and children, one cannot compare his to a conventional samsaric life, for such were his realizations and motivations that he could move through a householder's routine unstained. He is like a lotus in the mud, free from defilement. When someone suggested to Marpa's disciple Milarepa that he should marry in emulation of his teacher, Mila replied: "Marpa is like a lion, and I like a fox. If the fox tries to jump as high as the lion, he only breaks his back."

In Marpa's mind all phenomena were perceived as a Buddhafield, all sentient beings as enlightened deities, and all sounds as Dharma teachings. Thus, for him samsara constituted an enlightened state, and confusion was recognized as having the nature of pristine wisdom. He fully achieved Buddhahood, the Vajradhara state, in one lifetime.

Marpa translated many teachings into Tibetan, especially Mahamudra and Vajrayana texts. These he transmitted to a great number of disciples, particularly the four known as the pillar disciples. Among these Milarepa was to be the most renowned.

The version of Milarepa's life contained in this volume takes a somewhat different form from that found in some other texts, though it does not contradict them, for great teachers have different life stories according to the way they are perceived by different disciples. For example, while some of his students saw Mila as walking, others saw him meditating, still others saw him giving teachings, and yet others saw him as ill—all at the same time!

Milarepa held the practice lineage and became one of the key inspirations for Dharma followers, regardless of the sect to which they belonged. Because of his direct perception of samsara, his great renunciation, and his willingness to endure hardship, he achieved the realization of all the great Buddha qualities and became an instrument for perpetuating the Dharma in Tibet by effortlessly composing *vajra doha* songs. As he himself predicted, his fame was spread by the Dakinis. In our time his life story is available in many languages, and has become a healing force for beings disheartened by samsara. He is perhaps the best-known Buddhist figure after Shakyamuni himself.

Milarepa transmitted the stainless, nectar-like teachings to numberless disciples. Among them, Gampopa has been likened to the sun, while Rechung Dorje Drakpa was compared to the moon. In the case of Dharma Lord Gampopa, he combined both the Kadampa and Mahamudra lineages.

At this point we must switch our attention for a moment to Atisha, a prominent master at Nalanda University, who brought the Kadampa lineage to Tibet. Born into an upper-class family in Bengal (India), Atisha was untouched by worldly enjoyment because he saw clearly the nature of the samsaric state. Journeying to Serling (Golden Island) he received the Bodhisattva's vow and teachings from Lama Serlingpa, Dharmakirti. He also received teachings from Nagarjuna's lineage (profound view lineage) from the Asanga lineage (profound action lineage) and the Naropa lineage (profound blessing meditation practice lineage). Because of his strenuous study and practice, combined with the Bodhicitta motivation he so cherished, Atisha became an ornament of this world.

When the time arrived for Dharma to enter the land of Tibet, Atisha journeyed there at the request of King Lha-Lama Yeshe Öd and Jangchub Öd, and for thirteen years gave teachings which produced many disciples, including the great Geshe Drom Tonpa. In addition, to satisfy the King, he wrote the text known as the *Lamp for the Path to Enlightenment.*

Dharma Lord Gampopa, who was the next holder of the Kagyupa lineage, received Atisha's complete Kadampa teachings including the Lam Rim from Geshe Chagri Gongkawa, Chya-yulwa, Nyukrumpa, Maryulwa Loden Sherab, and others. Like an ocean which encompasses the waters of many rivers, this great being ceaselessly sought opportunities to study and practice in order better to benefit others. Thus it was that in hearing the name of Milarepa his mind was moved with conviction and the determination to reach the master whatever the sacrifice. Staying with Milarepa for three years, he studied the major Vajrayana teachings including the Six Yogas of Naropa, Chakrasamvara, Vajra Yogini, Hevajra, Guhyasamaja and others. He fully accomplished his studies and realizations, and in particular he perfected his mastery of Mahamudra and Tummo. Indeed, his mind became inseparable from the Vajradhara state.

After completing his study, Gampopa went to Dagla Gampo as foretold by Milarepa. There he began giving teachings and meditation instruction to disciples gathering from all directions like geese flocking to a lotus lake. As prophesied by the Buddha in the *Samadhi Raja Sutra,* he attracted many thousands of disciples, as well as no less than five hundred Bodhisattvas. In this way he made the name of the Dagpo Kagyu renowned in the three worlds.

It was with Gampopa that the four branches of the Kagyupa arose. These are: the Phagdru Kagyu founded by Phagdru Dorje Gyalpo, the Karma Kagyu founded by Dusum Khyenpa (Karmapa I), the Tselpa Kagyu founded by Shang Tselpa, and the Bahram Kagyu founded by Darma Wangchuk.

Gampopa wrote many important texts according to both the Sutra and Tantra teachings. These include: the *Four Dharmas of Gampopa*, the *Co-Emergent Wisdom*, the *Precious Rosary of the Excellent Path*, and the *Jewel Ornament of Liberation*, this last being the first Lam Rim commentary printed in Tibet. All these constitute the essence of the Kadampa and Mahamudra lineage offered for the benefit of future generations. Gampopa himself said, "In the future those who wish to see me can study the *Jewel Ornament of Liberation* and the *Precious Rosary of the Excellent Path*. It is the same as seeing me directly." That this is possible is because the complete essence of Gampopa's teachings and advice on compassion and wisdom is contained within these texts. If we study and practice them thoroughly and keep them in our heart, it is the same as meeting with the Buddha or Lord Gampopa himself.

After Gampopa's passing, his heart-son Phagmodrupa continued the lineage. Before meeting with Lord Gampopa, Phagmodrupa, under the guidance of many well-known masters, studied such aspects of knowledge as the sciences of art, logic, medicine, language, and metaphysics (inner meaning). In particular, under the Jetsün Sakyapa he made a thorough study of the Lam Dre teachings, and became renowned for his vast and profound wisdom in these areas. He could also remain for days meditating in the state of bliss, clarity and non-conceptualization.

Due to karmic connections, along with fortuitous causes and conditions, Phagmodrupa received the opportunity to meet with Dharma Lord Gampopa, the Great Physician. During one of their discussions Phagmodrupa recounted his achievement in the meditation state. Lord Gampopa, who at the time was stirring a bowl of tsampa, held out a piece of dough and said, "This dough is more useful than your realization." At that moment all Phagmodrupa's pride was released. Lord Gampopa then instructed him directly, pointing out the nature of mind. Within a few days Phagmodrupa fully actualized the direct realization of Mahamudra. The skin of the ordinary state was suddenly peeled away, and at that moment Phagmodrupa said: "All my other great teachers lacked the one word necessary." Thereafter, Phagmodrupa received the complete Lineage teachings and meditation instruction. In accord with Gampopa's intent he emphasized the five-fold path of Mahamudra (bodhicitta, yidam deity, the four kayas of guru yoga, mahamudra and dedication) which encompasses the complete teachings of the Buddha, both sutra and tantra.

Phagmodrupa established a monastery in Central Tibet, fully transforming that area into a sambhogakaya Buddhafield. He gathered many thousands of disciples, among whom were eight great Kagyupas who established the Drikung, Taklung, Lingre (or Drukpa), Trobu, Martsang, Yerpa and Shukseb Kagyu orders. He also wrote several major texts, including the *Phagdru Thadru*, and commentaries and explanations of sutra and tantra teachings. The four major and eight great Kagyu lineages, acting like brothers in one family, benefitted countless sentient beings in different parts of the world.

Phagmodrupa's successor was Lord Jigten Sumgön, who is the embodiment of the Buddhas of the Three Times and a reincarnation of Arya Nagarjuna. He appeared at an auspicious time and place for acting as an inspiration to those determined to be free of samsara. Early in his life he met with great masters, received all aspects of the teachings, and eventually encountered Lord Phagmodrupa, from whom he received the complete lineage teachings. To integrate these within his mind he practiced day and night until he attained Buddhahood in the Echung Cave at the age of thirty-five. His wisdom enabled him directly to perceive the very subtle levels of cause and effect, and to become renowned as the master of interdependent origination. At the request of humans and non-humans he established a monastery at Drikung, thus becoming the founder of the Drikung Kagyu order. His teachings there were geared to his hearers' faculties and level of understanding, and he easily cut through cultural differences and dogma, revealing the universal law of causes and conditions. Though he had hundreds of disciples, he never excluded any beings from his heart, wishing only to dispel their suffering and establish them in freedom from samsara. The embodiment of wisdom and compassion, he cut the link of their negative propensities. In this way he is like a medicine healing all the diseases of suffering, like unstained nectar transforming the afflicting emotions into wisdom, like a moon cooling the heat of samsara, like a sun dispelling the darkness of confusion, like a wish-fulfilling gem fulfilling through pure teachings all beings' desire for peace and happiness, like a warrior conquering the enemies of suffering, like a bridge leading from samsara to nirvana, like a ship crossing the ocean of samsara, like a parent tending his children at sacrifice to himself, and like a loyal friend upon whom all can rely. Manifesting in different forms, he benefits beings tirelessly until the end of samsara. If one takes him as a root guru, he promises to bless one and lead one to enlightenment.

Lord Jigten Sumgön wrote many commentaries and explanations, especially the four volumes known as *Inner Profound Teachings* in which he gives meditation instruction and advice, five volumes of general teachings, and teachings on Tummo. One of his foremost works, the *Gong Chik*, contains all the essential aspects of Vinaya discipline, Bodhicitta and Tantra. This text has many commentaries, both detailed and concise, by such masters as Sherab Jungne, who was Lord Jigten Sumgön's own disciple, the Eighth Karmapa, the Fourth Shamarpa, and the Drikung Dharmakirti. Lord Jigten Sumgön's disciple, the scholar Ngorje Repa, also wrote *Thekchen Tenpe Nyingpo* (Essence of Mahayana), a complete Lam Rim teaching of both sutra and tantra.

From this great being until the present day there is an unbroken lineage of Drikung Kagyu teachers whose histories are detailed in another Tibetan text.

Though there are many life stories of the great spiritual masters, this present volume stands apart from many in that it was written by a being who had accomplished both scholarly achievements and a high level of personal realization. Dorje Dze Öd, a reincarnate Bodhisattva, was a heart-son of Palden Ritrö Wangchuk, himself a chief disciple of Lord Jigten Sumgön, who caused the lineage teachings to flourish in the area of Mount Kailash (Western Tibet). Born in the city of Kyanglung, close to Mount Kailash, Dorje Dze Öd took monk's vows at the age of thirteen, became a bhikshu at nineteen, and thereafter studied all aspects of knowledge including the Root Vinaya Sutra, the Abhidharma, the Kriya Tantra, the Charya Tantra, Yoga Tantra and Anuttarayoga Tantra. When he attended Palden Ritrö Wangchuk at Jangchubling (Drikung Thel) he instantly felt as if he were meeting a very close friend. As Dorje Dze Öd was perceived to be a proper vessel, Palden Ritrö gave him all the teachings and instructions until, with practice, he realized Mahamudra, saw the Lama as Vajradhara, and was established in the non-returning state. He was fully qualified to write different commentaries, and so was the life-holder of the Buddha's teachings.

In later years Dorje Dze Öd would go to Purang (Western Tibet) and gather a large number of disciples, becoming an object of refuge for both gods and humans. His more gifted disciples perceived him in miraculous ways. Once, when he was performing the Bodhicitta ceremony, three hundred horses with riders suddenly broke into the assembly, terrifying the people. Those disciples having pure vision saw that as the Lama entered into meditation, he became the Thousand-Armed Chenrezig, protecting the whole assembly and causing the horsemen immediately to turn back. After Dorje Dze Öd finished the teachings, one of his attendants asked, "What was the meaning of all those horsemen?" to which the Lama replied: "The local deities of Tise and Naknyil were trying to create obstacles, but I routed them."

After completing his Dharma activities, Dorje Dze Öd formed the intention of entering parinirvana, saying: "The Dakinis have asked that I go to them." At that time his realized disciples received different visions: some saw parasols made of rainbows in the sky, and some heard celestial music. One disciple, Zhonnu Öd, saw five-colored light streaming upward from the crown of the Lama's head.

It is not surprising, therefore, that in Dorje Dze Öd's compilation of the lives of the Lineage ancestors we find teachings representing both the ordinary state and the enlightened view. It is our privilege to be able to peruse them, recognizing that herewith we are being given the opportunity to tread the path of the great masters. For us to study and practice diligently, sacrificing temporary benefit for absolute freedom, until we achieve the same result as they.

May all sentient beings be magnificently blessed
so that our mind may follow the Dharma;
May all sentient beings be magnificently blessed
so that the Dharma becomes the Path;
May all sentient beings be magnificently blessed
so that the Path removes error;
May error dawn into pristine wisdom.

The Supplication to the Kagyu Forefathers

by Lord Jigten Sumgön

NAMO GURU

The unchanging Clear Light of Dharmakaya is
great bliss.
The assembly cloud of the Buddhas of the Three
Times who possess the Two Bodies[1]
Establish all beings in the state of great bliss.
I prostrate to Lama Vajradhara.

The Body of Mahamudra is the union of
nonduality.
Your limitless billions of emanations
Ripen all those to be trained.
I prostrate to Lord Tilopa.

Through enduring inconceivable hardship,
You pleased the Great-Bliss Lama, the source of
good qualities.
You achieved the supreme and common attainments
without exception.
I prostrate to glorious Naropa.

---

[1] Dharmakaya and rupakaya. The dharmakaya is the ultimate achievement of Buddhahood. The rupakaya is a Buddha's physical form, which arises for the benefit of others.

In the Forest of Medicine, you dispelled the sickness
of the three times.
With various, unpredictable bodies of illusion,
You benefit others through your great compassion.
I prostrate at the feet of Lord Maitripa.

Your mind does not move from the state of Clear
Light.
You manifest the good qualities of the secret
mantra without exception.
You ripen all beings by way of the Vajrayana.
I prostrate to Lord Lhotrakpa.[1]

You accomplished the ultimate essence
By way of the three kinds of pleasing.[2]
The Precious Lama is the crown jewel of the
world, including dakas, dakinis, and gods.
I prostrate at the feet of Jetsün Mila.

Maitreya, the Regent, the Lord of Compassion,
Performs the profound activities of the Buddha's
teachings.
You are the chief lamp of the world dispelling the
darkness of ignorance.
I prostrate to glorious Dipankara.[3]

The Buddha predicted your coming in this age.
You accomplished all the intentions of the Buddha.
Great Being, you spontaneously attained the Body.
I prostrate to peerless Gampopa.

The glorious, precious Lord of Beings[4]

---

[1] Marpa the Translator.

[2] Making offerings to one's guru, serving him, and following his instructions.

[3] Atisha, the Indian teacher who founded the Kadam lineage. Atisha was regarded as an emanation of Maitreya, the coming Buddha, and his teachings were brought into the Kagyu lineage by Gampopa.

[4] This and the remaining verses of praise are addressed to Phagmodrupa, Lord Jigten Sumgön's teacher.

Possesses the Two Purities[1] of the stainless Dharmakaya.
The lord of samsara and nirvana is glorious Vajradhara.
I prostrate to the nondual body of the lama.

The precious teachings of the Buddhas of the Three Times
Are profound, peaceful, unelaborated, unchanging Clear Light.
By that, all those to be tamed are ripened and freed.
I prostrate to you who expand the teachings.

In the center of the mandala
Of the clear, nondual Wisdom-Mind
Arise the reflections of the objects of knowledge of the three times without exception.
I prostrate to the Supreme-Birth Speech of you who have full understanding of degrees of ability and dormant qualities.

The ocean of all good qualities
Of samsara and nirvana without exception
Arises without effort for those who attend you.
I prostrate to you who are a great, unending treasure.

Like the fire at the end of the kalpa,
You consume all the fuel of bad deeds and obscurations without exception.
You annihilate all the enemies of samsara, the Four Maras.[2]
I prostrate to you, the hero victorious in battle.

---

[1] That which is pure from beginningless time and that which is pure of temporary obscurations.

[2] The mara of mistaking the skandhas for a self, the mara of seeking pleasure, the mara of death, and the mara of the afflicting emotions.

For whoever recollects you with faith,
Uncontaminated great bliss blossoms fully.
You exhaust the sufferings of samsara without exception.
I prostrate to you who are a marvelous source of blessings.

From within the unelaborated Clear Light,
You fully realize the very subtle causes and effects,
The essence of the interdependence of the objects of knowledge of the three times,
And the supreme intention of the Buddhas of the Three Times.

Through inseparable emptiness and compassion,
You dispel all the sicknesses of the six realms of samsara without exception.
I take refuge in you who are a King of Physicians.

You are the King of Great Bliss, unchanging in the three times,
You abide in the three worlds without enjoying nirvana.
You are the unceasing embodiment of compassion.
You are the tireless Great Sage.
Through your great compassion, you see all (beings) as your sons.
You do not abandon even those who are in great difficulty.
Through your compassion, you join with happiness even those who harm you.
Through exhausting the (fiction of a) self, you fully purified the three spheres.[1]
You are the one friend, the source of marvelous compassion.
May I never part from you, the peerless lama.

[1] Actor, action, and that which is acted upon.

By not parting from you, Precious One,
May all sentient beings of the three times, equal in number to the limits of space, who have sunk into the ocean of suffering,
Fully develop uncontaminated great bliss,
And may they be established in the state of Vajradhrik.[1]

This was composed by Lord Jigten Sumgön.
DZAYANTU

This was translated by the Ven. Khenpo Könchog Gyaltsen with the assistance of Rick Finney at the Tibetan Meditation Center, Washington, D.C., in October 1987.

---

[1] Another name of Vajradhara.

Vajradhara

OM SVASTI
I prostrate to the Lord of teachings,
The crown of the victorious banner of realization,
Spontaneously established,
Possessing the two-fold purification
Inseparable from the kingly great bliss body and the
Buddhafield,
Unceasingly manifesting the spontaneous stream
of activities
According to the need of practitioners.
The glorious Vajradhara body,
Inseparable from the three bodies,
Is the Lord Vajradhara
Who ripens and liberates all sentient beings.
No one can express the entire story of his life;
Yet I will write as much of an account
of the Kagyu lineage
As can be understood by ordinary people.

The Lord of the three worlds and the King of Dharma, Vajradhara, is the embodiment of the Buddhas of the Three Times, the nature of the Triple Gem, and the essence of the three kayas of the Buddha. Until the ocean of samsara ends, he ripens and liberates all sentient beings.

The Lama is the Buddha

The *Chöten Tsekpa Tantra* tells us:

Prostrate to the Lamas,
The embodiment of all the Buddhas,
And the root of the Triple Gem,
Having the essence of the Vajra Holder.

And the *Dompa Gyatso* says:

Pay homage at the lotus feet of Vajradhara,
Whose body is precious as a jewel,
Who by his kindness
Causes great bliss to arise in a moment.

In the *Dompa Jyungwa* it is written:

The Lama is the Buddha and the Dharma;
Likewise, the Lama is the Sangha.
The Lama is glorious Vajradhara;
The All-Creator is he.

Less fortunate beings who lack the eye of devotion wonder how Vajradhara appears as a spiritual master. For those who think in this way the *Vajra Tent* offers this verse:

I am Vajrasattva
Who manifests the body of a master;
To benefit all sentient beings
I remain in an ordinary body.

Therefore the precious Lama is the Buddha,
Whose body, speech, and wisdom mind
Pervade all samsara and nirvana,
And remain unceasingly throughout the three times.

In general, the Buddhas of the Three Times cannot fully recount even in an entire kalpa the qualities of him whose every activity of body, speech, and wisdom mind is adapted to the needs of each sentient being. In particular, in this fortunate kalpa there will appear a thousand and two

Buddhas. Especially for this degenerate age there manifested a Buddha filled with limitless compassion. In India there appeared a mass of his disciples who compiled the teachings known as the Six Ornaments of Jambudvipa, as well as great yogins. In Tibet, the Land of Snow, there appeared the great Dharma kings and the great masters and ministers. Later came Atisha and his lineage, and all the great Kagyupa masters. These are the manifestations of the precious Lama Vajradhara. Even the Buddhas cannot fully recount the life stories of all these beings, and if they cannot describe the root and lineage lamas' qualities and activities, who can do so? Yet, as my Lama instructed me, I will write that part of their life stories which can be understood by ordinary beings.

Simply by hearing the precious teachings of the Kagyupa, one is blessed by all the root and lineage Lamas, and by the Buddhas and Bodhisattvas. The Dakas and Dakinis gather like a cloud, and the Dharma protectors remove all inner and outer obstacles. As a lamp dispels the darkness, the practice of these teachings dispels the false and afflicting emotions. Like a wish-fulfilling gem, so will the practice of these teachings help one to fulfill all wishes. Like a medicine which neutralizes all poison, the practice of these teachings neutralizes the poison of moral defilements. Like the attainment of the sky treasure siddhi, the practice of these teachings confers limitless peace and happiness in samsara and nirvana. Like the waxing moon, all the qualities increase; like the rising sun overwhelming the light of fireflies, the teachings overcome even the qualities of the Sravakas and others; like a precious wheel, the teachings lead to the omniscient state of Buddhahood; like the precious elephant which bears heavy burdens with ease, the teachings dispel the suffering of the mother sentient beings, limitless as the sky; like the precious steed, the teachings enable one to attain Buddhahood speedily; like the precious jewel, the teachings illumine the darkness of ignorance; like the precious minister, the teachings enable one to discriminate between samsara and nirvana, cause and effect; like the golden science of alchemy, the teachings transform all negativity into attainment; like the universal king, the teachings enable humans and non-humans to join together happily, free from even the thought of discord.

The quality of the path, and the wheel of the endless fruit of body, speech and wisdom mind cannot be expressed. In brief, this Lineage teaching allows us to achieve the ordinary and extraordinary attainments and quickly to realize complete Buddhahood. This is the path of devotion, about which the *Hevajra Tantra* says:

> The co-emergent wisdom
> Which cannot be expressed
> Can be found nowhere.
> It can only be realized
> Through ultimate devotion to the Lama
> And through one's own collection of virtue.

And the *Guhyasamaja Tantra* says:

> Even if one has committed the five heavy negative karmas,
> Killing millions of sentient beings and Brahmins every day,
> Yet if he follows this Teaching
> And has devotion to the Lama,
> He will doubtless become realized.
> But he who has no devotion to the Lama
> Will not become realized even if he practices.

The *Uttaratantra* says:

> The ultimate meaning of self-arising
> Will be realized through devotion.
> The light-radiating sun
> Cannot be seen by him who has no eyes.

The teaching which can be realized through aspiration-devotion, and which cannot be described in written words, is transmitted only from ear to ear, and from heart to heart. It is this teaching which Vajradhara has given to the great saint and emanation, Tilopa, who in turn gave it to Naropa, who gave it to Marpa Lotsawa in the South. Marpa gave it to Milarepa, who gave it to Dagpo Lharje (known as Gampopa). Gampopa also received the teachings of Atisha, who had three lineages: the profound view lineage, the profound action lineage, and the blessing experience lineage.

The profound view lineage was given by Arya Nagarjuna to Chandrakirti, who gave it to Rigpe Khuchuk, who gave it to Kusali Chewa, who gave it to Kusali Chungwa, who gave it to Atisha.

The profound action lineage was given by Lord Maitreya to Asanga, who gave it to Vasubhandu, who gave it to Arya Namdrul De, who gave it to Soso'i Kyewo Namdrul De, who gave it to Chok-gi De, who gave it to Dulwai De, who gave it to Khenpo Yangdak Namnang Zä, who gave it to Singhabhadra, who gave it to Rinchen Zangpo, who gave it to Gunamitra, who gave it to Lama Serlingpa, who gave it to Atisha.

The blessing experience lineage was given by Vajradhara to Tilopa, who gave it to Naropa, who gave it to Saint Dombipa, who gave it to Atisha.

Atisha had many disciples, but his lineage was given to Geshe Tompa, who gave it to Naljorpa Chenpo who gave it to Geshe Nyukrumpa, who gave it to Gampopa. Also, Geshe Tompa gave the teaching to Geshe Chen-ngawa, who gave it to Geshe Chya-yulwa, who gave it to Gampopa. Gampopa gave it to the glorious Phagmodrupa, who gave it to Lord Drikungpa (Lord Jigten Sumgön). From Lord Jigten Sumgön this teaching spread to all the great Drikung Kagyu lineage holders in Central, Western and Eastern Tibet.

All the Buddhas of the Three Times
And all the Kagyu Lamas
Are the emanations
Of the Lama, Glorious Vajradhara.
By making offerings to the precious Lama

One makes offerings to all the Lamas.
If he is pleased, all are pleased,
And one achieves the supreme attainment.
Arya Nagarjuna said:
Refrain from all other offerings;
Make offerings only to the Lama.
By pleasing him
One attains omniscience, the ultimate attainment.
The short-cut path of Vajrayana
Is the combination of the interdependence
Of object, motivation and matter.
The glorious Vajradhara said:
It is far superior to make offerings
Even to one pore of the Lama's skin
Than to make offerings to the Buddhas of the Three Times.
This is the essential point.
Therefore, make offerings to him
Of body, wealth and practice.
Of the three, the practice offering is superior.
In particular, he who wishes to hold the lineage of Vajradhara
Should perform the practice offering.
He who has accomplished the practice action
Is the activity of the Lama.
This is the life-root of the Buddha's teaching
And is cherished by the Kagyu Lamas.

What does devotion mean?
The glorious Lama has said:
To one who grows in confidence
The Lama is the embodiment
Of the three kayas of the Buddha.
Whoever sees the Lama's activities
Understands the turning wheel of Dharma.
He who accomplishes the practice
Is a proper devotional vessel.

The blessed, glorious Vajradhara, because of the inseparability of the three kayas, pervaded all the realms of samsara and nirvana, ripening and liberating all the sentient beings. It is said in the *Inconceivable Secret Sutra:*

> As emptiness pervades all phenomena,
> Likewise his body pervades;
> As his body pervades,
> So does light;
> As light pervades,
> So does his speech;
> As his speech pervades,
> So does his wisdom mind.

And in the *Don Nyepar Köpai Gyaltsen,* a commentary by Lord Jigten Sumgön, it says: "The Buddha as Dharmakaya possesses limitless excellent qualities. In particular, he has thirty-two separated qualities,[1] ten strengths, four fearlessnesses, and eighteen unassociated dharmas. By these he sees clearly and without error the past, present and future in his wisdom mind. He also possesses thirty-two ripening qualities which are the thirty-two major marks. When he was on the path to Buddhahood, he gathered innumerable accumulations of virtue and merit which caused these ripening fruits to appear. All the Buddhafields appeared to this dharmakaya body, which in turn pervades all the Buddhafields. Thus he benefits and liberates countless sentient beings through his body, speech and wisdom mind of endless qualities, the source of the wheel of inexhaustible ornaments.

The Buddha's body appears to a greater or lesser degree to each of the Bodhisattvas at the different levels of the path according to their degree of realization. This type of appearance is called the body of quality, or the sambhogakaya of the Buddha, which is described frequently in all the sutras and shastras.

---

[1] meaning: separate from impurities such as afflicting emotions; hence, eternally pure.

The activities of the self-nature of dharmakaya are free from all elaborations and boundaries, and forever remain. For the other condition[1] the Buddha cultivates mind on the path to enlightenment, and by the force of his aspirations variously manifests his body, speech and wisdom mind according to the understanding of sentient beings, effortlessly and continually until the end of samsara.

Appearing as horses, elephants and chariots,
Oxen, lions and rabbits
And other containers
In both peaceful and wrathful forms,
He establishes all beings
In the cessation of suffering.
A single utterance of Vajradhara
Pervades the language of gods, nagas, yakshas and
vampires,
And the languages of humans,
And the ocean of different languages of all other
sentient beings.

Even if he teaches in one language, all understand him in their own languages, each according to his level. In this way he benefits countless sentient beings and completely understands their different needs.

The sage appeared as Brahma, Vishnu, and the sixty-four viewers according to the disposition of the sentient beings of the six realms.

The victorious ones taught the view of
Sravakas and the Pratyekabuddhas,
Chittamatra, Madhyamika and others
According to the level of understanding of each.

The vehicle of the gods and Brahma;
Likewise, the vehicle of the Pratyekabuddhas
and others

[1] sentient beings.

Were taught by the Buddha
To liberate unripened beings.
Until there is an end to afflicting emotions
There is no end to vehicles.
These various views
Lead to the peace of nonduality.

The profound activities of the dharmakaya,
The interdependence of self and other conditions,
Appear definitely,
As is explained in all the sutras and shastras.

The Buddha

(circa 620 B.C. *- circa 543* B.C.*)*

Skillful compassionate one born into the family of the Shakyas,
You conquered the hordes of Mara, which others could not.
Your body is splendid like a mountain of gold.
To you, the King of the Shakyas, I prostrate.

—*Lord Jigten Sumgön*

Within each major kalpa (age) there are four minor kalpas: the emptiness kalpa; the manifestation kalpa; the maintenance of the universe kalpa; and the destruction kalpa. Each of these kalpas in turn contains twenty intermediate kalpas, giving a total of eighty intermediate kalpas. During sixty of these (pertaining to emptiness, manifestation and destruction) no Buddha will appear. In the present kalpa, which is the first of the twenty intermediate kalpas, one thousand two Buddhas will appear. Of these, four Buddhas have already manifested: Krakuchhanda, who appeared when the life span of humans lasted eighty thousand years; Kanakamuni, who appeared when the life span of humans lasted forty thousand years; and Shakyamuni, who appeared when the life span of humans lasted one hundred years, and when they were marked by defilements and engaged in quarrelling. Indeed, their minds were like threads which are so hopelessly knotted that even highly realized beings cannot disentangle them. Still, out of his great compassion Buddha Shakyamuni consented to appear among them in order to lead them out of their blindness. In the *Uttaratantra* the phases of his existence are described in this way:

> Realizing the nature of samsara with compassion;
> Looking upon samsara without separating the mind from Dharmakaya;
> Manifesting in various emanation forms;
> Previously born in the Tushita Heaven;
> Descending from that Heaven;
> Conceived and born on earth;
> Expert in the creative arts;
> Enjoying the kingdom;
> Renouncing, and enduring hardships to approach the heart of enlightenment;
> Subjugating maras and achieving enlightenment;
> Turning the wheel of the enlightenment teachings;
> Entering into Parinirvana;
> Manifesting these activities until the end of samsara, the impure realm.

1. THE TUSHITA HEAVEN AND DESCENT

Before descending to earth, Buddha Shakyamuni was born in the Tushita Heaven as Devaputra with great clear mind and profound recollection. Seated on the lion throne, he gave teachings to all the gods. At this time he heard the celestial sound of the cymbals, and the songs of the Buddhas of the Three Times, perfectly invoked, addressing him thus: "In samsara, burning with the fire of emotions, you, great warrior, pervade the clouds. The falling rain of your ambrosia pacifies the afflicting emotions of those who are not gods."

Hearing these and other words, he looked for the five sights—the continent called Jambudvipa; the six cities such as Champaka; the Shakya clan which, for seven generations, has not declined through intermarriage; a mother named

Mahamaya, who was free from the thirty-two negative qualities; and a time of the five increasing degenerations in which people suffer greatly and become objects of compassion, for they are difficult to tame, hold wrong views, have a declining life span, are defiled by the five mental poisons, and gain wealth through impure means. Seeing these things, he said to the gods: "By these signs the sentient beings in Jambudvipa show their afflicting emotions and their enjoyment of negative action." When he said this, the gods replied: "All of Jambudvipa is in ruins because of the six dialecticians, the six followers, and the six meditators. Therefore, do not go there." Devaputra refused to listen, saying: "I will blow the conch shell of impermanence, beat the gong of emptiness, and roar with the sound of selflessness." He then empowered Maitreya to take his place on the throne, and declared three times to the six realms of the gods that he was descending to this world. Then he manifested as the precious elephant having an immense, though glorious and gentle, body with six trunks. He was adorned with the golden nets and a beauteous red hat, and gave forth a pleasant odor because of the medicinal herbs he ate.

2. ENTERING THE MOTHER'S WOMB

In the middle of the night of the fifteenth day of the second month at the time of the full moon, when Mahamaya was in retreat, the Lord Buddha entered her womb through the right side. Mahamaya then dreamed that a mountain had become her pillow, that the sun was rising within her body, and that she was giving teachings to many sentient beings. She felt light and at ease. In the months to come she had many other auspicious dreams, and experienced bliss and freedom from afflicting emotions.

3. BIRTH

After ten months, the moment arrived for giving birth. Mahamaya was passing by the Lumbini garden when, quick as a flash of lightning, she grasped a branch of the laksha tree with her right hand. The child emerged from her right side, and Brahma and Indra descended to earth to make offerings, wrapping him in a pure silk cloth. After the gods and nagas bathed him, the child took seven steps in each of the four directions. At that time he revealed many jewel treasures and fulfilled the wishes of his father so that he became known as Siddhartha (the Fulfiller of Wishes).

To pay homage to the yaksha Shakya Phel, the Bodhisattva sat on a chariot throne made of four precious jewels, and proceeded to the city of Kapilavastu. Here were assembled some of the Shakya clan who, being untamed, respected no one. But when the Bodhisattva passed, they immediately grew docile so that he became known as Shakyamuni (the Tamer of the Shakyas). When he neared the temple of Shakya Phel, the god came out and did prostrations. Thus, he also became known as the God of Gods.

As his mother passed away seven days after his birth, thirty-two nurses were appointed to care for him. All the Brahmins and astrologers prophesied that if the child renounced the kingdom, he would become a Buddha; otherwise, he would become a universal monarch.

One day a rishi called Krishna, along with his nephew, came to the kingdom from the Himalayas. King Suddhodana asked: "Why have you come here?" and the rishi replied: "Great king, I have come to see your son."

> The sage and liberator of sentient beings
> I have come to see.
> What kind of prediction
> Have others made about him?

King Suddhodana replied: "He will become a wheel-turner king." The rishi then said: "Listen Lord of the Earth. Those who say so are confused of mind. In this degenerate time there will be no wheel-turner."

> The treasure of the Teaching
> Contains all the virtues.

He will achieve Buddhahood,
Becoming victorious over all the faults.

The King, seeing the rishi's eyes fill with tears, said:

Why are your eyes filled with tears?
Is there any danger that the child's life
Will come to an untimely end?
Please tell me if there is any negative sign.

The rishi replied:

Even were a rain of vajras to descend from the sky
on this child,
They could not harm a hair on his body.
He is a great saint.

"So why are you crying?" the King said. The rishi replied:

Lord of Men, meeting with this Dharma treasure
I die without fulfilling my wish.
I know I cannot enter into nirvana.
Seeing my faults, tears come to my eyes.

Later, this rishi's cousin, whose name was Mejin, became a monk of the Buddha and was called Kathayana.

4. EXPERT IN THE CREATIVE ARTS

Adorned with the ornaments,
He became expert in astrology and literature.
When he departed the city,
He meditated in samadhi
Under the shade of the jambu tree,
Praised by the six sons of the gods.

5. ENJOYMENT IN THE KINGDOM

When his father saw him under the shade of the jambu tree, he praised him in this way:

Sage, when you were born
And meditated in samadhi,

I twice prostrated at your feet,
O liberated one.

In time, all the Shakyas requested that the Bodhisattva marry, but he replied:

Born of the fault of desire,
Marriage, like a poisonous leaf, is the root of
suffering, conflict and resentment.
It is not wise to stay near woman.

Later, in considering the matter, he said:

The previous Bodhisattvas who have appeared
Had wives and children.
I will follow their path.

So saying, he agreed to take a wife. "What kind of consort do you wish?" they asked. The Bodhisattva set down the necessary qualities for his princess and gave the list to his minister, saying: "If you find such a woman, bring her to me." When the minister took the note to the daughter of Shakya Lakna Bechon, she asked him: "Why do you come to me?" He said:

The son of Suddhodana,
Supremely beautiful,
Adorned with the thirty-two special marks
And possessing glorious attributes,
Has named these qualities
Which are acceptable to him in a queen.

She replied:

Brahmin, I possess all these qualities.
This supreme being can become my husband.
If he agrees, do not delay our union.

King Suddhodana asked that she be brought to the palace, but her father, thinking that the Bodhisattva was not skilled in athletics, refused to give his daughter to Shakyamuni. To overcome his father's disappointment, Shakyamuni entered a contest from which he emerged the victor. When he competed in archery, everyone was astonished by his talent. The Bodhisattva then said:

> This is the heart of the earth
> Where all the previous Buddhas were seated,
> Remaining in peace.
> The ego-less wisdom arrows
> Have destroyed the enemy of afflictions
> And torn the nets of wrong view.
> Thus they achieved nirvana, peace, and the precious enlightenment
> Free from impurity.

The Shakya Bechon then offered his daughter to the Bodhisattva, who in addition accepted other queens and their retinues, totalling eighty-four thousand in all.

6. *RENOUNCING THE KINGDOM*

At this time the Bodhisattva was invoked in music and song. As the rishi predicted, the father had a dream of the son's renunciation. Becoming frightened, he heaped yet more worldly treasures on his son and appointed guards to watch over him. But one day the Bodhisattva's attendant Dunpa drove his chariot in the eastern, southern and western directions where he saw aging, sickness and death. Seeing such suffering, he was greatly moved and said:

> What is the use of youth
> Which is ultimately destroyed by age?
> What is the benefit of health
> Which will only end with illness?
> What is the good of wisdom in life
> If this life lasts not forever?
> Aging, sickness and death follow each other inevitably.

In the northern direction he saw a monk, and feeling deep devotion he asked his father if he might be allowed to take vows. But his father refused. Then, the son asked the father to grant him the wish of not being tortured by the three sufferings. But clearly his father could not fulfill this wish either. Instead, he again surrounded his son with further worldly comforts and protection.

One night, when all his attendants were asleep, the Bodhisattva thought that he should leave the palace. Thus, he called to Dunpa, saying:

> Awaken, and quickly fetch my magical steed
> Ngakden.
> I intend to search for the garden of hardships
> Visited by previous Buddhas seeking enlightenment.
> I know that this will please all the sages.

Dunpa replied:

> This is not the hour to go to the garden.
> No one holds malice toward you here;
> You have no enemies,
> So why do you need a horse at midnight?

The Prince replied:

> Dunpa, you have never disobeyed me,
> So do not do so now as we prepare to separate.

At last Dunpa brought the horse, but the horse would not allow the Prince to mount him. The Prince told him:

> Ngakden, this is the last time
> That you will carry me.
> So take me without delay
> To the garden of hardships.
> After achieving enlightenment
> I will quickly fulfill the needs
> Of all sentient beings
> Through the rain of samadhi.

As his father lay sleeping the Bodhisattva circumambulated him, and rode off in the night saying:

> Until I achieve the supreme path of all the Buddhas
> I will not return to this city of Kapilavastu.

Within two sessions (half a day) he covered a distance which normally takes twelve days. Alighting from his horse, he removed his ornaments, gave them to Dunpa and dismissed him and Ngakden. But Dunpa objected: "It is not right that you should remain alone." The Prince replied:

All beings come into this world alone;
Likewise do they die.
During this life they also suffer alone.
There are no friends in samsara.

He then cut his hair in front of the fully pure stupa, and returned to Dunpa. Indra, manifesting as a hunter, brought monk's robes which the Prince exchanged for his fine garments of silk. He then made a bowl from the leaf of the karavira tree and set out to see King Bimbisara to equalize the virtue.[1] The King, feeling great devotion, addressed the assembly:

Adorned with the supreme signs
And many marks of perfection,
He walks a short distance ahead.
Gaze upon him, O wise men.

As the King and Siddhartha walked together the King spoke of the luxuries of samsara, and on returning to his palace staged many entertainments. But Siddhartha said to him:

I am not interested in worldly pleasures.
Even if this entire earth and its oceans
Were filled with the seven types of gems,
Men would be dissatisfied.
It is like burning firewood in summer.
So all desires lead to attachment and hatred.
It is difficult to cross the ocean of suffering.
O King, the status of kingship
Is like a muddy swamp;
It is the root of pain and fear.
The ignorant alone desire it.

---

[1] Tibetan phrase for begging

7. UNDERGOING THE HARDSHIPS

Following the five ascetic rishis, Siddhartha underwent hardships for six years by the banks of the Nairanjana. So great were his austerities that the ribs of his back could be seen. The gods, gazing on him, thought he would soon die, and so they lamented:

> The son of Shakya, the essence of sentient beings,
> When in the Tushita heaven
> Would have done well to remain and give teachings.
> But he promised to liberate sentient beings
> And now it seems he will die.

And they told Mahamaya that her son, Siddhartha, would soon pass away. Hearing this, the mother descended from the heavens and made this lamentation:

> When my son was born in the garden of Lumbini
> Fearlessly, like a lion, he took seven steps,
> Looked in the four directions and said:
> This is my final birth.
> You have not fulfilled this pleasing prophecy;
> I see the words of the rishi Krishna unrealized
> That you would achieve enlightenment.
> All I see is the impermanence of death.
> Who will give life to my only son?

Siddhartha replied:

> This earth may crumble;
> The sun, moon and stars fall away.
> Yet even if I were an ordinary being
> I would not die.
> Soon I will achieve Buddhahood.

Then he realized that the path of extreme austerities would not enable him to fulfill his vow, so he determined to meditate on building strength of body. Rishi Deva, who had been the Bodhisattva's friend before he renounced the kingdom took pity on his condition and told two village women, Gamo and Gatopma, to bring him offerings. When he partook of their milk porridge, the color of his body transformed into pure gold. His five disciples, thinking that he had renounced the path, abandoned him. The Bodhisattva asked the two women how the merit of their offering could be shared, and they replied:

> Whatever accumulations of merit are created by these gifts,
> O renowned one, fulfiller of all wishes,
> We offer to you.
> May you achieve the ultimate state
> And fully accomplish your excellent thought.

8. *APPROACHING ENLIGHTENMENT*

When the Bodhisattva was approaching enlightenment, the gods created a road of golden sand, sprinkled it with sandalwood-scented water, and strewed flowers on the ground. In this way they made many offerings.

The Bodhisattva then addressed Tashi, a seller of grass:

> Tashi, quickly give me some kusha grass;
> It will be of great use,
> For today I will subdue the maras with their retinues,
> And will reach peaceful, precious enlightenment.

He made an offering of this smooth grass, which was green like the neck of a peacock, and spread it under the bodhi tree with the roots facing the tree. On this he sat, saying:

> Even if my body dries up
> And my skin and bones disintegrate,
> Yet will I remain in this seat
> Until I achieve enlightenment,
> Which is hard to find, even during many kalpas.

Thus he promised.

9. SUBJUGATING THE MARAS

From his forehead, the Bodhisattva radiated a light known as the Subjugation of the Assembly of Maras. Because of this invocation, all the groups of sinful maras, who delight in negative actions, gathered to his left. The hundred-handed said:

> My body has a hundred hands,
> And even one can shoot one hundred arrows.
> I will therefore pierce the body of practitioners.
> Father, rejoice, come forth;
> Do not lag behind.

Those who gathered to his right delighted in positive action, and were known as Great Discrimination Mind. They praised him, saying:

> The body of him who meditates on loving kindness beyond samsara
> Cannot be harmed by poison, weapons or fire.
> Such weapons, if thrown, will be transformed into flowers.

It was accomplished as they said. Thus, the male maras could create no obstacles; neither could the female maras deceive him. In this way he defeated all the maras.

10. ACHIEVING ENLIGHTENMENT

In the first part of the night, he achieved the four stages of samadhi and the state of super-awareness. In the middle watch of the night, he achieved the clairvoyance of recollecting his previous lives; and in the last hours of the night he achieved the stainless wisdom of the end of afflicting emotions. He then realized in a moment the nature of the twelve links of interdependent origination (the twelve nidanas), both in their arising and cessation, as well as the four noble truths. Thus, in a moment, he achieved enlightenment, the perfect Buddhahood.

11. *TURNING THE WHEEL OF THE TEACHING*

Lord Buddha reasoned in this way:

> I have found a teaching like ambrosia,
> Profound, peaceful, free from conception,
> Luminous, uncreated.
> If I tell of this teaching,
> No one will understand.
> So I shall stay in the forest
> Without speaking.

Bringing offerings, Indra requested the one-thousand-spoked golden wheel with these words:

> Like the moon free from eclipse,
> Your mind is completely liberated.
> Please awaken the victors of battle
> To kindle the light of wisdom
> And destroy the darkness of the world.

Brahma then appeared and requested:

> Go wherever you will, O Sage,
> But please give the teachings.

To them the Lord Buddha replied:

> All beings are chained to desire
> And remain immersed in that state.
> Therefore the teachings I have found
> Will be of no benefit,
> Even if I offer them.

Thus he refused to give the teachings. Again Brahma requested:

> The teachings previously given in Magadha[1]
> Are all impure and false.
> Therefore, Sage, open the door of ambrosia.

---

[1] Central India

For many lifetimes Brahma had cultivated his mind and accumulated great merit so that he could request the teachings from the Buddha. For this reason the Buddha finally agreed to do as he wished, saying:

The sentient beings of Magadha
Are full of faith and pure devotion.
They are ready to hear the teachings;
I will therefore open the door to ambrosia.

So he proceeded to Varanasi to give the teachings to the five disciples. On the way, he met rishi Nyendro who said: "You are radiating light and clarity. Who is your teacher? From whom did you take your monk's vows?" The Buddha replied:

I have no master;
I am the self-born Buddha,
Victorious over negative action.
Therefore, Nyendro, I am self-victorious.

Nyendro then asked: "Where are you going?" The Buddha said:

I go to Varanasi,
To the city of Kashika.
There I will kindle the teachings
In sentient beings
Who are as blind men;
I will beat the drum of the teaching
For sentient beings
Who are as deaf men;
I will cause the rain of teachings to fall
On sentient beings
Who are as lame men.

As he approached Varanasi, the five disciples who had previously abandoned him determined to insult him when he would come. As soon as he arrived, however, they paid him homage. Then the Buddha turned the wheel of the Dharma three times in succession.

12. ATTAINING PARINIRVANA

Lord Buddha went to Kusinagara near the Hiranyavati River. He blessed all the sentient beings, each in their own language, as he thought of them all as his own sons, saying that if any doubts or hesitations were arising, they should question him during these, his last moments. Those gods, demi-gods and humans who loved the Dharma gathered the finest offerings and supplicated him with these words:

> All the sentient beings,
> Tortured by the disease of afflicting emotions,
> Are separated from the skillful physician of the Dharma.
> Lord Buddha, the blessed One,
> Do not abandon us.

The Buddha replied:

> The Buddhas are Dharmata;
> Therefore they remain, saying nothing.
> Dedicate your lives to awareness
> And protect your thoughts through mindfulness.
> Renounce all non-virtuous actions;
> Be content and happy.

This he said, along with many other teachings. And at midnight he passed away. Brahma and all the Buddha's principal disciples lamented:

> The aspiration of the previously blessed ones
> Has passed beyond samsara, leaving us.
> All of us, gods and humans,
> Are now without a leader.

In this way they made many expressions of sorrow.

At this time Mahakashava was meditating in the peaceful samadhi at Vulture Peak Mountain. Therefore, he did not learn of the Buddha's passing for seven days, but when he heard of it, he, too, came to Kusinagara and said:

Alas! Noble blessed one,
I am tortured by suffering.
The compassionate one did not wait for me.
Why have you attained parinirvana so fast?

The Buddha passed away in his eighty-second year. His body was cremated, and the relics divided into eight parts: the first portion was reserved for the people of Kusinagara; the second for the people of Sapara; the third for the people of Kampaka and Buluka; the fourth for the people of Ramawa and Drodhava; the fifth for the people of Chinudvi; the sixth for the Shakya of Kapilavastu; the seventh for the Litsavi of Vaisali; and the eighth for King Ajatasatru. The vase containing his body was given to the Brahmin Bola. The Brahmin Drevo built a stupa, and the ashes were given to the Brahmin's son Pipayana. For these he built a stupa at a site known as Pipala. One of the Buddha's teeth was kept in the realm of the thirty-three gods; one was kept in Rabtugawa in the Gandharva country; one was given to Vazitam, the King of Kalinka; and one was given to the King of the Nagas in the city of Rama.

Tilopa (988–1069)

Vajradhara has appeared to highly realized and advanced beings, teaching the four kinds of tantra within the vidyadhara category. When one teaches the sutras [Buddha's discourses] one should explain the history of the Buddha; when one teaches the shastras [commentaries by accomplished masters] one should recount the life story of the writer; and when one gives the instructions one should relate the history of the lama's lineage.

The lama is supremely important for the giving of instruction; therefore the sutras and tantras explain the qualities necessary in a lama. It is very important to search for a qualified lama. And he, in turn, relies on the teachers of the lineage. The faults which can arise in lamas are: impurity in keeping the three vows; preoccupation with the worldly life; the karma of attracting evil spirits; indifference to the path of devotion; adherence to the substance of the law rather than to its essence, and others. One should avoid these faults.

From Vajradhara or Buddha Shakyamuni until now, all the teachers are the emanation of the Buddhas. They are without fault and adorned with all the good qualities. So one should seek such a teacher. The precious Kagyu lineage embodies these qualities.

The history of Vajradhara has been recounted, so here begins the life story of Tilopa, comprising four aspects: (1) his life in human form; (2) emanating Chakrasamvara; (3) manifesting as Chakrasamvara, and (4) embodying the Buddhas of the Three Times. Of these aspects the first has thirteen divisions.

I. HIS LIFE IN HUMAN FORM

A. *Manifesting as a Human Being and Overpowering the Dakinis*

In East Bengal in a city called Zako lived a family of three: the father was known as the Brahmin Salwa; the mother was known as the Brahmin Saldenma; and the daughter was known as the Brahmin Saldron. As no son had been born to them, the man and woman made offerings and prayed to the worldly gods, the triple gem, the spiritual friends (gurus) and Chakrasamvara. In this way a son was born. When he was shown to astrologers and others who read signs, some recognized in him the marks of a god, others the marks of a human being, and still others the mark of a Buddha. None could agree on who he was:

> We do not know if this child
> Is a god, naga, or yaksha.
> Still, guard this excellent being with care.

The boy was given the name Brahmin Salyö.

When he was growing up, a fearsome, ugly woman came to care for him. She said, "There is no place where one can avoid death." The boy's mother therefore asked her, "What can I do for him?" And the woman replied, addressing the boy:

> Herd buffalo
> And read scriptures.
> There you will find the prophecies of the Dakinis.

With this she disappeared.

One day, while the Brahmin Salyö was herding buffalo

and reading the scriptures under the shapa tree, the woman appeared again, this time asking his name, the country of his birth, and the name of his parents. "My country is Zako in the East. My father is the Brahmin Salwa; my mother is the Brahmin Saldenma; my sister is the Brahmin Saldron; and I am the Brahmin Salyö. This tree is the shapa root and I am tending buffalo to earn my living, as well as practicing the Dharma by reading scriptures." She replied: "This is not how it is." He asked: "Then what is the truth?" She replied: "Your country is Oddiyana in the North; your father is Chakrasamvara; your mother is Vajrayogini; your brother is Pantsapana, and I am your sister, Bliss-giver. If you want to find the true buffalo[1] go to the forest of the bodhi tree. There the stainless Dakinis hold the ear-whispered teachings." He replied: "If I go there, the Dakinis will pose obstacles and prevent me from succeeding." She said:

Yogi, you can get the teachings.
You have received the predictions
And kept the samaya vows.

Realizing that she was a Dakini he said: "The path is dangerous and I do not know how to traverse it." In reply she gave him a crystal ladder, a jeweled bridge, and a coral-handled key, saying: "I give you my blessings; depart without hesitation."

The ladder and the bridge spanned the gulf
And the key opened the locks.

Fearlessly he journeyed to Oddiyana in the North and approached the iron wall of Gandhola. Using the Dakini's bridge, he crossed a poisonous lake, and with the ladder climbed the iron wall. The temple of Gandhola had three gates. Opening the first, he found the stainless Dakinis of outer nirmanakaya emanations. These manifested myriad fearsome forms, with unpleasant sounds and threatening gestures to cause him fright.

---

[1] meaning: his real mission.

We are the stainless Dakinis
Who desire flesh and blood.

But the yogi said:

Even your frightening gestures and threatening sounds,
O fearsome Dakinis, cannot make the hairs of my body
Stand on end.

Hearing this, all the Dakinis fell into a faint, and when they regained consciousness they begged his pardon. As Tilopa entered the courtyard, the Dakinis said:

We are to you as the butterfly to the lamp;
The butterfly hopes to extinguish the lamp,
But instead dies in the light.
Just so, we hoped to harm you,
But you overpowered us.

One among them continued:

I am just an ordinary being, without authority.
If I do not ask our leader's permission to let you in,
She will eat my flesh and drink my blood.
Therefore, precious one, please do not think unkindly of me.

With this she disappeared inside the temple. Then the Loka Karma Dakinis, the middle or sambhogakaya emanations, appeared and said:

We are the Loka Dakinis
Who eat flesh and drink blood.

Making the three threatening mudras, Tilopa overpowered the body, speech and mind of these Dakinis, saying:

O great fearful Dakinis,
Even you cannot make
The hairs of my body stand on end.

Hearing this, all the Dakinis fell into a faint, and when they regained consciousness they said:

> We are to you as flies to a lamp.
> You have overpowered us.

The chief among them continued:

> I am a Minister, yet have no authority.
> If I don't ask her permission to let you in,
> Our Queen will eat my flesh and drink my blood.
> Please do not think unkindly of me.

With this, she disappeared inside the temple and spoke to the Queen, who permitted Tilopa to enter. Immediately he went into the meditation state without paying homage to the Queen. At this, all the Dakinis became angry and said:

> She is the blessed one,
> The mother of the Buddhas of the Three Times.
> Let us beat him
> Who shows no respect.

But the blessed mother said:

> He is Chakrasamvara,
> The father of the Buddhas of the Three Times.
> Even a rain of vajras falling on him
> Could not destroy him.
> Therefore I will give him the teachings.

Thus, he received the teachings of the prana and many others which are unrecorded. Still, he was not satisfied. Then the blessed mother said: "Who are you, who sent you here, and what do you want?" Tilopa replied:

> I am Pantsapana,
> My sister, Determa, sent me;
> I want the perfect teaching,
> The stainless bliss, the great secret
> Of the ordinary and extraordinary.

The blessed mother said:

> In my three treasures
> There are three wish-fulfilling gems,
> Co-emergent wisdoms
> Which dispel the darkness of ignorance.
> I will give these to you if you understand the signs.

In the three treasures are three signs of body, speech and mind: the self-arising body of co-emergent yab-yum; the seven-syllable self-arising emerald gem in the three-pointed Dharmakara of vajra speech; and the five-pointed vajra jewel of the self-arising mind. Tilopa recognized these, besides seeing the three secret tantra treasures which he requested in general:

> In the secret treasure of body, speech and mind,
> the three wish-fulfilling gems,
> I request the view, meditation and action
> And samaya teachings of self-liberation.

The Dakinis replied:

> The secret treasure of body, speech and mind,
> The three wish-fulfilling gems,
> Are sealed to the great yogi
> Who was prophesied, and who kept the samaya.
> Though you are fortunate,
> You may not be able to open the door.

Thus, they answered in general.
Tilopa then addressed the blessed mother in particular:

> From the body treasure of Tsakali
> I request the common wish-fulfilling gem;
> From the speech treasure of jeweled scripture
> I request the samaya wish-fulfilling gem;
> From the wisdom mind treasure of mudra
> I request the wish-fulfilling gem of the mode of
> abiding.

The blessed mother said:

> From the body treasure of Tsakali
> The common wish-fulfilling gem
> Is sealed with the lock of the prophesied one.
> It cannot be opened to you who are not prophesied.
> From the speech treasure of jeweled scripture
> The samaya wish-fulfilling gem
> Is locked by the samaya keeper.
> It cannot be opened to you who do not keep the samaya.
> From the wisdom mind treasure of mudra
> The mode of abiding of the wish-fulfilling gem
> Is sealed by the realized yogi.
> It cannot be opened to him who is unrealized.

Tilopa replied that he had the three keys necessary.

> In the forest of the shawa garden
> The Dakini gave me the keys and prophesied:
> You who were prophesied kept the teachings;
> You who are realized, bring the teachings.

All the Dakinis mocked him and said: "The one who made this prophecy is an emanation of a mara.

> A blind man cannot see
> Even if he is shown form;
> A deaf man cannot hear
> Even if he listens to noise;
> A mute cannot speak
> Even if he is told to utter sound;
> A crippled man cannot move
> Even if he is commanded to walk.
> So there is no truth in you
> Who are deceived by maras.

Tilopa replied:

> A lie is a false word.
> When falsehood ends
> There is no lie.

It was not a mara speaking to me,
But a Dakini.

And he repeated that he had the keys to open the three secret treasures which are sealed:

If I divide these three keys,
I have the self-liberation key of samaya
Which opens the door to the tantra of Zalavara,
And to the mental vow of the secret word of the Dakinis,
And to the light of wisdom which dispels the darkness of ignorance,
And to self-awareness, self-arising, and self-clarity.

I have the key of spontaneous experience
Which opens the door to the mind-as-such,
Self-appearing clarity which is ever unborn,
The great prediction of the Dakinis.

I have the key of experience of the realized yogi
Which opens the door to the non-appearance of non-objective mind,
Without even a particle of unmindfulness,
And to Mind-as-such, Dharma-as-such, and Dharmakaya.

When he said this, all the Dakinis were pleased and held a ganachakra feast. Along with the sindhura vajra wisdom mandala, they gave him the four empowerments by which he achieved the two attainments. They also gave him the ear-to-ear and mind-to-mind lineage teachings with the blessings of the wisdom Dakinis who said:

Father, the blessed one,
Chakrasamvara, the supreme bliss,
Tilo, the Buddha, Lord of Sentient Beings,
We offer you the three wish-fulfilling gems.

They gave him all the teachings of the Hearing Lineage: in general, the teachings of the *Chakrasamvara Tantra*; and in particular, the secret meaning of the quintessence. They also transmitted to him the *Ocean of Samvara*, the *Ocean of Vajra*, the *Ocean of Heruka*, the *Ocean of the Dakinis*, the *Ocean of Action* and the *Ocean of Activities*, as well as the *Tantra of Jyorwa Shi Khagyor*, the *Tantra of Heruka Bhadra*, the *Tantra of Nyingpo*, the *Tantra of the Vajra Dakinis*, the *Tantra of Dechok Dorje Trengwa*, the *Tantra of Dakini Sangwai Zö*, and the *Tantra of Vajradhara Self-Appearance*. These were the thirteen tantra teachings given to him. Thus, he achieved the first stage, and attaining the heavenly realms he soared to the sky, saying:

> In space like a bird
> Fly without obstacles, Prajnabadra.
> In the pervading emptiness
> Of the element of appearance
> Fly, awareness-wisdom.

All the Dakinis requested that he remain with them.

> Where will you go, precious one?
> Please remain here for our benefit.

Refusing them, he said: "I will have different families of disciples. I must therefore leave you for this purpose.

> I, the yogi, will go to Tsukgi Norbu Monastery
> For the spiritual sons
> Naropa, Ririkasori, and others.

Just as he was disappearing, a formless Dakini gave him the nine Dharma subjects with their sounds and signs: "Loosen the knot of the mind by ripening liberation; act like a sword striking the water; chase the sun of realization which is the material of samaya; see samaya in the mirror of your mind; see that the light of awareness is wisdom; turn the wheel of the channel and wind net; see the outer mirror equalizing taste; see the mahamudra of self-liberation; hold the jewel of the great bliss speech." Thus he was given the nine teachings. Realizing them, he said:

> In the temple of the illusory body
> Place the sacred teachings of the formless Dakini.

Keep the steel of unexpressed speech.
Fly, O bird of the clear light mind.

And he proceeded to the Crest Ornament Monastery.

This shows how Tilopa as a human being overpowered the Dakinis, and how he received the teachings.

B. Acting as a Non-human Teacher

The Saint Tilopa became famous by receiving the teachings directly from the Wisdom Dakinis in Oddiyana. When he was asked who his Lama was, Tilopa replied:

I have no human teacher;
My Lama is the Omniscient One.

Looking down from the sky, the Dakinis said:

Tilopa, who realized the two truths
And is expert in the five aspects of knowledge,
You have no human teacher;
All your Lamas are omniscient ones.

When the people heard that Tilopa did not have a human lama, they lost their faith in him.

C. To Put an End to Non-devotion, Tilopa Shows That He Has a Human Teacher.

The great yogi Tilopa received two Buddha lineages, and four lineages of the realized yogins. Thus, he held six lineages. Among the Buddha lineages he received from Vajrayogini, mother of the Buddhas of the Three Times, was the hearing lineage teaching which was not recorded. This he received in Oddiyana in the North. He also received and realized the tantra of the secret mantra from Vajrapani at the Cemetery of the Burning Flame in the East. From the four yogins, he received the following teachings:

The Teachings of Arya Nagarjuna

In Bhalenta in the South at the time that Tilopa was a shepherd there, Nagarjuna was practicing with the aim of achieving the precious vase attainment. After he had done so, Tilopa came upon him and from him received the instructions of the clear light and illusory body from the father tantra of Guhyasamaja. Nagarjuna appointed Tilopa King of that area; so he was called Nada Tilo. Outside the kingdom were many non-believers, but within the kingdom everyone felt strong devotion for Tilopa. Riding an elephant and carrying a sword and shield, he struck all the trees, saying: "Enter the battle." At once, all the trees became soldiers, as did the grass and the bushes. Thus, those who formerly lacked devotion toward Tilopa developed deep trust. When there was an invasion of this country by Persians, Nada Tilo imbued his subjects with fearlessness. Climbing on a giant trunk, he radiated a bright light from his shield which blinded the entire army, along with their horses and elephants. When he raised his sword, men fled in every direction:

> Turn back the battle of Duruka,
> The shield and sword achieved their goal.

The Teachings of Lawapa

From Rolpai Dorje, a disciple of Lawapa, Tilopa received the instructions of Clear Light and Bardo from the teaching of Hevajra.

The Teachings of Luipa

Tilo received the entire Chakrasamvara teachings from the Nampar Gyalwa of the Luipa Lineage.

The Teachings of the Great Brahmin Saraha

Tilo received the entire Mahamudra teachings from Shawari. These are the lineage teachings received from the four yogins. Some say that from the Dakini Kalwazangmo he received the instructions of Karmamudra, Phowa, and Bardo from the *Dompa Gyatso Tantra*, and that from Acharya Charyawa he received the Tummo instructions, the practice of the ground, path and fruition from the *Chakrasamvara Tantra*.

Charyawa, Ludrub, Lawapa, and Kalwazangmo
Are the four Lamas of my lineage.

D. Achieving the Attainment of Residing in Heaven

In the East Tilopa became realized through pounding sesame seeds. He sang this song:

The ignorant do not know
That oil is the essence of the sesame seed;
Likewise, not knowing the branches of
interdependence,
They cannot extract their essence.
Just so, the co-emergent wisdom
Resides in the heart of all sentient beings;
Yet it cannot be realized
Unless it is pointed out by a Lama.
Pounding the shell of sesame
Releases its essence;
Likewise, the meaning of suchness
Is revealed by the Lama's instructions.
Transformed into one nature
Is the inseparability of all objects.
Kyeho! Marvelous it is to see clearly in this moment
The depth of meaning
For which others journey far.
There is no need for the antidote wisdom;
There is no path or stage to traverse;
There is no goal to achieve.

On hearing these teachings, a great assembly under the five Pantsapana leaders were liberated in a moment of the afflicting emotions, and all achieved the attainment of residing in Heaven. Thus, the entire place was emptied of inhabitants.

E. The Great Quality by Which Tilopa Overcame a Powerful Yogin

A King named Metok Lingpa requested on behalf of his

mother that all the Panditas and Yogins perform a ganachakra feast. They agreed that this was the highest path to accumulate virtue, and all attended and built the mandala. When a powerful yogi who was leading the assembly sat on the throne, a lady of ugly appearance arose from the midst of the yogins and pointing to him, said: "You cannot lead the meditation." The assembly asked: "Then who should lead?" She replied: "My brother." "Where is he now?" they asked. "He is in the Blazing Cemetery." The assembly set out to seek him, and found him swinging from the hair of a horse's tail which was suspended from the little toes of corpses piled on the branch of a tree. He was blue of appearance, with blood-shot eyes, wearing cotton undergarments. They requested that he come to the feast, and when he arrived he and the yogi sat together on the throne and began engaging in a contest. Each built a shrine for worship and then tried to destroy that of the other by his miracle powers. Tilopa succeeded in destroying the yogi's shrine, but the yogi could not destroy Tilopa's. Then both men manifested in many different forms, each carrying a corpse on its back. The corpses were then transformed into the materials of the ganachakra feast. Through his meditation, Tilopa transferred all his corpses to the cemetery, but the yogi could not do the same. Then Tilopa turned his body inside-out and from each pore manifested a palace of mandala deities, complete with cemeteries. He also manifested Jambudvipa in which there resided many Buddhas benefitting all sentient beings. Then, riding on snow lions, he brought the sun and moon down to earth and galloped over them. The Yogi could not match this feat, and so was roused to great devotion for Tilopa. Everyone asked: "Who is this amazing yogi?" Tilopa replied:

> I am Tilopa, the realized yogi,
> Free from effort in whatever I do.

Then he led the meditation, and the other yogi begged his

pardon, requesting the teachings. The powerful yogin Lodrö is now in the Oddiyana country.

F. Subduing the Heretics

Seeing a heretic doing harm to the Buddha's teaching, Tilopa said to himself: "It is time to subjugate this being." He therefore agreed to enter a debate whose outcome would determine which man's path would prevail. The king acted as mediator in this debate on language, logic and other subjects. As in the building and destroying of the mandala shrine, the heretic stopped the sun in its course and Ru (Tilopa) caused it to set. Then he halted the sun, but the heretic could not cause it to set. Ru said, "Cut your locks and enter my path." But the yogin became angry and radiated flames in his direction, saying:

> I can shake the three realms;
> There is no yogin I cannot terrify.

Tilo then manifested a larger flame, and sent both it and the heretic's fire back to him. Thus, the heretic's belongings were completely burned, even to his thick mane of hair.

> I am Tilopa,
> Who has achieved omniscience.

The heretic developed great devotion, and with all his disciples did prostrations, offering a mandala and requesting teachings. Thus the assembly were liberated. The heretic became known as Yogin Nakpo Kewa and thereafter resided in the Central Wood Forest Cemetery.

G. Meeting the Barmaid

Entering a tavern, Tilopa said, "Bring me some beer." The barmaid replied, "Give me some money first." Tilo drew a line where the rays of the setting sun fell on the ground, saying, "When the sun passes this line I will give you the money." As he drank the beer he transformed himself, sometimes into a cat, sometimes into different yogis, and sometimes back into his original form. In this way he drank the contents of seven cellars. When he was asked for the money again, he entered into samadhi and manifested enough casks of beer to replace all those which he had drunk. He then stayed the sun in its course, and all the beer was sold. In this way, the barmaid and her companions developed great devotion. Addressing Tilopa, she said:

> You are a precious being,
> So please allow us to be your disciples.

He then transmitted the Vajrayogini practice teachings, liberating the barmaid and other beings in that very life. From that day, the barmaid, who became known as Yogini Nyimai Öd, resided in Sosaling Cemetery.

H. Subduing the Magician

The King of Sosaling and the magician Rakya Dewa were enemies. The magician therefore sent a magic army to defeat the people surrounding the palace. The King, realizing he was the victim of sorcery, became alarmed and assembled his ministers to determine what to do. Just then, an ugly woman appeared among them, asking, "Why are you gathered here?" They replied, "We are trying to think of ways to end this war." She said, "I know what to do; let us go to the King." When she was in the King's presence, she suggested that he seek help from Tilopa. Through samadhi meditation, Tilopa emanated myriad armies who vanquished the enemy and arrested the magician. The magician said:

> Precious one, you rely on the teachings.
> Therefore, how can you wreak such destruction?

Tilopa replied:

> Killing magic beings is no sin
> Because they have no mind.

Thus, the magician developed devotion and requested the

teachings. From that day he became known as Yogin Luchye Denma and resided at Haha Cemetery.

I. Manifesting Numerous Forms

Tilopa manifested as a hunter and a butcher who, by his activities, caused the other hunters and butchers of the region to lose their means of livelihood. But having completely realized the ultimate, he knew there was nothing to kill.

J. Showing the Evident Cause and Effect

A heretic, holding the view of the Lokayatas (atheists of ancient India), was preaching this doctrine to all the people of the Rada country. A Buddhist scholar refuted his arguments, saying that cause and effect exist. But it could not be determined which of the two men was right because there was no judge present. When Tilopa arrived in the midst of the debate, the men asked him to act as judge. At the end, Tilopa said, "He who acknowledges cause and effect is the victor." The heretic then said, "I wish to debate with you." Tilopa defeated him by his extraordinary insights, and gave him the teachings. Then the heretic said, "Since I don't see cause and effect directly, I don't accept your doctrine. If it is true, please show me directly. Only then will I accept the Buddha's teachings." With a snap of the fingers, Tilopa showed the heretic the burning tortures of the hell realms. The heretic saw a copper pot filled with molten metal, but empty of human beings. He asked the guardian of hell, "Why are there no beings in this pot?" The man replied, "In the Rada country in Jambudvipa there is a heretic who doesn't believe in cause and effect, and who is creating negative karma by spreading wrong views. After his death we will cook him in this pot!" The heretic then said to Tilopa, "It may be true that one is born in hell through negative karma, but perhaps it is not necessary to engage in virtuous actions." Tilopa said, "Come, I will show you." In a moment Tilopa took him to the Heaven of the Thirty-Three Gods.

There, in each god's palace was a divine couple—a god and goddess. In one palace, however, was a goddess standing alone. The heretic asked, "Why has she no consort?" The goddess replied directly, "In Jambudvipa there is a being who is just now changing his view, understanding cause and effect, giving up non-virtuous action and practicing virtuous action. After his death, he will be reborn here." Thus, the heretic developed deep devotion. Tilopa said, "Sinful beings, motivated by negative karma, suffer the mental phenomena of hell, but virtuous beings, motivated by positive karma, enjoy the mental phenomena of the higher realms." He then gave the heretic the teachings and liberated him. From that day he became known as Yogin Dina, and resided in Palkyiri.

K. Subjugating the Butcher

A butcher was taking the lives of many animals and giving their meat to his son. Tilopa, seeing that it was time to tame him, transformed the meat into the cooked flesh of the butcher's son, meanwhile hiding the son himself. When the butcher took the lid off the cooking pot and saw his son's flesh, he began to weep. Tilopa said, "If you cease taking life, I will restore your son to you." The butcher agreed and Tilopa returned his son to him. The man purified his negative karma, promised not to engage in any further wrong action, and developed devotion. Tilopa gave him the teachings and liberated him, saying:

> The result of one's negative actions
> Will return to oneself.

In this way Tilopa chose him as a disciple. From that day the man became known as Yogin Dechye Gawa and resided in the land of the Rakshas.

L. Subjugating the Singer

Once there was a skillful singer who was in the habit of entertaining the assembled crowd. When Tilopa arrived he said to the man, "Why are you howling so?" The singer became angry and said, "Let us engage in a singing contest." The singer knew only worldly songs. With enlightened voice Tilopa sang many celestial songs. The singer developed deep devotion and asked to be his disciple:

> Where, precious one, do you come from?
> You have subjugated me.

Tilopa replied:

> I am the singer Tilopa
> Inhabiting the entire world of Brahma.
> I come here as a beauteous singer:
> Now I wander off, directionless.

Tilopa then gave him the teachings and liberated him. From that day the man became known as Yogin Yangdan, and resided in Nagara.

M. *Subjugating the Powerful One*

A man named Nyima was so powerful that he could bind all phenomena. Many people gathered about him, though they feared his power. Tilopa manifested pretended anger toward him, and in return the man cast a spell on him. Tilopa then killed the man's Dharma protectors and all his retinues. The man suffered so greatly that Tilopa looked on him with deep compassion, saying: "I am happy because I am the victor, but you are suffering because your retinues are dead. Yet others are suffering in the same way because of your negative actions. If you promise to stop engaging in negative karma, I have a way to restore the dead." The man agreed, and Tilopa brought back the consciousness of those who had been killed, restoring them to the man. Thus, he developed strong devotion. Tilopa said:

> I, the realized yogin Tilopa
> Have killed no one.

He then gave the man teachings and liberated him. From that day he became known as Yogin Nyida and resided in a city known as I Mi Tsundha.

II. APPEARING AS A MANIFESTATION OF CHAKRASAMVARA

Tilopa took the vows of a monk at the temple on the grounds of the Blazing Cemetery of Lakshetra, in the Ashoka garden, near the river Salanadi, because the Abbot there was his uncle and the Acharya his mother. He became known as the Bhikshu Kalapa. In the morning he meditated in a small hut; in the evening the monks gathered and said ritual prayers. Occasionally they had to do the monk's purification renewal practice, and were punished if they violated the discipline. Tilopa did the opposite: Early in the morning he killed a mass of locusts on the road, separated their heads from their bodies, and heaped them up in two piles; in the evening he went to a tavern and ate the barley residue left over from making beer. His uncle, Dawö Zhonnu, who was in charge of the monastery, could no longer tolerate such behavior. He and other monastery officials spoke privately to Tilopa and told him to cease his unconventional behavior. They also warned that if he missed the purification renewal practice he would be severely punished. But Tilopa went out and killed more locusts. At one point he was seen by the King who was journeying toward the monastery for ceremonial prayers. The King was so shocked that he asked, " Who is your Abbot and who your Acharya?" Tilopa replied:

> The place is the Ashoka garden.
> My uncle is Abbot and my mother Acharya.
> I am Bhikshu Kalapa.
> Many millions of kalpas ago
> I spoke with the victorious Shakyamuni,
> Nagarjuna, Aryadeva, and Vajradhara.
> I have travelled to a hundred Buddhafields
> And I have seen the one hundred faces of the Buddha.
> I have attained the blissful level
> And have understood the interdependence of cause and effect.
> I have realized the Dharmakaya of Dharmata.

Even the great Saraha
Cannot match my realization.
I have not killed any sentient beings.

Thus he sang, and with a snap of the finger caused all the locusts to spring to life and fly away in radiant light. Then everyone understood that Tilopa was an emanation of Chakrasamvara. He became widely known and everyone felt deep devotion for him.

III. APPEARING AS CHAKRASAMVARA HIMSELF

With gentle discipline Tilopa went out begging and saying prayers. Seeing him, King Dawa respectfully made offerings and asked him about his parents and other details. Tilopa said:

I am Tilopa,
Born in a family of Brahmins,
Without father or mother.
I have no Abbot or Acharya;
I am the self-born Buddha.
I have no spiritual master.
My knowledge of the arts of sound and logic
Is self-arisen.
I am inseparable from the body, speech, and wisdom mind
Of Chakrasamvara.

In this way it became widely known that he was Chakrasamvara himself.

IV. SHOWING HIMSELF AS THE EMBODIMENT OF ALL THE BUDDHAS

The King Metok Lingpa, who felt deep devotion, was accepted by Tilopa as a disciple and liberated. The King performed a great ganachakra offering, invited many panditas and practitioners, and built a mandala. When Tilopa asked to lead the assembly, the guests all entered into samadhi, each having a different view of Tilopa. When they asked who he really was, he answered, "I am exactly as each of you sees me."

My body is Hevajra;
My speech is Mahamaya;
My mind is Chakrasamvara;
My limbs are Dragyunakpo;
My fingers and toes are Vajrabhairava;
My channels are the four-seat vajra;
My winds are the vajra mala;
My drops are the secret treasure;
My ushnisha is Sangye Thöpa;
All these together are Kalachakra,
The great bliss Sangye Nyamjor.
My mind is co-emergent wisdom,
Self-arising in the first moment,
I am the unborn Buddha of the past.
Unceasing in the second moment,
I am the Buddha yet unborn and not-appearing.
Spontaneously established in the third moment,
I am the unborn Buddha of the present.
My pores are a limitless Buddhafield.
In these abide the body, speech and wisdom mind
Of the Buddhas of the Three Times.

He then proceeded to the Crest Ornament Monastery.

All the great yogins learned of his renown and realized him as the embodiment of the Buddhas of the Three Times. He became known as Prajnabadra. His secret name was Dechen Dorje (Vajra of Bliss). He was also known as Thog Med Dorje (Unobstructed Vajra), Dewai Khorlo (Wheel of Bliss), Kalapa, and Tilopa.

Naropa (*1016-1100*)

There are four aspects to the life of the great saint Naropa, the heart-son of Tilopa:

I. the outer aspect: enduring the hardship of searching for the outer prophecy, he is recognized as a proper vessel;
II. the inner aspect: enduring the hardship of the inner practice, he reveals the meaning of the signs;
III. the secret aspect: enduring the hardship of offering the cherished body, he kindles the light of bliss; and
IV. the ultimate aspect: enduring the hardship of obeying orders, he achieves the result.

I. THE OUTER ASPECT

The first, or outer aspect, consists of two parts: (A) the quality of the proper vessel, and (B) the explanations to realize the superior qualities.

A. *The Quality of the Proper Vessel*

In the town of Zambu at Shrinagara lived the King Shiwai Gocha and the Queen Palgyi Lodrö, who had a daughter, Palgyi Yeshe. Since they had no son, they prayed and made

offerings to the Triple Gem and others. Finally, a son was born to them whom they showed to the sign readers. The sign readers said:

> This one is like the son of Suddhodana;
> If he stays in the world,
> He will become the lord of humans;
> If he renounces the world,
> He will achieve enlightenment and the two accumulations
> In this lifetime.

And so he was named Prince Kuntu Sangpo. As he grew older, he asked his parents' permission to become a monk, but they refused his wish. In reply, the Prince said:

> Whatever we do, if it is done without Dharma
> It becomes a source of suffering.
> Therefore I go to obtain the precious Teachings.

He then journeyed to Kashmir, to study with the master Arya Akasha, and received the lay (upasaka) ordination. Thus he was called Upasaka Akashagarbha. In Kashmir he studied the Dharma and was well trained in the five aspects of knowledge [creative arts, medicine, language and sound, logic, and metaphysics or inner meaning]. But this displeased his father who wished him to marry. He said, "What is the use of Dharma if one disobeys one's parents?" The Prince replied, "All the six realms of sentient beings are our natural parents, not just one or two beings. But if you find a lady of deep intuition and pure discipline, devoid of the faults of heretics and learned in the teachings of the Mahayana family, let me know." The King sent his ministers searching in all directions for such a person and at last, in Eastern Bengal, they found a maiden, the daughter of the Brahmin Kargyal, Brahmin Drimedma, who possessed the necessary qualities. They therefore requested her hand. But the Brahmin Kargyal said, "We Brahmins, though considered heretics, nonetheless are possessed of great compassion, whereas your king, though a Buddhist, sometimes engages in evil deeds and shows less compassion than we. Therefore I will not grant you my daughter's hand." But the King's Minister insisted, and finally the Brahmin agreed.

The maiden was brought to the kingdom and the two were married, but after a time the Prince became so sad that he said:

> Worldly life is filled with limitless faults;
> Therefore, I must renounce it.

He made his feelings known to the Princess, and she agreed not to be an obstacle in his path. At the Happy Garden Monastery the Prince took the vows of a novice monk from Khenpo Sangye Kyab and Master Yeshe Öd. And so he was called Sangye Yeshe. Later, he was fully ordained in Kashmir by the Abbot of Surgang, Chökyi Lama, and the teacher Chökyi Yeshe, and by the Secret Master Chökyi Changchub. And so he became known as Chökyi Gyaltsen. From there, he went to Pullahari Monastery where he stabilized his study and practice. There he was called Netan Tanpa Zinpa (Holder of the Teachings).

At Nalanda he was appointed Northern Gatekeeper upon the passing of Khenpo Nyimai Dorje. Whenever he debated with heretics, he emerged victorious:

> The evil debater
> Who searches for the relative meaning
> Will be grasped with an iron hook.
> The sword of the knowledge of sound and logic
> Cuts the root of the evil debater,
> And the trusty lamp of the Buddha's Teachings
> Dispels the darkness of the evil debater's ignorance.
> The wheel device of the pith instructions
> Destroys the city of illusion;
> The supreme jewel of the three noble vows
> Purifies the stain of wrong action.
> Sharpen the sword of wisdom
> Before the great scholar-king in Nalanda;

Cut the root of the tree of heretics;
Plant the victory banner of the Buddha's Teachings.

And so he was called Jigme Trakpa (Renowned Fearless One).

At Nalanda University he became Chancellor and gave teachings and monastic vows, as well as meditation instruction. One day there appeared a woman with thirty-two ugly signs—brown hair standing on end, a bulbous forehead, wrinkled and pitted face, coarse eyelashes, bloodshot, watery eyes, flat nose, twisted, gaping mouth, pendulous lips and buckteeth, lolling tongue, goiter, pendulous ears, coarse, green skin, trembling, gnarled hands, and a hump on her back. Sneezing and yawning, crying and laughing, limping and leaning on a walking stick, she asked, "Do you know the words of the Dharma, or the meaning of the Dharma?" Naropa replied, "I know the meaning," and the woman wept. Then he said, "I know the words of the Dharma," and she laughed with joy. Then he asked, "Who understands the meaning of the Dharma?" She replied, "My brother." He said, "Please take me to him." She said, "Pray, meditate and search." With this she disappeared.

By seeing this woman of the thirty-two ugly signs, he understood the thirty-two negative qualities of samsara in their outer, inner and secret aspects. By outer aspect it is meant that the thirty-two subtle and gross causes and effects of samsara give samsara the nature of suffering; by inner aspect it is meant that there are thirty-two impure components to the body; by secret aspect it is meant that in the thirty-two channels of the body there are thirty-two vital energies. Through meditation on these, one can achieve the co-emergent wisdom. Realizing the truth and its opposite, he said:

The mind, deluded by the appearance of samsara,
Sees the faults of others with the senses.
It is darkened by the prison of samsara;
It is made intolerable by the fire of samsara;

It is caught in the spider web of samsara;
It is stuck in samsara as the bee is in nectar;
It is encased in samsara like a silkworm in a cocoon.
There is no substance to the hollow tree of samsara.
Samsara is like the moon's reflection in water,
Without essence;
Samsara is like an animal chasing a mirage;
He who desires samsara falls into a pit.
Samsara is like being trapped in the jaws of a
crocodile;
Samsara is like wandering in the land of the rakshas;
Samsara is like a poisonous snake which destroys
anyone who sees or touches it;
Samsara is bordered by the precipice of karma;
Samsara is like a wave in water, or fog;
Samsara is tied by the lasso of karma;
Samsara is bound by the seal of karma;
Samsara is the density of darkness;
Samsara is the deep mud of the three poisons;
Samsara is the dance of impermanence;
Samsara is the enchantment of this life;
Samsara is the shadow of birth and death;
Samsara is a merciless hunter;
Samsara is snared by the hound of death;
Samsara is a vast, sorrowful field of grasping and
fixation;
Samsara is the galloping horse of the eight worldly
dharmas;
Samsara is caught by the iron hook of desire;
Why should I not search for the Lama
While I have this precious, impermanent body?

Thus he gave away all his treasures, his Dharma texts and other belongings, saying: "Now I will search for the perfect Lama." But his three pandita friends, who were also gatekeepers of Nalanda University, requested that he remain. The Western Gatekeeper, Jetari Trale Namgyal, said:

The root of the teachings
Is the community of the sangha;
In giving up the community,
The teachings disappear.
Please remain with us.

The Eastern Gatekeeper, Pangyakara Gupta, said:

The root of Dharma
Is the morality of the community;
In giving up morality,
The teachings disappear.
Please remain with us.

The Southern Gatekeeper, Nakpo Tulshuk, said:

The root of the teachings
Is the friend vowed to discipline;
In giving up friendship,
The Dharma disappears.
Please remain with us.

Then the five hundred panditas of Nalanda with one voice requested:

We are ignorant, uncomprehending,
Without the great scholar-physician of Dharma.
Therefore, blessed Jigme Trakpa [Naropa]
Remain here for our sakes.

Thus they requested. Naropa replied:

The end of birth is death;
The end of meeting is parting.
All accumulation is consumed.
Therefore, how can I find a path without death?
One may be trained in sound, logic and various commentaries,
Schooled in the five aspects of knowledge,
Learned in the ocean of teachings.
But without a qualified Lama

One cannot quench the suffering of one's thirst.
The essence blessing of ambrosia
Of the ocean of tantras
Does not satisfy one's mind
Without the attainment of the Lama's blessing.
Even with the quality of miracles, psychic powers and such
One cannot see the ultimate meaning.
Therefore, whatever happens,
I will search for the holy Lama
With the help of Hevajra.

Thus, he refused their request.

I search for the Lama
By renouncing the meaningless activities of this life.

Wearing his robes and carrying a staff and begging bowl, he set out towards the East. Suddenly, a celestial voice was heard:

There will be a prophecy
Of the Lama Buddha
With the help of Chakrasamvara.
Go, there you will find the Lama Buddha.

On hearing this he said:

Henceforth, why should I not do Chakrasamvara practice?

So he built a grass hut at the Flower Cloth Cemetery. After he had recited the seven-syllable mantra of Chakrasamvara[1] seven hundred thousand times, the earth shook, lights radiated, pleasant odors filled the air, and other miracles occurred. Two Dakinis appeared (some say in a dream, some say directly) and prophesied:

Search in the East for the Lama Buddha Tilopa;
This Lord of non-duality, bliss-wisdom,

---

[1] OM HRI HA HA HUM HUM PHAT

This Lord of sentient beings,
This emanation of Chakrasamvara
Will be found there.

By this prediction he realized that Tilopa was his Lama for seven lifetimes. So he said: "Why should I not search for the prophesied Lama?" He then searched for Tilopa for one month, but could not find him, so he said:

I could not find the prophesied Lama Buddha,
I must be deceived by maras.

Again he heard a celestial sound which said:

Search for the Lama.
You will find him
If you do not remain in the mara of laziness.

So he continued his search, enduring the twelve lesser hardships:

1. Travelling along a narrow precipice between a rocky place and a river, he encountered a leprous woman. "Please step aside," he said, and she replied:

All is inseparable and unending,
Without boundary or conception.
With thoughts of clean and unclean
You cannot find the Lama.

So saying, she disappeared with a snap of the fingers and Naropa fell unconscious. When he regained consciousness, there was no precipice or leprous woman to be found.

2. He then wandered into a desert where he saw a dog whose body was crawling with maggots. As the dog blocked the road, he stepped over him, and the dog said:

All the sentient beings of the six realms
Have the nature of one's parents.
Without cultivating great compassion
And entering into the Mahayana path
You cannot find the Lama, even if you search.

He said, "How is this true?" The dog replied:

> You cannot find the Lama
> As long as you regard others as inferior.

With this he disappeared.

3. Continuing his search, Naropa met a man pounding another's head. He asked: "Have you seen Tilopa?" The man replied, "Please help me to pound this man's head and I will tell you." Naropa thought, "I cannot pound the head of a man," and he refused. The man said, "In the teachings on great compassion, if one does not pound the head of ego with the hammer of egolessness, one cannot find the Lama," and with a snap of the fingers he disappeared.

4. Again Naropa continued his search. This time he met a man pulling out the intestines of another and chopping them with a sword. He asked, "Have you seen Tilopa?" The man replied, "Help me to chop these and I will tell you." When Naropa refused, the man said:

> If, with the sword of unborn Dharmata,
> You don't cut the continuous intestine of samsara,
> You cannot find the Lama.

With this he disappeared.

5. Naropa continued his search, and meeting a man cleaning the inside of another's body, he asked, "Have you seen Tilopa?" The man replied, "Help me with this cleaning and I will tell you." Naropa refused and the man said:

> If, with the continuity of the profound teaching,
> You don't wash the impurity of mind's thought
> To achieve self-liberation from samsara,
> You cannot find the Lama.

With this he disappeared.

6. Naropa continued his search, asking some people he met along the road if they had seen Tilopa. They replied,

"Go and ask the King." When he did so, the King replied, "Marry my daughter and become my subject." Naropa accepted the King's daughter, who later left him and went on her way. Naropa became angered and cast a spell from the fifty-first chapter of the Chakrasamvara teaching, whereupon a celestial voice was heard saying:

> Aversion and hatred,
> Dependent on desire,
> Were born in the lower realms.
> How can you find the Lama?
> Are you not deceived by the illusory being?

The kingdom then disappeared.

7. When Naropa continued his search, he met some ladies and asked them if they had seen Tilopa. They replied, "There is a hunter in the mountain forest. Ask him." There, he saw many wild animals and met a black-skinned hunter who was chasing them with bow and arrow. Feeling great compassion for the animals, Naropa said:

> Plant the OM on the hunter's bow.[1]

The man explained his kind of hunt:

> The arrow of the non-attachment illusory body
> Is drawn from the bow of the clear light experience.
> On the mountain of the self-cherishing body,
> In the forests of samsara-habit,
> I, the hunter, wish to kill
> The wild beast of grasping and fixation.
> Tomorrow I will go down to the city and beg.

With this he disappeared. Naropa thought: "Tomorrow Tilopa will appear in the city."

8. Naropa continued his search, going to the city where he asked for Tilopa. The people replied, "We do not know him,

---

[1] meaning that the bow should be prevented from acting as a weapon

but there is a beggar inside that hut named Tilopa," and they pointed out a man to him who was burning lice in a fire. Naropa circumambulated him and did prostrations, asking, "Are you Tilopa? Please accept me as your disciple and give me the teachings." Tilopa replied:

> For all the sentient beings of the three realms
> In the pervasive path of Dharmata
> The concept of lice arises.
> Self-born and self-nurturing,
> If you do not kill such lice,
> How can you find the Lama?
> I am the fisherman Gyatso.

With this he disappeared.

9. Naropa thought he might find Tilopa near a river, so he journeyed on, meeting two elderly householders plowing the field. Their two sons were gathering up ants from the ground, and the woman was fishing. When Naropa asked if they had seen Tilopa they replied, "First, it is the hour to eat, so let us prepare food." The woman cooked a fish and offered it to him, but Naropa refused to eat it. With a snap of the fingers the old lady caused the fish to fly up in the air and said:

> If you do not eat the fish-like afflicting emotion of thoughts,
> Which run after enjoyment,
> How can you find the unborn Lama?
> It is hard to have a Lama
> When the mind is bound by thought.
> I depart now to kill my parents.

With this she disappeared. Naropa thought, "Perhaps tomorrow I will meet someone who is killing his parents."

10. Naropa was determined to continue his search, whether or not he found the teacher. On the way, he met a man who was impaling his father with a stick and locking his mother in a dungeon. When he asked the man about Tilopa, the man replied, "If you help me to kill my parents, I will then help

you." When Naropa refused, thinking such an action would create heavy negative karma, the man said:

> If you do not kill the parents of grasping and fixation
> Which are the cause of birth in the ocean of samsara,
> How can you ever find the Lama, even if you search?
> I depart now to watch the spectacle.

With this he disappeared. Naropa thought, "Tomorrow I will see a man watching a spectacle."

11. Naropa continued his search. In a country inhabited by one-eyed men, he saw corpses fanning themselves, blind men peering, deaf men hearing, dumb men speaking, and lame men running. When he asked one of the one-eyed men if he had seen Tilopa, the man replied, "Generally, I have not seen Tilopa. If you truly wish to search for him, attend the lineage Lama in your heart."

> In the proper vessel of the devoted disciple
> Devotion and confidence should grow within the mind
> And raise the sword of the realized view.
> The meditation horse of bliss and clarity gallops;
> The action knot of grasping and fixation is loosened;
> The sun of self-clarity grows warmer.
> Blaze the fire of the great bliss experience
> And look on the realization of the wish-fulfilling gem.
> The dumb speak, saying nothing;
> The deaf hear, understanding nothing;
> The blind see, perceiving nothing;
> The lame run, standing still;
> And the lifeless unborn ones fan themselves,
> Creating the wind without basis.
> The one eye is the single taste of all.

In this way he manifested the signs of Mahamudra. Naropa, not understanding his meaning, thought of asking to be his disciple, but the man disappeared.

12. Again Naropa continued his search, this time in a mountain known as Awakara in Parata Gyen. Although he met these emanations of the Lama, he grew discouraged, thinking: "I have not seen the Lama because of my negative tendencies which have not been purified." And he sang this lament:

> Though following the prophecy of the Dakinis
> And giving up the place
> Where the root of all the teachings is,
> Separating from friends who have the three vows
> And disregarding the advice of my counsellors,
> I have not found the Lama, even by enduring mental suffering.
> This body is creating obstacles.
> Therefore why not search for the Lama
> By giving up this body?

With this he raised his sword and tried to kill himself. But from the sky a voice spoke:

> By killing the Buddha
> How can you find the Lama?
> Mendicant, perhaps I am the being you seek.

Naropa looked into the sky and wept. Overcome with emotion, he folded his hands at his heart and said:

> Like a cloud in the sky, you are always changing.
> I, though searching, could not find the precious one.
> Alas! Will you not look on me with compassion?
> Allow me to follow you.

Tilopa replied, "From the beginning I have followed you like a shadow. But because of your obscurations you did not see me. Your name will be Drime Ziji (Stainless Dignity).

> You, Drime Ziji,
> Are the wish-fulfilling tantra,
> The secret teaching of the Dakinis.
> Now you have become a proper vessel for the precious instructions.

Thus he spoke, and chose him as his disciple. Then Tilopa gave him the Nine Teachings of the Formless Dakinis which are the great qualities of the family of the proper vessel.

B. The Four Explanations to Realize the Superior Qualities

1) Vajradhara Explains Non-returning:

The sign of bliss
Showing the source of bliss,
That which shows the path of enlightenment
To all sentient beings,
The Lord of beings,
Possessor of the eye of Dharma
Is non-returning.

2) Explanation by the Yidam Deity:

At midnight in the Pullahari Monastery, Chakrasamvara said:

The Lama (Naropa) is like a great tree
Which has the nature of the unborn body;
He is attended by disciples, like birds.
Naropa possesses the unborn body.
The Lama is like a great river
Which is the stream of the stainless teaching;
He purifies the stain of afflicting emotions.
Naropa possesses the inexpressible speech.
The Lama is like space
Which is like the sun of wisdom,
Free from obscuration.
He dispels the darkness of all sentient beings.
Naropa possesses the non-conceptual mind.

3) The Lama Also Explains the Disciple as a Proper Vessel:

All the disciples of Tilopa then asked, "You are a great saint, immaterial like a cloud in the sky. Therefore, whom should one attend if one searches for peace?" Tilopa said:

Naropa, unforgetting recollection,
Attended me during twelve hardships;
He has my suchness.
The future searcher of teachings
Will attend Naropa
If he wishes to have the realizations.

4) Naropa, Himself, Explains the Self-liberated One

The path of Mahamudra
Not objectified in the mind,
Free from elaboration and inexpressible,
Realizes the primordial wisdom
With the unobstructed mind.
Because of this
There is no need to ask anyone.
I am the self-liberated yogin,
The appearance of nonduality.

This ends the outer aspect, in which Naropa was recognized as a proper vessel by enduring the hardship of searching for the outer prophecy.

II. THE INNER ASPECT

Enduring the hardships of practice, Naropa reveals the meaning of the signs. The inner aspect has two parts: (A) opening the maturing path empowerment, and (B) kindling the light of method of the liberation path.

A. *Opening the Maturing Path Empowerment*

Sitting on an empty plain, Tilopa began pounding pegs into the ground. He remained silent, his mind in the nondual state. Naropa did prostrations, circumambulated him, and making mandala offerings requested instruction. Tilopa then manifested thirteen signs whose meaning Naropa understood and explained:

To the Lama, who is like a precious gem,
One should have unchanging faith and devotion.

One's mind should be clear as a crystal,
And drink the stream of the stainless instructions,
Loosening the knot of the eight dharmas of this life.
Many water vessels have but one taste;
Appearances are like a rainbow,
Without real substance.
The Dharmakara is unborn;
The reflection in the mirror is emptiness-bliss.
The Dharmakaya drop exists in oneself;
The knot is free from expression, thought and speech;
The dumb explain details without words;
The tree ripens the fruit naturally.

Tilopa said:

You explain the thirteen knots of signs.
You are a being who understands the signs,
The wish-fulfilling gem of the secret Tantra,
The secret teachings of the Dakinis.
Look at the mirror of wisdom teachings,
The empowerment which ripens those who are not ripe.

Naropa said:

How can I, who am blind, see,
Obscured as I am by the darkness of ignorance?

Tilopa replied:

Look on that which cannot be seen.
In the nature of the unseen
Liberate those without liberation.
The yogin will be liberated
By seeing the meaning.

Naropa said:

Retrieve the precious gem of the mind
From the ocean of samsara
By depending on the ship of the Lama.

Seeing the maturing path
I, the yogin, am happy.

Tilopa, seeing that Naropa was attached to the teachings, said:

The instructions are only a sign,
Leading to yet greater happiness.
Do not be attached to the teachings of the Lama.

Tilopa then gave the vase empowerment to Naropa's body, showing the contents and container as the mandala of the enlightened deities, or as appearance without existence. He then gave empowerment to his speech and showed undefiled bliss. He next gave the wisdom empowerment to his mind and showed the self-awareness co-emergent wisdom. He finally gave the empowerment to the three gates and showed the inexpressible mahamudra. Setting fire to the edge of a piece of cloth, he caused the entire cloth to go up in flames. When he asked Naropa if he understood, Naropa replied, "In one moment the Third Wisdom Empowerment burned the afflicting emotions of samsara as a flame does a piece of cloth."

So Naropa was liberated by developing non-attachment. At this time he said:

The meaning of empowerment,
Like the spark of a fire,
Burns the cloth of afflicting emotion.
I am content.

B. Kindling the Light of Method of the Liberation Path

By undergoing the twelve major hardships, Naropa receives the teachings.

1. Jumping from the roof of the Otantra temple, Tilopa said, "If you want teachings, come after me. If I had a disciple, he would jump from this roof." Naropa thought, "He must be telling me I should jump." When he landed, he

felt intense pain. Hearing his moans, Tilopa said, "What has happened to you?" Naropa replied:

> This clay pot of a body, fully ripened,
> This broken vessel is like a corpse.

Tilopa said:

> This clay pot of a body, self-cherishing,
> May be broken, Naropa.
> Look at the mirror of the mind
> Through the lineage
> Of the wish-fulfilling gem of the Secret Tantra,
> The Secret Teachings of the Dakinis.

At this time he was given the wish-fulfilling gem of the teachings of the four lineages. On these he meditated one year.

2. Naropa made an offering again, did prostrations and requested further teachings. Tilopa said, "Come after me," and Naropa followed. Tilopa then asked him to jump into three giant loads of burning sandalwood which were heaped up. When Naropa emerged from the fire badly burned, Tilopa asked, "What has happened to you?" Naropa replied:

> The wheel of the sandalwood fire
> Brings pain to the body, inseparable from the flame.

Tilopa said:

> The fuel of the body of self-cherishing
> May be burned, Naropa.
> Look at the mirror of the samaya mind,
> The wish-fulfilling gem of the Secret Tantra,
> The Secret Teachings of the Dakinis.

At this time he was given the instructions of the wish-fulfilling samaya. On these he meditated for one year.

3. Naropa again requested further teachings and Tilopa said, "Make a bridge with your body over this river filled with

leeches." Naropa obeyed so that Tilopa could cross the river, but he fell into the water. Tilopa said, "What happened to you?" Naropa replied:

I fell into the water;
Leeches go through my body,
Therefore I suffer, without any choice.

Tilopa said:

The river of body-cherishing
May be drowned, Naropa.
Look at the mirror of the common mind,
The wish-fulfilling gem of the Secret Tantra,
The Secret Teachings of the Dakinis.

At this time he was given the complete teachings of the generating-arising process.

4. After one year Naropa again requested further teachings and Tilopa said, "If you need teachings, bring me a bamboo stick, fire and oil." Tilopa then poured oil on the bamboo, heated the stick in the fire, and pierced Naropa's body in many places. When Naropa cried out in pain, Tilopa said, "What has happened to you?" and Naropa replied:

This body is composed of the knot of grasping and fixation.
Therefore I suffer.

Tilopa said:

The knot of this karmically ripened body
May be destroyed, Naropa.
The Secret Teachings of the Dakinis
Are the wish-fulfilling Tantra.
Look in the mirror of the mental heat and bliss.

At this time he was given the complete instructions for Tummo.

5. After one year Naropa again requested further teachings, and Tilopa, who was residing in a cave, told him,

"Bring me cooked rice." Naropa went off and begged rice from a family entertaining a large company of guests. When he returned and offered it, Tilopa smacked his lips with pleasure, ate heartily, and said, "Bring me more." Naropa said, "They may not give me more." In reply Tilopa gave him a mirror, a chain, a vase filled with water, and a pot, with the instructions, "If they are unwilling to give you more, take it by force." Naropa returned to the same place and saw that the guests had gone outside. Entering the empty house, he came upon a pot of rice which looked even more delicious than that which he had been given before. This he took away with him.

Seeing what he was doing, the guests chased him. But Naropa threw the mirror at them, which was transformed into a lake, separating him from the angry throng. When they continued to follow in their boats, he threw the chain at them, which was transformed into a mighty mountain. Still, the people followed him, climbing the mountain. He then threw the vase of water at them, which was transformed into an enormous river. But the crowd crossed the river. Then he threw the pot at them, which was transformed into an iron hut in which he hid himself. Unable to enter, the people built a sandalwood fire around the hut. When the heat became intolerable, Naropa left the hut and the people fell upon him, beating him fiercely. Just then Tilopa appeared, saying, "What has happened to you?" Naropa replied:

I have been pounded like rice
And squeezed like a mustard seed.
Therefore I suffer.

The copper of this karmically ripened body
May be beaten, Naropa.
The Secret Teachings of the Dakinis
Are the wish-fulfilling Tantra.
Look in the mirror of the mental dream.

At this time Naropa was given the instructions of the dream which is the self-clarifying confusion.

Tilopa said:

6. After a year Naropa again requested further teachings. Just then a Princess was carried past in a sedan chair, and Tilopa asked Naropa to pull her down and drag her about. When he did so, the King's ministers fell on him, beating him nearly senseless. Tilopa said, "What has happened to you?" Naropa replied:

The minister, like an artist lacking compassion,
Grinds me to powder as he would his paint.
Therefore I suffer.

Tilopa replied:

This mountain of a self-cherishing body
May be broken, Naropa.
The Secret Teachings of the Dakinis
Are the wish-fulfilling Tantra.
Look at the mirror of the unchanging object.

At this time Naropa was given the instructions of entering into the Phowa Trong-jug siddhi.[1]

7. After one year Naropa requested further teachings and followed Tilopa onto an empty plain where a man was carrying a load on his back. Tilopa commanded Naropa, "Chase this man and beat him." When Naropa tried to obey, he found that the man kept retreating like a mirage. Seeing Naropa's exhaustion, Tilopa said, "What has happened to you?" Naropa replied:

I am like an animal chasing a mirage.
Chasing that which does not exist, I suffer.

Tilopa said:

The continuity of the three realms of samsara
May be cut, Naropa.
The Secret Teachings of the Dakinis

---

[1] consciousness transference

Are the wish-fulfilling Tantra.
Look in the mirror of complete liberation from
illusion.

At this time Naropa was given all the instructions of the illusory body, the self-liberating eight worldly dharmas, and other teachings.

8. After a year Naropa requested further teachings. Tilopa said, "Follow me." While they were on the road there appeared a Minister leading his bride on an elephant. "Abduct the bride and drag her on the ground," Tilopa said. "Then I will give you the teachings." When Naropa had carried out Tilopa's order, the Minister beat him almost to the point of death. As Naropa lay on the ground crying out in pain, Tilopa appeared, blessed him, and dispelled his suffering.

9. After a year Naropa made a mandala offering and requested further teachings. Tilopa said, "If you want the teachings, follow me." When they reached an empty plain, Naropa saw a richly adorned Prince riding a chariot which was guarded by many soldiers. Tilopa said, "Steal the Prince's ornaments and pull him from his chariot by the hair. Then I will give you the teachings." When Naropa obeyed, the Prince's guards fell on him with arrows and stones. When Naropa was near the point of death, Tilopa appeared, blessed him, and dispelled all his suffering.

10. After a year Naropa made a mandala offering and requested further teachings. Tilopa said, "Seek a consort and I will give you the teachings." Naropa found a beautiful woman of devoted temperament with whom he lived happily for a time, but later she made many difficulties for him. Tilopa appeared and asked, "Does all go well with you?" Naropa replied:

I suffer, laboring constantly
Under the grasping and fixation
Of dual appearance.

Tilopa said:

In the non-duality of samsara and nirvana
Labor may exist, Naropa.

11. After a year Naropa requested further teachings. Tilopa said, "If you want the teachings, offer me your consort." Naropa obeyed, but the woman showed her attachment for Naropa by giving him a sideways glance. Making a show of anger, Tilopa beat the woman, but still Naropa remained tireless in his devotion. Nor did there arise in him wrong view; indeed, the merit of offering his consort to Tilopa caused him to rejoice. Tilopa asked, "Does all go well with you?" Naropa replied:

Without expectations
I offer the wisdom consort
To the Lama Buddha.
Therefore I, the yogin, rejoice.

Tilopa said:

In the great path of Dharma-as-Such
It is well to be happy, Naropa.

III. THE SECRET ASPECT

Enduring the hardship of offering the cherished body, Naropa kindles the light of bliss. The secret aspect has two parts: (A) blazing the light of bliss, the twelfth trial; and (B) blazing the light of stainlessness.

A. *Blazing the Light of Bliss*

12. After enduring these major sufferings for twelve years, Naropa made a mandala offering and requested further teachings. Journeying to a place shrouded by a dust storm, he settled the debris with his own blood and made an offering heap of his eyes, nose, tongue and limbs. Then Tilopa appeared and asked him, "Do you fare well, Naropa?" Naropa replied:

The mandala of this contaminated body
Is offered to the Lama.
I, the yogi, fare well.

Tilopa said:

The contaminated, essenceless body
May be offered, Naropa.
The Secret Teachings of the Dakinis
Are the wish-fulfilling Tantra.
Look in the mirror of the nondual mind.

Naropa said:

I am blinded by the darkness of ignorance;
How can I see?

Tilopa replied:

Look at that which cannot be seen.
Within the unseen
The yogi, seeing the meaning, is self-liberated.

After going through the twelve hardships, Naropa was given the Phowa teachings. Until this time he had experienced only minor sufferings. Hereafter, he experienced no mental suffering, thus becoming like Sadaprarudita.

B. Blazing the Stainless Light

Naropa remained within that which cannot be seen and was liberated within the unseen. Offering his realization to Tilopa, he said:

The precious gem of the mind
Depends on the vessel of the Lama.
Liberated from the ocean
Of the Three Realms of samsara,
I, the yogin, fare well,
Seeing the meaning of nonduality.

Realizing that Naropa was attached to the substance of the teachings, Tilopa said:

> The method of proceeding
> From joy to greater joy
> Is to be unattached
> To the substance of the Lama's teaching.

Naropa replied:

> Liberated in the unseen by non-grasping,
> Burning the cloth of afflicting emotions
> With the spark of nonduality,
> I fare well.

Thus he achieved the effortless Mahamudra realization, the twelve interdependent links and their reverse order.

IV. THE ULTIMATE ASPECT

Enduring the hardship of disobeying orders, Naropa achieves the result. The ultimate aspect consists of two parts: (A) directly achieving the realization of the fruit, and (B) receiving the prophecy of the Lama.

A. *Directly Achieving the Realization of the Fruit*

Naropa received all the teachings, did prostrations, and departed.

One day Tilopa appeared in the sky and said:

> By sitting, the blind cannot see form;
> By sitting, the dumb cannot speak;
> By sitting, the deaf cannot hear;
> By sitting, the lame cannot walk;
> By sitting, the root of the tree cannot remain stable;
> By sitting, one cannot realize Mahamudra.

Naropa understood that he must now put the teachings into action. Taking up an empty skullcup, he set out to beg. On the road he met a child who was expert in reading the signs.

This child gave him a burning sword. When Naropa put the sword in his skullcup, it melted and he ate it. Everyone was amazed and the news travelled until it reached King Dawang. To test Naropa and see if he were truly a realized yogi, the king caused a large army to advance on him. Making the threatening mudra, Naropa destroyed the entire force. The King then sent a drunken, raging elephant to Naropa, which Naropa also killed with the threatening mudra. As the King and the entire country mourned the death of the elephant, Naropa asked that a hole be dug in which to place the beast. Through the practice of phowa siddhis, he then caused his consciousness to enter the elephant's body, thus ending the sadness of the people. In this way his fame spread in all directions, and the King, offering him his daughter, reverently requested the teachings.

When Naropa engaged in hunting and other activities, the King said, "I will provide you with whatever you need, so please cease hunting." But Naropa refused to listen. The monks of Shravaka told the King, "If you continue to make Naropa the object of your reverence, we will go elsewhere." So the King allied himself with the monks and agreed to persecute Naropa. First, however, they asked the King's daughter to leave, but when she refused to do so they bound her to Naropa with cords. They then hurled weapons at the two, shouting curses at them, and hitting them with hammers. The crowd even made a fence of swords and wheels around them and created a sandalwood fire, but Naropa and his consort, unaffected, began dancing.

After seven days, when everyone thought that Naropa and the Princess must be destroyed even to their bones, they went to check. But the two were floating in space in union in the Heruka form, holding the bell and vajra, having the nature of the rainbow body. Naropa said:

> The wheel of sandal fire
> Helps to burn the tree trunk of ego;
> The wheel of weapons
> Helps to cut the continuous rope of samsara;

The wheel of harsh words
Helps to build the armor of patience;
The knot of the karma of hatred
Helps to loosen the knot of the three poisons;
The hammer of morality
Helps to pound the demon of ego.
Taking the life of others carelessly,
If not against the three vows
And not a cause to be born in the lower realms,
Is the great company of Naropa's action.

The King then had a dream in which he fell through a crack in the earth to a hell-realm where he stayed for many years.

Shot by the bow of the eight worldly dharmas,
The arrow of the Lama
Sent me to the three lower realms.
This I saw in my dream.
I beg the pardon of the Lama for my errors.
Just as King Ashoka purified his negative karma,
So do I ask to be forgiven my intolerable error.

The life of King Ashoka clarifies the meaning of King Dawang's dream. The latter asked Naropa, "What was the most meritorious action King Ashoka performed in his life?" And Naropa replied, "In a single morning he built ten million stupas consecrated by ten million arahats, containing ten million relics of the Buddha." The King then asked, "And what is the heaviest negative karma one can perform?" His teacher said, "To divide the sangha, burn temples, or let the mind be burned by the fire of grasping and fixation; also, to show disrespect toward the Lama, revile him, use the wealth of the sangha wrongly, divide the country, gain one's livelihood by selling precious texts, and decline the antidote of wrong view. All these constitute the most negative actions, which will cause one to be reborn in the hell realms for seventy-two thousand, five hundred kalpas. Those who are realized or are dumb, or who act for a purpose, or who are subject to forces greater than they experience less negative results. He also explained how negative karma can be purified: Abandon your attachment to country, purify negative karma, and realize the meaning of the unborn.

King Dawang again begged Naropa's forgiveness for his behavior, saying, "The result of my actions appeared in my dream. So I beg forgiveness for all my faults. Please consent to purify me." Naropa replied:

> Loosen the knot of this life's eight dharmas;
> Annihilate the forces of darkness and ignorance;
> Dry the mind of the three poisonous samsaras;
> Kindle the wisdom light of the regretful mind;
> Confess in the unborn state.

Thus, by Naropa's blessing, King Dawang was liberated. This was the accomplishment of performing the action.

B. Receiving the Prophecy of the Lama

Tilopa appeared in the sky saying:

> Not being accepted by the Lama and Dakinis,
> Not developing the experience and realization,
> Not being liberated from yearning,
> Do not perform action, Naropa.

Naropa asked:

> Then should I listen to the teachings?

Tilopa replied:

> Listening to the teachings
> Is like drinking salt water.
> It cannot free one from desire, Naropa.

Naropa asked:

> Then should I preach the teachings?

Tilopa replied:

> By the elaboration of the word
> One cannot realize the meaning of suchness, Naropa.

Naropa asked:

> Then should I practice meditation?

Tilopa replied:

> By liberating oneself from attachment
> One need not engage in the meditation experience.

Naropa asked:

> Then, again, should I perform the action?

Tilopa replied:

> When you are free from outer fixation and inner grasping
> There is no need to perform action, Naropa.

Naropa asked:

> Then should I realize the view?

Tilopa replied:

> Not perceiving non-observation,
> There is nothing to see in reality, Naropa.

Naropa asked:

> Then should I achieve the result?

Tilopa replied:

> When one is free from the duality of hope and fear
> There is no fruit to achieve, Naropa.

Naropa felt confused, and said:

> The nature of form is appearance;
> It is not inherently born.
> If something exists, there is reason to act.
> If it does not exist, is there the need to act?
> This self-awareness—
> Blissful clear mind—
> Is nothing but emptiness.

If it exists, there is a reason to be attached.
But without existence, what is the use of grasping?
This mind, self-aware and empty,
Is free from the duality of extremes.
There is reason to experience if there is meditation.
What is there to experience since there is no
  meditation?
In the great bliss
Of the spontaneously accomplished one,
If there is virtue and non-virtue
There is a reason to ripen the result of happiness
  and suffering.
In the nature of the equality state,
Why accept virtue and reject non-virtue?

Tilopa replied:

Until you realize the nature of the unborn,
The interdependent origination of appearance,
Do not abandon the chariot wheel
Of the two accumulations, Naropa.
When the master shows the path of unborn mind
There arises a multi-colored appearance.
Release the mind like a crow from a ship
And experience enjoyment, Naropa.
In the mind-as-such, self-awareness and clarity,
If you do not realize interdependent arising
You will be bound by the experience of attachment,
  Naropa.
In the unborn, free from elaboration,
Freely enjoy.
If you realize this temporal experience
Of recollection and introspection as illusion,
Be carefree, Naropa.
Various are the thoughts of grasping and fixation,
The cause of birth in the darkness of samsara;
Cut directly whatever arises
With the sharp axe of realization, Naropa.

If one attaches the mind
To the enjoyment of form, sound and others,
One is like a bee stuck in honey;
Be free of grasping, Naropa.

Again Tilopa said:

In the nature of the vajra body
All the paths and bhumis are accomplished.
Subjugate the maras in the four wheels
By the meeting of positive interdependence of
mind and body.
In this one lifetime
Realize in an instant the co-emergent wisdom;
Perfect the unity of clarity and emptiness.
By meditating simultaneously on the five stages
All the energy of the recitation of the vajra word
Comes into the path directly.
One will achieve all the qualities respectively
And accomplish the four bodies and five wisdoms.

Naropa said:

I see my errors dimly, like the moon.
It is deep, the mud of the three-times samsara.
The knot of karma is tightly bound
By harmful thought.
The heap of darkness-ignorance is dense.
Wrapped in the cocoon of worldly pleasure,
Stuck in the honey of grasping,
Meditation disappears like clouds,
Or like writing in water.
Scattered is the experience of turtle hair,
Vanishing is the realization of sky-flowers.
So how can the blind give up grasping?

Tilopa prophesied by singing the song of the six vajra dharmas:

In the Pullahari Monastery,
In the monastery of nonduality,
In the illusory body,

Burn the fuel of dream-habit
With the tummo of wisdom-fire, bliss-heat;
Release the thought of grasping and fixation.
In the inexpressible monastery
Of the great bliss Mahamudra.
Cut the continuity of envy in the bardo
With the sharp sword of realization
Of inherent co-emergent wisdom;
Release the grasping of perception-attachment;
Traverse the secret path of the wish-fulfilling gem;
Cut the root of the tree of eternal view;
Explain the sign of the dumb;[1]
Cut the continuity of samsara by magnificent blessing;
Recognize the mother and son like old friends.[2]
Kyeho! This is self-awareness wisdom
Which is beyond words and not an object of the mind.
I, Tilo, can show nothing.
Just understand the intrinsic self-awareness.
Do not bring non-observation into the mind.
There is not even a dust-particle of recollection
In the mind-as-such, self-awareness.
I, Tilo, have shown nothing.
All that is unborn
Is self-awareness, self-clarity, emptiness.
Emptiness is free from birth and cessation;
Why should there be doubt?

Thus Naropa was liberated and said:

The path of Mahamudra
Is non-observation in the mind.
The mind, free from elaboration, inexpressible,
Free from obscurations, and seeing wisdom,
Has nothing to ask of anyone.
I am the spontaneous, stainless, self-liberated yogin.

---

[1] refers to dispelling the nihilist view

[2] refers to the meeting of one's practice with the clear light

Thus Naropa achieved the highest realization. Then Tilopa prophesied the coming of Marpa Lotsawa, who would be a proper vessel:

> By the self-liberated sun of wisdom
> At the Pullahari Monastery
> The fortunate one from the Land of Snow
> Dispels the darkness of Mati
> And pervades by the light of wisdom.

Tilopa then sealed this prophecy with three commands: "Do not preach in the assembly; do not debate with heretics; do not give empowerments to the King. From Tibet, the Land of Snow, will come a man to whom you should give the teachings."

After a time Naropa's friend Riripa requested that he give teachings for the benefit of all sentient beings:

> Give up the mind of solitary peace and such,
> Like Shravakas and Pratyekabuddhas;
> Dispel the darkness of all sentient beings
> By the Dharma light of Naropa.

Another friend, Kasoripa, made the same request:

> Dharma physician, Naropa,
> By the medicine of the precious teachings
> Dispel the pain of the afflicting emotions
> In all suffering sentient beings.

Tilopa said:

> That which is unborn, Dharma-as-such,
> From the sky of Dharmakaya
> Produces the continuous rain of Dharma
> Which ripens the crop of sentient beings.

Thus he allowed Naropa to give teachings.

Naropa said:

> By the order of the Lama Buddha
> Coming together with the words of my vajra brothers,

I offer far and wide
The nourishment of the essence of Sutras and
Tantras.

Thus Naropa agreed to give teachings, and with that Tilopa disappeared into the sky.

The different names by which Naropa was known are: Samantabhadra, Upasaka Akashagarbha, Shramanara Buddha Jnana, Bhikshu Dharma Dwa Za, Abhayakirti, Nödän Ziji, and Shri Naropa.

The Four Great Dharma Kings of Tibet

THE LIFE STORY OF THE FOUR GREAT DHARMA KINGS OF TIBET

In this kingdom of the Land of Snow,
In the meaning Sutra and Tantra,
Lord Buddha prophesied and praised
The four forefather kings.
The first discovered, the second started,
The third established, and the fourth highly and
profoundly established
The development of the precious Buddha's teaching.

Discovering the Dharma

The finding of the teachings concerns King
Thothori Nyantsen
Who abides in the palace of Yumbu Lhakang.
At the same time in Magadha in India
A King called Za sat under the bodhi tree.
Through his offerings and supplications
Varjasattva appeared before him in the sky,
And a rain of Dharma texts fell.

At the same moment in Tibet

King Thothori received these texts[1]
Known as the Sutra of the Ten Virtuous Teachings
Written by Bedhurya.
There also fell to earth a crystal stupa.
King Thothori could not distinguish whether these
Belonged to Dharma or the Bon religion.

So he named them *The Awesome Secret*,
And kept them on a jeweled throne,
And made lavish offerings to them.
By that magnificent blessing
The King regained his teeth which had fallen out,
His hair became dark again,
And he lived to the age of one hundred twenty.
He then wrote this final testament
At the time of his death:
My sons and grandsons
Should open my sacred treasures from time to time,
Make offerings to them and pay homage.
His sons and grandsons all listened and obeyed.
By this power the kingdom prospered.
King Thothori was an emanation of the Bodhisattva
Samantabhadra.

Starting the Development of the Dharma

The starting of the teachings concerns
Avalokiteshvara
Who manifested as King Songtsen Gampo.
When he was four years old,
He ascended the throne of the Land of Snows.
At that time the King's Minister had a son
Known as Thonmi Sambhota.
The King gave this boy two jars of gold dust
And sent him to India, the source of knowledge,

[1] The transfer of the texts from one King to the other was accomplished through a miraculous hurricane which blew the precious manuscripts from India to Tibet.

To study language.
Here he met Lejin in the South.
After he had completed his studies,
He returned to Tibet
And translated the *Megaratna Sutra, Pundarika Sutra,*
The *Rinchen Thok*, the *Dzungchok Drangnga*,
And the *Le-namje*.
He created the thirty characters of the Tibetan language.
The King's four closest Ministers
Learned language from him for four months.
Then the King made a written declaration to his entire kingdom
About the ten virtuous actions
And the need to abandon alcohol, the root of many ills.
He emanated the Bhikshu Shila Akara Mati from his forehead
And sent him to India.
When the Bhikshu returned to Tibet,
He brought with him an eleven-headed, eight-handed statue of Chenrezig
Fashioned out of snake-heart sandalwood,
And, separately, a piece of this sandalwood.
From the Tala mountain he brought a piece of gorshisha wood;
From an island in the ocean he brought a handful of grass;
From the Chöten Padma Khorlo in Keru city
He brought two handfuls of relics belonging to three Buddhas.
He also brought a part of the bodhi tree,
And two jars of sand from the Holy Land.
From near the Naranjana river he also took sand
And several precious objects, as well as milk
From a cow which ate incense.
These ten very precious objects he brought back

And offered to the King.
Out of them the King built
An eleven-headed Chenrezig image.
The daughter of the Nepali King,
An emanation of the wrathful Tara known as
Lhachik Tritsun,
Was invited to Tibet.
The Nepali King sent her with the image of Vajra
Akshobhya,
A Maitreya dharmachakra,
And a Tara image made of sandalwood.
To house these the Princess built the Rasa Trulnang
temple.
The daughter of the Chinese Emperor,
Kong Jo, an emanation of Tara,
Was also brought to Tibet.
Her father sent her with a Shakyamuni Buddha
image,
And to house this she built the Ramoche temple.
Songtsen Gampo built twelve other temples as well,
In the four directions of Tibet.
At last, in his eighty-fourth year he went to Rasa
Trulnang temple,
And with Tritsun and Kong Jo
Did prostrations before the image of the great
compassionate one.
Together, the three said:
This great compassionate one
Is inseparable from us.
Therefore, whoever has devotion and faith in us
Should also make offerings to the great
compassionate one
So that all his wishes might be fulfilled.
The King said: In five generations
There will come a Dharma King
Who will establish the Dharma strongly.
Four generations after his parinirvana

Will come a King bearing the name of an animal,
Who will destroy the teachings.
For this he will be reborn in the hell of continuous suffering.
After that, for many generations
The Dharma will be maintained,
And there will be myriad devoted practitioners
Who will honor the Buddha's relics.
In this Land of Snow,
At the end of the five hundredth period,
The Buddha's light will be rekindled
And the Dharma will be strongly re-established.
Thus the King and Princesses predicted,
And like water dissolving into sand
They dissolved into the heart of the great compassionate one.

Establishing the Dharma

King Trisong Deutsen,
A manifestation of Manjushri,
Was enthroned in the Ox Year at the age of thirteen.
He encouraged the growth of the Dharma
And promoted the building of Samye Monastery.
At that time certain Ministers hostile to the Dharma
Created obstacles to his Dharma activities.
So the King sent a messenger with six jars of gold dust
To invite Shantarakshita to come from India;
And when he was twenty years old
The King sent another messenger with two jars of gold dust
To invite Padmasambhava to come from India to Tibet.
In the Tiger Year he built Samye Monastery;
In the Horse Year the building was completed;

In the Sheep Year it was consecrated.
In the same way he built many other monasteries and temples.
Then the King sent a messenger with twelve jars of gold dust
To invite Vimalamitra from India.
Later he invited Kamalasila,
And in the same way many other great masters.
These masters and many great translators met
And rendered a number of Dharma texts from the Sanskrit.
They were fully confident in and devoted to the Triple Gem;
Thus, the development of the Buddha's teaching progressed.

Firmly Establishing the Buddha's Teaching

The King Ralpachen, the emanation of Vajrapani,
Built Ushangdo Monastery
And invited many great masters there.
Together with many scholars
He translated myriad Dharma texts
Which had not been undertaken by his forefathers.
He also edited translations that had been done before,
And deeply venerated all the objects of refuge.
Therefore we owe a great debt to this succession of Kings.
At the time of King Lang Darma
The objects of refuge were destroyed
And the Dharma declined like the setting sun.
At that time Tsang Rabsal, Shakyamuni of Ngok, and Yo Gejung
Fled to the mountain known as Dam Tik
With a mule laden with texts.
They were followed by Gongpa Rabsal,

A being of exceptional intellect.
To him they gave the complete teachings before their death.
The King Lang Darma was assassinated by Lhalung Palgye Dorje,
And after two generations
Four men from Ü and two from Tsang in Central Tibet
Became disciples of Gongpa Rabsal.
Their followers in turn caused the community of monks
To flourish in Ü and Tsang.

Developing the Dharma in Western Tibet

When the great Bodhisattva Yeshe Öd became King,
He built an excellent monastery
In Shangshung Troling,
As well as Spontaneous Wish-fulfilling Monastery
In Khoehar in Purang.
He also built Nyarma Monastery in Mar-Yul
And Tapo Monastery in Chiti,
And sent many gifted children,
Including Lotsawa Rinchen Zangpo,
To India, the source of knowledge,
To study Sanskrit and the Dharma teachings.
He encouraged all his subjects
To become practitioners
And offered his entire kingdom
For the increase of Dharma.
Thus, the teachings were established in Western Tibet
Where they flourished widely.

Marpa
1012–1099

Naropa had numberless disciples, but among them the most highly realized numbered one hundred eight, along with twenty-eight yogins who could perform the glorious actions, and four heart sons. Of the last, the principal disciple was Lord Marpa Lhotrakpa.

There are three phases to the life story of Marpa:

I. the quality of obtaining the prophecies;
II. the quality of undergoing hardships related to family; and
III. the quality of the experience of samadhi.

I. OBTAINING THE PROPHECIES

The quality of obtaining the prophecies has two aspects: (A)the prediction of himself as a manifestation, and (B) the prediction of himself as a proper vessel

A. The Prediction of Himself as a Manifestation

In the Sutras the Buddha stated, "In the Gyedan city Chöphel will benefit the teachings." And Padmasambhava prophesied in his *Revealed Hidden Treasure,* "In future times there will appear a limitless emanation of great compassion.

At Peser in Lhotrak will appear a man called Marpa Lodrö."

A man known as Lashö Yonten Bar went to India to study Sanskrit. While in a primitive place he was attacked by a robber and tied up. When the breath had nearly left his body, a lady rode by on a jackal, and by merely glancing at the robber caused him to become immobile. Lashö Yonten Bar said, "You are the all-compassionate one." And the woman replied, "I came here seeing that you were close to death. Where do you come from?" "I come from Tibet and am journeying to India to study Sanskrit and become a translator," he said. "My brother Dombi Heruka manifested as Marpa Lotsawa and benefitted many sentient beings. Do you know him?" she asked. The man replied, "I have heard his name, but I have not met him." She then gave him two rocks, one black and one white, saying, "When you find that you are in a situation of danger, cast these on the ground." Wherewith she departed.

Dombi Heruka is the manifestation of the Buddha
himself.
Of him it is said in the *Namchak Barwa Tantra*:
There are ten wrathful forms to tame with wrath;
Eight bodhisattvas to tame with compassion;
Eight excellences to tame by inferior means;
And eight great yogins manifested for practitioners
in this life.

B. The Prediction of Marpa as a Proper Vessel

Tilopa said, "By the self-liberated wisdom sun at Pullahari Monastery dispel the ignorance of Mati and let the light of wisdom prevail. In the Dharmakaya, Dharma-as-Such, nothing is born. By the stream of Dharma activities, ripen the fruit of sentient beings." Riripa said, "Renounce the desire for your own tranquility, like the Shravakas and Pratyeka Buddhas. By the light of Naropa's teaching, dispel the pain of afflicting emotions caused by the sickness of all sentient beings."

II. THE QUALITY OF UNDERGOING HARDSHIPS RELATED TO FAMILY

In Chukhyer in the valley of Lhotrak there lived a clan known by the name of Marpa. The father was named Marpa Wangchuk Öser, whose own father, in turn, was named Könchog. The mother was Gyamo Dode. To them were born five children, two older and two younger than Marpa.

Agreeing to send Marpa to Drogmi Lotsawa at Nyungu Lung Monastery in Latö Mangkhar, the parents gave him a black horse known as Senghe Khadang, bearing a saddle made from the sengdeng tree, a silken blanket, a large silver ladle, a fine piece of turquoise, and a text containing the eight thousand verses of the *Prajnaparamita* written in gold. Marpa was also given many other precious objects with which to obtain the teachings. But as Drogmi Lotsawa was reluctant to give teachings, Marpa received few from him. However, he learned Sanskrit and spoke with certain Indian scholars who inspired him to journey to India for further study.

Meanwhile, Drogmi Lotsawa returned Marpa's horse, which he sold for six sang of gold. He then journeyed to Nepal and met the teacher Chither, who gave him the four seed Tantras and the Dharma protectress Vetali, as well as the Phowa Trong-jug, the Hevajra empowerment and the related Tantra teachings. In all, Marpa stayed in Nepal for three years to accustom himself to the heat. During this time he became friendly with Nyö Jungpo (a Tibetan translator) in whose company he journeyed to India. Nyö went to Eastern India and Marpa went to the West in search of a Lama.

In the West, in the city of Lakshetra, he came upon Pandita Yeshe Nyingpo, who gave Guhyasamaja teachings. But before obtaining these he had to cross a poisoned lake. He therefore went to a man who lived in a small village in the forest, offered him a gift, and asked how he could cross the lake safely. The man applied juice from an herb to Marpa's entire body, but still the poison of the lake caused Marpa's skin to shed like that of a snake.

Once he had arrived, Marpa received the Guhyasamaja, Illusory Body, Clear Light and many other teachings. Later, many yogins like the elder and younger Kusulu assembled at a ganachakra feast. One yogin rode in on a jackal and another appeared on a giant cat. When they were asked who they were, the yogins said, "We are Kantapa and Pentapa, disciples of Naropa." Marpa then received teachings from them, especially from Pentapa, remaining in that place five years.

By this time all that he had brought with him was nearly used up, so he went to Nepal and met men bringing supplies from Tibet. From there he returned to India and met many lamas, in particular Yeshe Nyingpo and Pentapa, who treated him with great kindness. To each of them Marpa offered a mandala made with one sang of gold. Pentapa was so pleased that he took Marpa to meet Naropa at Pullahari Monastery.

At that time there were four Gatekeeper scholars in Nalanda: the Eastern Gatekeeper was Shantipa; the Southern Gatekeeper was Ngaki Wangchuk Drakpa; the Western Gatekeeper was Sherab Jungne Bäpa; and the Northern Gatekeeper was Pullaharipa (Naropa). Pentapa pointed out Naropa as the peerless one among them, and so it came to pass that Marpa met Naropa, offering him a gold mandala and requesting the teachings. Naropa manifested the nine deities of Hevajra and gave Marpa the empowerment, as well as teachings and instructions related to the Hevajra tantra.

Later, Marpa met Lord Maitripa in the East, near the Ganga River at Radiant Flower Monastery atop Blazing Fire Mountain. From him he received Hevajra teachings, Töpa Lurlang, and the essence of the Mahamudra. He then returned to Naropa and requested the Mahamaya teachings. Naropa said, "Though I am expert in this teaching, I must send you to another lama who possesses the essence of the teaching." Pleased with the ganachakra feast Marpa had offered, Naropa turned to three of his realized disciples and said, "This Tibetan will travel to an island in the poisoned lake to receive Mahamaya teachings from Shiwa Sangpo [Kukuripa]. One of you should protect him from the dangers of poison; one should protect him from the dangers of wild animals and other obstacles; and one should protect him from the dangers of humans and non-humans." The three accepted, and Naropa supplied Marpa with the offerings he would need for the empowerments. "You must travel for two days in water coming up to your knees," he said. "But each night you will find a place to rest, free from danger." When Marpa at last arrived, he found a man seated under a tree, whose body was covered with hair, whose face resembled a monkey, and whose eyes were red. "Who sent you here?" the man asked Marpa. "Where are you going? What do you want?" Marpa replied, "I am sent by Naropa to meet Shiwa Sangpo and receive the Mahamaya teachings. Are you Shiwa Sangpo? Please give me the teachings." "Naropa may have studied a lot," the man said, "but he is not a spiritual master; he may have meditated, but he has no experience; he may protect vows, but he has no morality. If he knows the teachings he should have given them to you. This is a demon's island. I kill and eat whoever comes here," and with that he bared his fangs. Marpa thought, "Such a realized being as Naropa, and this man is challenging his greatness!" and he was displeased. Again he said, "If you are Shiwa Sangpo, then give me the teachings." Shiwa Sangpo smiled and said, "Are you angered that I am challenging the name of Naropa?" Marpa replied that he was. Shiwa Sangpo then declared, "That is a sign that Naropa is your root Lama. Now, let us go," and he led Marpa to his dwelling place. For two weeks he gave Marpa the empowerments, and then said, "When you return, you will be able to do so through thought alone, by the power of my blessing. Simply make supplications." Marpa did as he was instructed.

When he had returned, Naropa said, "Have you completed your mission?" And when Marpa replied that he had, Naropa said, "Shiwa Sangpo may be learned, but he is not a spiritual master; he may have meditated, but he has no experience; he may protect vows, but he has no morality. He is nothing but a being wrapped in hair." Marpa thought: "It must be the nature of these highly realized beings to challenge each other." Naropa then asked, "Are you angered?" and Marpa replied, "No, I am not." Naropa declared, "This is a sign that I am your root Lama, but in truth Shiwa Sangpo is also a great teacher." Naropa then gave Marpa the Mahamaya teachings again and they were the same as Shiwa Sangpo's.

Once Marpa went to a town where he met Nyö. The two challenged each other to a debate over the teachings they had received. When Nyö was defeated he asked, "Who is your Lama?" Marpa said:

> To the inferior he is but a form;
> To the profound he is a mantra;
> But to the ultimate, the yogi of the Dharma
> Is the Lama who shows the path of liberation.

Naropa then gave Marpa the Guhyasamaja.

Before he left for Tibet, Marpa performed a ganachakra feast. While offering the torma with his right hand, Naropa placed his left hand on the crown of Marpa's head and said, "You will have to return to India once more, and this will be the sign:

> The flower being of the sky
> Rides on the horse of the barren woman's son,
> Which is reined with the hair of a turtle.
> With the dagger of a rabbit's horn
> He kills the enemy of the Dharma expanse.
> The dumb speak and the blind see;
> The deaf hear and the lame run;
> The sun and moon dance and the conch shell sounds;
> The wheel and a small child spin."

Marpa then journeyed to Bodh'gaya to make offerings, and there met Nyö. Together they went to see Lama Bhalingsarya who transmitted the teachings of the Tantras of Manjushri,

Yamantaka, Hevajra, Nama Sangiti, and Guhyasamaja. Marpa remained there seven years, thus staying in India twelve years in all.

With Nyö, Marpa went to Nepal where he met the son of Lama Drogmi, who expressed amazement at his realizations. In reply, Marpa sang a song about the wondrous teachings he had received. Then he came to Latö Tshoshi (Western Tibet) where he paid homage to Drogmi. Many people gathered to watch the three translators as they sat side by side. Drogmi thought, "If I had given Marpa all the teachings and empowerments when he first came to see me, he would have become my disciple and follower." In this way he was filled with regret.

Then Marpa travelled to Central Tibet where his great teachings caused talk of him to spread widely. At that time gold was being mined in Namra, so Marpa received many golden offerings.

III. THE QUALITY OF THE EXPERIENCE OF SAMADHI

This section has six aspects: (A) revealing and invoking the sign, (B) the prophecy of seeing the Lama, (C) blowing the breath of compassion, (D) being chosen by the Lama as predicted, (E) showing himself as self-liberated and (F) revealing his gift of samadhi.

A. *Revealing and Invoking the Sign*

From Phenyul came Marpa Golek who offered Marpa Lotsawa ten sang of gold and forty sang-worth of silks and other precious items. At this time Marpa revealed the signs as predicted by Naropa:

> The flower dakini of the sky
> Rides on the horse of the barren hearing lineage
> Which is reined with the inexpressible turtle's hair.
> With the horn of an unborn hare
> She kills the preconception in the Dharma expanse.

With the inexpressible unspoken speech of the
dumb Tilo
Blind Naro liberates, seeing the unseen meaning.
The lame discrimination of the deaf Naropa
Neither comes nor goes
On the mountain of Dharmakaya, Dharma-as-Such.
From the Hevajra of sun and moon
The dancing is the taste of the many;
The fame of the shell pervades in the ten directions,
Blowing toward proper vessels.
The wheel is Chakrasamvara,
And the child is non-grasping.
The wheel of the hearing lineage spins.

B. The Prophecy of Seeing the Lama

Marpa returned to India bearing sixty sang of gold. On the way he traversed Nepal, where he met his previous teachers and made offerings. Learning that Naropa had entered the action[1] he journeyed to the city of Lakshetra in the West and asked for Yeshe Nyingpo who was staying in a forest, attended by a woman of low caste. "When she comes to gather water," he was told, "ask her if you may see him." When she arrived, he made his request. Pointing to a large jar of water she was holding, she said, "Use one-third of this water to bathe, and one-third for drinking." After Marpa had finished bathing, the washing water fell back into the vase and transformed into his white seed-essence (bindu). The woman then performed a yogic exercise over the vase and from her secret place emanated a stream of red seed-essence. After the two essences had merged and Marpa bathed in the water again, all his preconceived thoughts dissolved. And when he drank the water and looked into the vase he saw the full assemblage of the Guhyasamaja deities.

Then Yeshe Nyingpo appeared and Marpa did prostrations

[1] meaning: achieved the stage where he could dissolve or reappear at will

before him. Yeshe Nyingpo asked, "Are you liberated from the bondage of afflicting emotions? Are you purified? Have you realized the meaning of suchness?" He then gave him the four empowerments, the teachings of the illusory body, the clear light and others.

From there Marpa returned to the island in the boiling, poisonous lake to the South where dwelt Shiwa Sangpo. Together they performed a ganachakra feast during which a woman brought in a corpse. She cut the skull from the head and in it mixed the urine of Shiwa Sangpo with the blood of the corpse. This samaya fluid was then offered to all the assembly, and when it was brought to Marpa, it was boiling. Looking into it, Marpa saw the mantra syllables of the Mahamaya and realized the yogin of the profound mantra. At the ultimate he realized the meaning of the Suchness and remained seven days in stainless samadhi. While in this state, he also studied the meaning of the four yogas and received the teachings of Gyuma Sangyü. After this he performed a ganachakra feast for one month, and Shiwa Sangpo said:

> I dreamed that the glorious Naropa
> With the glance of an elephant
> Radiated the light of the sun and the moon
> Toward Tibet from his two eyes.
> So you will meet Naropa.

Thus predicted Shiwa Sangpo.

A Dakini then led Marpa to the East where Lord Maitripa was staying at the Cemetery of Blazing Fire Mountain. There, all the corpses, though moldy, putrid, and half burned, laughed, whistled, and made other sounds. The fire of the cremation ground, which was dark green, created a cloud of smoke in the sky which caused an epidemic wherever it travelled. For this reason the place is called Blazing Fire Mountain Cemetery.

When Marpa saw Maitripa sitting under the shade of a nyagrota tree, he performed an offering to please the Dakinis, as well as a mandala offering to please the Lama. With one-pointed mind he made supplications and received the Töpa Lurlang Tantra, the Hevajra Tantra, and the Mahamudra teaching. Thus, he was established in the nature of the original mind.

At this time the glorious nonduality Avadhutipa (Maitripa) accepted Marpa as a disciple and gave him the four empowerments of the inner profound signs. As a result, he progressed through the basic ground motivation, achieved the stainless samadhi, attained the unchanging state for seven days, and established the ground path, the three kayas. Different signs appeared: inanimate objects came to life; two red emanation jackals accepted a torma; the Formless Dakinis of the upper, lower, and middle realms began speaking; and all of space was pervaded by local Dharma protectors making music. Maitripa prophesied that Marpa should go to the Land of Snow in the North where there would be many proper vessels.

There Marpa celebrated a ganachakra feast for a month, and Maitripa said:

I dreamed of a captain sailing a ship
And raising the jewel atop the victorious banner;
Of a youthful girl glancing in a mirror
And a bird flying and raising a banner.
You will meet Naropa.

In the region of the Water Tree Rosary, Marpa performed a ganachakra feast one hundred times before Yogini Bone Ornament, from whom he took the teaching of the Four-Seat Vajra. Yogini Bone Ornament said:

I dreamed of someone blowing conch shells
From the peaks of three mountains:
Of the road leading from the three junctions of
the valley.
By the lamp blazing in the vase
The whole earth is illuminated.
You will meet Naropa.

Thus she prophesied.

For the novice attendant of Naropa, Sherab Sangye, and other of his followers Marpa performed the ganachakra feast, asking them to seek prophetic dreams. All obtained dreams containing signs that Marpa would meet Naropa. He then performed a ganachakra feast for a month with Gezul Sherab Sangye who said:

> I dreamed of leading a blind person
> From the great plain of suffering,
> And entrusting him to another
> Who dispelled the error of sightlessness
> By showing him the mirror of the mind.
> You will meet glorious Naropa.

Thus prophesied Gezul Sherab Sangye.

Then Marpa performed a ganachakra feast for a month before Riripa who said:

> I dreamed the same dream as the Dharma King.
> The noble family of the Dharma King
> Was supplicating the Brahmin Sangshap
> And established the noble virtues.
> You will meet Naropa.

Thus prophesied Riripa.

Marpa then performed a ganachakra feast for a month before Kasoripa who said:

> The mirror of Dharmakaya, Mind-as-Such,
> Is like the completely pure circle of the moon.
> This unshakable meaning
> Will be shown in Pullahari by Naropa.

Thus prophesied Kasoripa.

C. *Blowing the Breath of Compassion*

Marpa searched for a month, and when he arrived at Flower Heap Monastery, he dreamed that Lord Naropa was riding a lion atop a sun and moon disk in the heavens, surrounded by two consorts. When Marpa made the supplications, Naropa offered this reply:

I, Naro, have entered into the nonduality,
Being supported by two consorts
Revealing the signs of method and wisdom,
Riding on a lion,
And singing and dancing on sun and moon disks.
Are you not deceived by your deluded dreams?

That day when Marpa looked into the sky, he saw Naropa's form clearly like a rainbow, and he supplicated the master who made this reply:

If the steed of continuity, confidence and devotion
Is not spurred on by the whip of perseverance,
The wild beast of grasping and fixation
May be trapped and condemned to wander in the net
of samsara.

With this Naropa disappeared. Marpa ran after him, but though he caught sight of him, the vision of Naropa kept on retreating. Exhausted, Marpa lamented:

Alas, Lord, will you not, in your compassion,
look on me?
Will you abandon him who is without refuge?
I offer my life to the Lama.
Please heed this confused, ignorant one.

Thus he supplicated, looking into the heavens. In the mist of a dark mountain he saw the Lama and followed after him, entering into a rocky enclosure in the mountain. From the sky a voice came forth saying:

All things are like the appearance of illusion.
Clarity and emptiness are without definition.
Your mind is confused in its solitude.
This is the nature of the relative.

Naropa disappeared like a bird in flight and Marpa, who

could do nothing but gaze at the sky, said:

> Lord like a bird in flight,
> If I do not understand that which is without
> definition,
> I am like a dog chasing a bird's shadow,
> Wandering near the precipice meaninglessly, am I
> not?

Thus he spoke and leapt into the air with the thought: "The Lama goes to no definite place, so where can I search?" From out of space he heard a voice:

> Everything is unborn.
> In the Dharmata, Dharmakaya, Mind-as-Such,
> If one does not loosen the serpent-knot of
> hesitation,
> Then, like a two-pointed needle,
> One accomplishes nothing.

Marpa, following after Naropa's disappearing form, saw the Lama's body in space. Joyfully, he supplicated Naropa who said:

> The non-attachment body is like a rainbow.
> If one cannot see it in the unseen state,
> Then, like a blind man looking at a spectacle,
> One cannot realize its meaning.

Thus he spoke and disappeared.

Marpa then went to the Mountain of Darkness where he saw the Lama's footprint on the Marvelous Crystal Rock. He built a bridge for himself and saw a self-arising blossoming lotus at the River of Various Daisies. Later, he saw a white vajra of sandalwood at the Rock of Various Jewels, as well as three miraculous footprints. Climbing to the top of the mountain near the Flat Square Rock, he supplicated Naropa for seven days. When the Lama appeared, Marpa did prostrations and offered a ganachakra feast. Naropa stirred the nectar in the skullcup with a spoon made of a rib, and gave what was left to Marpa, who experienced the eight excellent tastes. Naropa said:

The great bliss enjoyment of one taste
Lies in the great vessel of bliss.
If one does not enjoy the great bliss,
The nectar of enjoyment will not appear.

Then Marpa searched for another month and saw the nine Hevajra deities on a sandalwood tree, as well as the eight-syllable mantra revolving at the heart center of the Yogini, and a footprint on the Crystal Rock. Supplicating further, he met Naropa in his actual body, and offering the Lama a gold mandala requested teachings. Naropa said:

If one does not offer the Dharmata mandala
On the ground of equality—
Appearance, pure from the beginning—
Then the jewel mandala of grasping
May be pulled into the life of samsara,
Is this not so?

So saying, he refused the mandala. Again, Marpa offered it, and Naropa threw it into the air, saying:

I offer this to the Lama
And the Triple Gem.

Marpa felt regret and Naropa, reading his mind, said, "If you need that gold, you can have it all." And with his miracle powers he retrieved the gold and returned it to Marpa. When Marpa sprinkled gold dust over Naropa, part of it fell onto his hair and part into his skullcup. The portion in the skullcup was transformed into nectar, which Naropa sipped. Then he stamped his feet and said, "If you want gold, I can turn this entire world into gold merely by touching it." Then he disappeared.

Again, Marpa searched and saw Naropa eating barley from another's bowl. He requested the teachings and Naropa, offering him the barley, said, "Eat this." But Marpa refused.

Naropa then said:

> The great bliss enjoyment of one taste
> Lies in the great vessel of bliss.
> If one does not enjoy the great bliss,
> One will not experience the vessel of great bliss.

So saying, he gave Marpa the essence of the Hevajra explanation and the direct teaching of Panchakula, as well as the detailed and brief teachings of the Precious Secret, the Co-emergent Teaching of Vajrayogini, and others. Then he said, "Go to Maitripa to review these teachings and obtain others." Marpa received further teachings from Maitripa and collected many texts. In this way the Tantras and other teachings descended from the lineages of both Naropa and Maitripa.

After collecting the texts, Marpa again sought Naropa and came upon him in the Forest of the Sengdeng Tree. Realizing his own pure mind as the appearance of the Lama, he said:

> In the meaning one should realize the non-going and non-coming.
> If one does not realize non-going and non-coming
> In the freedom from action, Dharmata clear light,
> One is like a wild beast chasing a mirage,
> And wandering on a plain without meaning,
> Is this not so?

D. Being Chosen by the Lama as Predicted

Marpa obtained the blessing by receiving Naropa's feet and hands on the crown of his head. Naropa supplicated Tilopa who appeared in the sky and blessed Marpa, saying:

> By the sun of self-liberated wisdom
> In the Monastery of Pullahari,
> Spread the light of wisdom
> To the being known as Lodrö,
> Who will dispel the darkness of ignorance in Tibet.

Since Tilopa so prophesied, Naropa said, "Let us proceed as the enlightened Lama ordered." So he and Marpa went on their way to Pullahari Monastery.

E. Showing Himself as Self-Liberated

As Naropa and Marpa went toward Pullahari Monastery the worldly Dakinis created obstacles because they could not tolerate Marpa's carrying away all their life-essence profound teachings to Tibet. Unable to dispel these obstacles, Naropa supplicated Tilopa:

My son prophesied by the Lama,
The proper vessel Marpa Lodrö,
Is beset by obstacles caused by the maras.
Please grant your blessings, Lord Protector.

There then appeared among the Dakinis a wrathful emanation of Tilopa, vast as space and bearing various weapons. In fear and trembling all the Dakinis folded their hands and said:

Wrathful body and fearsome speech
Bearing fearsome weapons,
We take refuge in the glorious body.
We are not obstructors.
After seven months the chariot throne will be prepared
For the glorious Lord Naropa.
And from the hall of Pullahari,
In the palace of the self-appearing Oddiyana,
We will welcome the prophesied self-liberated one.
After seven months we will invite Naropa
To Oddiyana on the chariot.

Thus they begged pardon of Tilopa who dissolved all his wrathful forms back into himself and transformed into the nature of rainbow light. From out of this light Marpa saw one-half of Tilopa's body and heard four verses of his teachings.

During his seven months at Pullahari Marpa received the Guhyasamaja teachings, the teaching tradition of Nagarjuna and his disciples, instructions on the one-session meditation of Rimnga, the meaning of the Great Supreme Glorious One, the empowerment of the Precious Secret, the blessings of the Secret Sindhura Vajra Wisdom of Vajrayogini, the instruction of the Four-Sign Empowerments of the Dakinis, and the blessings of the hearing lineage of Chakrasamvara.

> Beneath the foundation of Pullahari Monastery
> Are gathered the scattered Four Tantra Teachings:
> In the middle of the monastery
> Is established the meaning of the mother Tantra;
> At the summit of the monastery
> Is taught the meaning of the father Tantra.

From the nine teachings of non-form, five are taught and four should be received directly from Kasoripa. Kasoripa taught the Light of Awareness Wisdom, the Wheel of the Channel and Wind Nets, the Mirror of Outer Equalizing Taste, and the Precious Great Bliss Speech.

Marpa did prostrations and circumambulated Naropa, receiving the complete empowerment of the emanation mandala with blessings. He placed Naropa's feet on the crown of his head, requested the footprint, and performed the ganachakra feast with offering tormas. Naropa placed his left hand on Marpa's head and prophesied:

> The yogin who has seen the meaning of pervading
>   emptiness
> Will hold the jewel of the reigning King.
> The flower in the family sky will disappear,
> Yet the river of the teaching lineage will continue.
> Rim Nga has one meaning
> In the pervading Dharma-as-Such.
> Attachment, like scratches on a stone, disappears;
> Samsara, like writing on water, will vanish of itself.

"At your final transition I will come and lead you to the

Buddha land. In the future you will be reborn spontaneously in a lotus on Harikapa Island in the East of India. You will meet me at Shri Pravata in Southern India and will be called Indestructible Vajra Gupta. Through the action teachings you will achieve supreme attainment enlightenment in that life. You will have many disciples, some of whom will go to the heavenly abode for thirteen generations. The teachings with the supreme blessings will flourish." Thus Naropa prophesied. Then he said, "I will go to Oddiyana."

Marpa contemplated staying in India, but Naropa, who instantly read his thought, said, "Return to Tibet. We four yogis have given blessings in the four directions. Krishnacharya blessed the East; Nagarjuna blessed the South; Indrabhuti blessed the West; and I blessed the North, the Land of Snow. Therefore, do not tarry here. Return to your country. In the North there are many proper vessels." Thirteen Lamas connected to the Dharma teachings, including Lama Serlingpa, gave Marpa teachings and blessed him. In particular, the blessings of Naropa and Maitripa were unsurpassed.

In all, Marpa spent twenty years in India, twelve with Naropa and seven with Maitripa. Of the two, Naropa was a root Lama who was unequalled, the crest ornament, and the wick of the lamp.

During his return journey to Tibet Marpa spent time at Bodh'gaya, arriving during a great festival. In the day offerings were made by humans, and at night offerings were made by amanushas, gods, nagas, yakshas, gandharvas, kinaras, asuras, mahoragas, rakshas, and others. One night the crowd began shouting riotously, and the next morning a giant raksha, whose head measured sixteen feet across, was found dead. To calm the frightened people Marpa performed the Phowa Trong-jug and threw the body in the direction of the Tokmo Rock. Everyone manifested their gratitude.

Marpa then went to each of his Lamas to bid them farewell. The last was Shiwa Sangpo, who lived at Halaparpata in the poison lake. To him Marpa sang a long song which caused tears to come to the eyes of all who heard it. When

Marpa crossed the Ganga, two low-caste robbers, Shikyipa, began chasing him. Taking fright, he visualized the Lama seated on the crown of his head, whereupon he became invisible to the robbers, who turned back. Marpa felt boundless gratitude toward his Lamas, and grew in confidence and devotion for them all.

Marpa then went to a place near the Ganga called Paciltra, where he met a lady guarding an orchard. When he asked her for fruit, she replied, "Ask my mother." When he did so he found that the woman was a yogini. With the blazing mudra she caused all the fruits—grapes, apples and others—to fall to the ground. When Marpa opened one fruit and looked inside, he saw directly the fifteen perfected female deities from the Nectar Light tradition. Mother and daughter were both Dakinis.

Then Marpa journeyed to Nepal and at Ramadoli Cemetery joined certain yogins performing a ganachakra feast. They said, "We must hurry and finish this offering, since the Dakinis will come." Marpa felt disgust at their fear and thought, "How grateful I am that I have met such a teacher as Naropa; I must return to India."

At dawn Marpa slept briefly and had a dream in which a lady appeared before him wearing leaves. Placing her right hand on Marpa's head, she said, "Do not return to India, but continue on to Tibet. There, there are many proper vessels waiting. You will encounter no further obstacles on your way." Thus she prophesied and gave him the blessing.

In Nepal, in the Rinchen Tsül temple, Marpa received the practice of Nectar Light and the direct realization of Ralchikma from Lama Paindapa. At this time he had a dream in which he saw Lord Maitripa riding a lion in the sky. He created a song about this and sang it to Paindapa.

Further along, Marpa came to Lishokara, where he had a dream in which he saw two female Brahmins wearing the sacred thread, holding flowers, and reciting the Vedas. They said, "Go to the South, to Shri Parvata, and obtain teachings from the Great Brahmin [Saraha]." Marpa said, "I cannot get there," and they said, "Brother, have no fear. We will get you there easily." So saying, they placed him on a sedan chair and flew him through the sky to Shri Parvata. In the forest of the laksha tree, he found Saraha naked and covered with ashes, his hair knotted at the top of his head, a consort at each side. From him Marpa received the Mahamudra teachings. Later, he sang of this experience to Marpa Golek.

While all this was happening, Marpa Golek, who had pure devotion to the Lama, thought: "My Lama has still not returned to Tibet. Has he passed away in India or is he coming here? If he is coming, I should go forth to welcome him. So he set out and met Marpa at Kongphu. Marpa gave this disciple a ruby rosary of one hundred eight beads which had belonged to Naropa, and a vajra and bell which had belonged to Lord Maitripa. He also gave him the song of the Six Dharma Vajra Heart Teaching and others.

At Nyagro, at a place called Kong Karpo, he met the wealthy grandfather of Marpa Golek, who had founded a school of philosophy there. At the request of many disciples, he sang a song generally about his meetings with lamas in India and their different teachings, and particularly about his meeting with Naropa and the teachings he received from him.

Then he went to Lhotrak in the South where he lived the life of a hidden yogin. Ngok Shungpa, Metsönpo, Tsur Wangne and others gathered there and received many teachings. One day at Lho Layak, Marpa Tonse established a college and invited Marpa to come. On the way, he saw a farmer plowing a field. Marpa said, "Look here and see whether I have practiced bodhicitta or not." When he picked up a stone many ants crawled out, and when he cupped his hand they all crawled onto his palms.

F. *Revealing his Gift of Samadhi*

1. The skill of the lineage brings great fame

2. The skill of blessings brings the instructions of Mahamudra
3. The skill of samadhi brings mastery over prana and mind.

1. The Skill of the Lineage Brings Great Fame

Is the lineage not famous?
The Dakini possesses the Dharmakaya.
Is the grandfather not famous?
Tilo is the ultimate Buddha.
Is the Lama not famous?
Naro possesses the Dharma eye.
Are the teachings not famous?
I have three jewels not held by others.
Am I not famous?
I am the only heart-son of Naropa.

2. The Skill of Blessings Brings the Instructions of Mahamudra

Although all practitioners have a lineage,
If one has the Dakini lineage, one has everything.
Although all practitioners have a grandfather,
If one has Tilo, one has everything.
Although all practitioners have a Lama,
If one has Naro, one has everything.
Although all practitioners have teachings,
If one has the hearing lineage, one has everything.
All attain the Buddha through meditation.
But if one attains Buddhahood without meditation,
There is definite enlightenment.
There is no amazing achievement without practice,
But there is amazing achievement without practice.
By searching, all will find enlightenment,
But to find without searching is the great find.

Marpa said, "I will give the Mahamudra instruction without searching from others."

3. The Skill of Samadhi Brings Mastery over Prana and Mind

a) Mastery over unobstructed phenomena
b) Mastery over Trong-jug

a) Mastery over unobstructed phenomena. With the wind moving through the channels

Bodhicitta pervades the body;
Fully roused by the whip of one taste,
The Clear Light manifests, neither coming nor going.
The quality of the Lama belongs to the lineage.
The nature of samsara is free from basis.
The nature of appearance is unborn.
The nature of mind is unity.
One who always remains in the Clear Light
Will not see the city of Bardo.
Manifest the form body for others.
Unborn Dharmakaya is free from elaboration.

b) Mastery over Trong-jug. Generally, Marpa demonstrated the Trong-jug Phowa seven times in Tibet and once at Bodh'gaya in India. Once, a group of farmers set out with a yak to cut grass in the upper part of the valley. The yak died and Marpa said, "While I take a walk, cut the grass and make it into a bundle. The yak will soon stand up. When he does, place the bundle on his back." Soon the yak arose and the farmers loaded him with the grass. When they returned home, the yak again fell down dead, and the Lama returned.

At the time of giving the Four-Seat Teachings, Marpa said, "The Tantra is the auspicious interdependent path, so we should observe the signs and practice at once. Today I will offer you a spectacle, but whatever happens, do not remove my body." He then performed the Trong-jug before the lifeless body of a sparrow. In a moment the bird arose and flew to a nearby village where a group of children threw stones at him. Being thrown off course, he fell to the ground.

The monks immediately covered the bird with a cloth and brought him home. After a time the sparrow died and the Lama's consciousness returned to his body. Of this experience Marpa said, "Entering into an inauspicious form, I nearly embarked on a life filled with obstacles."

When Marpa gave teachings, the monks took turns making the mandala offerings. Once, when it was a young monk's turn, he stood near a pillar in order to protect the shrine from birds. When a pigeon came in, the monk threw a stone at him with such force that the bird died. So great was the monk's distress that Marpa came forward and asked him, "Is the pigeon dead?" When the monk replied that he was, Marpa said, "I will show you something." Slowly he fell over and the pigeon flew up into the sky. After some time, Marpa's consciousness returned to his body, and he said wearily, "In so inauspicious a body, it was difficult to detach my consciousness."

> In the bird form of the illusory body,
> Having the wings of unified experience,
> Exercise the skillful bird of the mind
> And meet the son and mother of bird and chicken.

An old dri died near a high cliff. When Marpa performed Trong-jug, his consciousness entered the dri, which came to the door of a farmhouse and said:

> Practice the teachings as the Lama tells you.
> The racing steed of channels, winds, and drops,
> Fully roused by the one-taste whip,
> Frees the dri from the cliff of danger.

When some hunters killed a deer, Marpa, performing Trong-jug, caused his consciousness to enter the deer's body. Entering a farmhouse, he said:

> Practice the secret teachings of the Dakinis
> As the Lama instructs.
> This fulfills all one's wishes.
> Find the wish-fulfilling deer.

Once, a patron invited Marpa to his house in order to honor him. When Marpa performed Trong-jug before a dead lamb, the lamb arose and said:

> By the vow of the secret heart of the Dakinis
> And the deathless wisdom nectar,
> The yogin of Dharma medicine
> Revitalizes the dead lamb,
> Causing it to dance.

Then the Lama, who was aged eighty-eight, and who was possessed of limitless qualities, passed away on the fourteenth day of the twelfth month of the Bird Year, when the sun rose on the mountain.

Jetsün Milarepa (1052–1135)

Lord Marpa of the Southern Cliff had many disciples, but among them ten are exceptional beings: Of these the earliest were Lokya Jungyel of Gyerphu and Marpa Golek; the other eight were Ngok Zhungpa, Me Tshonpo, Tshur Wangne, Lhaje Seringpa, Gyaton Shikpo of Trang, Marpa Chisawa, Nyangom Trangtak, and Jetsün Milarepa.

It was Ngok Zhungpa who established the lineage of the explanation and study of the teaching of the Tantra. While studying the Tantra of the Nyingma lineage from the spiritual master Gyerlungpa, he heard of the fame of Lord Marpa and went to him, offering a yellow horse and requesting the teachings. Later, he made three large offerings, the first being a one hundred eight volume set of the Sutras including three *Prajnaparamita* texts, the second being one hundred eight different kinds of valuable offerings, and the third being all his domestic animals, including seventy dri plus nomad tents, houses and even his dog. Still, Marpa refused to give him the complete profound teachings.

Meanwhile, Marpa was suffering from bloody dysentery which he had contracted in India because of the extreme heat. Thinking that the blood expelled by the Lama was a blessing, Ngok Zhungpa drank it with a silver spoon. When he saw this sign of devotion, Marpa realized that Ngok Zhungpa was a proper vessel, and gave him the profound instructions, especially the instruction of meditation on short 'A' (Tummo).

Me Tshonpo filled a large amount of land—as much as can be sown with twelve pints of seeds—with valuable objects of all kinds. First, he filled it with the eighteen different kinds of valuable offerings, then with the different kinds of domestic animals, and last with barley and armor.

Tshur Wangne offered one hundred eight volumes of texts and other valuable offerings. Ngok Zhungpa mastered the dream practice and Tshur Wangne mastered the Phowa, while Me Tshonpo mastered the Clear Light and the great saint Milarepa mastered Tummo. But among these heart sons, the foremost was the great saint and yogi, Milarepa.

There are four aspects to the life story of Milarepa: first, his meeting with Lord Marpa; second, his service of the Lama, who is pleased and gives him the teachings; third, the mastery of the ordinary and extraordinary attainments by practicing meditation in the service of the Lama; and fourth, his ability to ripen proper vessels.

I. HIS MEETING WITH LORD MARPA

The great saint lived in Gungthang in the Land of Snow, not far from Kyirong where rests a statue of the noble, great compassionate self-appearance (Chenrezig). He was of the clan of Khyungpo Mila: his grandfather was known as Mila Dorje Gyalpo, and his father as Mila Sherab Gyaltsen. His father married Nyangsama Karlek, and from this union there came forth three children: a girl, Peta; Tebchung; and Mila who at birth was named Mila Thöpaga.

Though the family enjoyed wealth and a good life, the father said: "Our lives are worthless if we have no Dharma." So when Mila was growing up, he was sent to the spiritual master Tsangpa from whom he received beginning instruction in the Dharma. Later on, he loaded his horse with six bundles and journeyed to central Tibet. From Lhaje Yeshe

Sung in Rukhulung he received the complete teachings of Yamantaka and the magical powers of the protector Sadong Marnak. These he practiced for eight years, achieving the signs. Then he went to Nyangtö Khore and received the teachings of Gyutrul from Bami Bhode Ratsa. In Nyangtö Gyankhar he received the Maha Ati teaching from Gyerton Wangne, and in Yuphug in Rong he received further Maha Ati teaching from Dreton Wangne. Then he set out for Yardrok Dor and from Marpa Jungne received teachings on the nature of mind according to the Sutras.

Once Marpa Jungne said, "Gungthangpa [Milarepa], you and I have no worth. You are merely listening and I am merely speaking. These teachings of Dzogchen, Gyutrul and others give a general idea of the view, but to experience the realizations is difficult. In Lhotrak resides a great master, Lord Marpa, a principal disciple of Naropa who endured many hardships for the teachings. Lord Marpa has the path of the blessing Tantra and the technique of auspicious interdependence. Should we not, father and son, proceed there?" These words awakened the connection which had existed between Marpa and Milarepa in previous lives, and by merely hearing them the great saint felt extraordinary devotion arise. Tears came to his eyes and the hairs of his body stood on end. He said, "Let us proceed."

So the master went forth with the disciple, but on the way Marpa Jungne became ill. "I can go no further," he said, "but you must continue." So the saint went on, experiencing hardships and hunger on the plain of Yardrok. He proceeded on his journey and approached Lhotrak.

II. AFTER MEETING WITH MARPA HE RECEIVES THE TEACHINGS AND INSTRUCTIONS

Mila continued without stopping and finally encountered Marpa in Khyenlung Monastery. He offered him sugar cane packed in goat skin and a piece of woolen cloth, saying, "I am from Gungthang and have no possessions. I am here because I fear the cycle of birth and death. Please accept me and grant me the teachings and necessities of life." The Lama replied, "I can do one or the other, but not both." Mila was satisfied and was allowed to enter the Lama's household. Thereafter he performed every kind of service for the Lama, including building, and even offered him his body. Thus he received the teachings.

At this time Ngok Zhungpa, Me Tshonpo, Tshur Wangne and others were also coming to receive teachings. Mila met them on the way to help them carry their many offerings, and with them he received Marpa's teachings and commentaries on the Tantras. His own offering consisted of a large covered jar and a fine woolen cloth. The Lama returned the cloth to him, saying, "Since you have no cloth, use this." But he accepted the jar, saying, "We must interpret the symbolism of this offering: first, it is precious and red in color, meaning that you will benefit from the Dharma and will have many spontaneous realizations; second, the jar has a stain on the outside, meaning that you will experience certain obstacles and endure hardship; third, the inside is empty, meaning that you will have difficulty finding a means of livelihood while you practice meditation." Later, all these predictions proved to be true.

Once there was a shortage of food due to an unusually hot summer and a modest harvest. So the Great Saint, Milarepa, went to sing in the city of Chukhyer for a crowd who remarked on the beauty of his song. For his skill he received a great quantity of barley which he offered to his teacher's wife. So pleased was she that she said to Marpa, "Although great offerings have been made to the Lama by the disciples Ngok Zhungpa, Me Tshonpo and Tshur Wangne, the offering of Great Magician (Milarepa) is the most meaningful. If there are teachings you lack, very well. But give him whatever teachings you possess." Still, the Lama was careful at this time to transmit only certain teachings.

As time went by, Great Magician grew strong from carrying stones, including some so large that they became known as the Giant Stones of Milarepa, since only he could lift them. For each stone Milarepa carried, Marpa gave him one teaching. One day Ngok Zhungpa said, "Since you are staying here, Great Magician, you have no need to hurry, but we have to return to our homes. So we would like to get the teachings before you." Milarepa replied, "You are hurrying to your homes, but I am also in a hurry—to achieve enlightenment. Look at my back." Then he showed them how it was covered with blisters from carrying so many heavy stones. The Great Saint then made a request to Marpa, saying, "I must practice meditation so please give me the essence of all the teachings in order that I may practice." So Marpa gave him the abbreviated form of the Six Dharmas of Naropa, the essence of the four Tantras.

One night Lama Marpa walked about his community to observe each of his disciples and determine if they were practicing.

Ngok Zhungpa was staring into a lamp and writing; Me Tshonpo was practicing meditation, and Tshur Wangne was meditating and looking at a small text which he had placed on his pillow. But when Marpa came to the place of the Great Saint, he saw that he had taken off his clothes and was in profound meditation with sweat pouring off his body. He therefore said, "Ngok Zhungpa will become a Master of the giving of teachings and explanations; Me Tshonpo will become a realized practitioner, and Tshur Wangne will become a meditation master. But Great Magician should not be asked to do physical work, for he will truly work hard to realize the whole of the meditation."

In all, Mila attended Lord Marpa for six years, eleven months, and was given all the teachings without exception. He thought: "I have received very profound teachings, yet I have not performed any service; indeed, I have taken the necessities of food and clothing from the Lama. On the other hand, Ngok Zhungpa and others offered the Lama all their wealth, so they must have received higher teachings than I. I must therefore go to them and obtain these teachings." Lord

Marpa read into his mind, so when Ngok Zhungpa was taking his leave, Marpa placed his vajra on the crown of his head and said, "Whatever teachings I have given you without exception should be given to Great Magician." Marpa then told Mila, "Ngok Zhungpa is a great being and is also a mature Dharma friend, so you must obtain teachings from him." So Great Saint went to Ngok Zhungpa, but while with him he saw robbers from Dol stealing Ngok Zhungpa's horses, sheep and other domestic animals. With his powers he cast hail stones from his fingers, causing the robbers to approach him humbly with offerings of chang, *Prajnaparamita* texts and many other precious objects.

Ngok Zhungpa gave Great Saint all the teachings without exception. Though he found a deeper meaning to the essence teachings, Ngok Zhungpa's long explanations were harder to understand than Marpa's more concise ones. As a result, Mila felt extraordinary devotion and deep confidence in Marpa. He thought, "In general Marpa expected offerings, yet in particular he accepted me, transmitting all the profound teachings without asking for service or precious gifts. I should perhaps go to Gungthang and gather some sugar cane for an offering, but Marpa has already received many precious objects, so my offering would appear as nothing. The supreme offering is the offering of practice. Therefore, to repay his kindness I should make an offering of my practice of the teachings he taught."

III. MILAREPA'S MASTERY OF THE ORDINARY AND EXTRAORDINARY ATTAINMENTS

Below the monastery of Ngok lies a cave known as the Cave of Mila. There Milarepa practiced meditation for one year without leaving his seat, while Lama Ngok Zhungpa supplied his food and other needs. After one year Milarepa experienced some blissful heat and calm abiding. He thought: "How long can I remain in the calm abiding state?" To test himself he made a butter lamp, placed it on his head, and meditated. In the morning when he arose from his samadhi, he had the impression of seeing a clear sky before him. He thought: "I am experiencing a special quality of meditation which I have not known before." Then he remembered: "The clear light appearance is not the sky, but the light of the lamp which I had forgotten upon my head!"

One night in a dream a lady appeared before him saying: "The blessings and attainments you have received are few. There are still obstacles before you. Go to the South near Nepal. There you will receive the blessings of the Dakinis, and will draw closer to the realization of the meditation." Then she lifted him up in a white cloth. Great Saint took the text given him by Marpa and journeyed to his own birthplace. His father had passed away long before. He met his mother and sister, and offered his house and all his properties to his first spiritual master. From there he went to Katse cave and meditated for four months. Then he went to Tsenyang cave and after meditating for some days, experienced the inner heat. He remained there three months while great inner heat and other qualities arose in him. Then he meditated in the Black Cliff cave.

One day while he was out walking, Mila noted that all the foliage in the farms below had grown yellow, as it was harvest time. Descending to the village to join the harvest celebration, he heard one of the crowd remark, "It is said that Mila Thöpaga, who was long a wanderer, now wears only a cotton cloth and is a good religious person. Is that true?" Another recounted, "It is said that Mila has meditated for four months together without any food and clothing, and has now achieved the realizations." Another said, "How marvelous! If we tried to see him, would we find him?" Another said, "He is here right now." As everyone held a different view, a dispute began which displeased Mila, but since the people were unsteady from drinking chang, he was able to make his escape back to the mountain.

Thereafter, Milarepa went to three caves on the White Cliff Rock to practice meditation. He then went to the rocky cave of Lingwa where a hostile demoness came to tempt him.

Later, Mila said, "There is no more danger at Lingwa Cave."

At that time Mila was eating nettles without salt or other seasoning so Gurib Lhabar of Rakma, hearing of Milarepa's fame, promised to supply him with the necessities. That winter he invited Mila to the Rakma region to meditate at Kyang Pal. From there Mila meditated at Jangchub Dzong, at the Sky Fortress Horse Tooth Cave of Naphu. It was here that he sang the Song of the Floating Southern Cloud. Then he went to the forest of Singha.

In Nepal a band of robbers stole from a band of yogins who said, "We are yogins; please do not steal from us." The robbers replied, "You are not yogins; the real yogi is in the forest. He is resistant to arrows." Later, Mila said, "The robbers of Nepal shot arrows at me, but they bounced right off."

Mila meditated in Nepal for four months, eating only fruit. At this time he sang the following song:

> Wondrous is the contented and solitary priest.
> Like the apes and monkeys who develop their agility,
> I, Milarepa, am practicing the art of meditation. . .

Afterward, Mila went to a cemetery of Suturi and performed a ganachakra feast with Dakinis in attendance. Later, when he was meditating in the solitary place of Gungthang, he saw a girl across the river tending sheep with her friends. They asked her, "What manner of man is this whom you have seen?" She replied, "He is a naked man." Mila thought, "I should go to them." But at that moment they disappeared and he thought: "Those are Dakinis."

Then Mila meditated in the Solitary Cuckoo Place. Gurib Dharma Tsa invited him to Naphu where he stayed for a time. An Indian lady wearing a golden earring prostrated before him and promised to provide his food for a month. Mila asked, "Where do you come from?" And she replied, "I come from the Pigeon Cave," and with that she flew away. In the morning Mila went to the cave and there saw a giant pigeon who circumambulated him seven times and did prostrations.

She then brought out forty jars of rice. Mila asked, "Are you bringing this for me?" The pigeon nodded its head. Mila remained there, meditating through the patronage of the pigeon. Then he meditated at the Tsikma Cave of Tsum. In the summer he stayed in the three caves of the White Cliff and in winter he went to Mang-Yul Rock and other places. At the White Place Pass there dwelt a yogin called Samten, whose retinue began criticizing Milarepa for his unconventional behavior and lack of Dharma knowledge. One day they approached him directly and said, "Since you are a good singer singer, please sing us a song." Thus he sang the following song:

> Like a snow lion cub,
> I have perfected nimbleness in my mother's womb.
> I have journeyed a long distance to the Southern Cliff[1]
> And met the Lord of the realized lineage.
> Hearken once more to the teachings of the Hearing Lineage,
> And practice the teachings in various solitary mountains.
> Why not be overcome by samadhi?

Hearing this, the yogi developed deep devotion for Mila.

Once Mila went to Sodugyenre in Ronphu. Some monks came to him, saying disrespectfully, "Yogin, you have no need of food or clothing. Please be an object of offering for us." So saying, they put him in a shrine and locked the door. But when they went outside, they saw Milarepa, and when they returned to the shrine, he was there as well. Seeing this, they recognized that he was a siddha and they developed deep devotion.

Mila also went to Nyanam and Mang-Yul Gungthang, becoming free of the need to travel in a physical form, and

[1]where Marpa resided

prodigal in his virtuous activities. Once, when he was staying at Zawog Cave, he saw from afar the son of Lama Lodrö who, though a small boy, was tending donkeys. When Mila sang a song, the child heard him and immediately went into meditation. All the donkeys returned to their huts.

The next day, Nyenchung Dorje Drak came to see the child at his home and asked, "Where did you go yesterday?" The child replied, "I heard a very beautiful sound which caused me to lose consciousness." The next day the child returned early with his donkeys to the place where Mila was staying. The Lama asked the child, "What kind of dream did you have last night?" He replied, "I dreamed that I went to the southeastern side of a meadow. A group of young women took a garland of flowers from a bowl and placed it around my neck." Mila said, "Will you follow me?" The boy agreed. Thus, the Lama accepted him as a disciple. When the child returned home, he said, "I can no longer look after donkeys. You must find someone else to take my place." The villagers said, "You were appointed to care for our donkeys because you are one of our own people." And his brother told him, "Do not tell us you are leaving. It is harvest time now. We need you. Return to your duties with the donkeys." However the boy returned to Mila's side and refused to go home. When they went to Palthan Plain, Mila carried him on his back because the walk was too arduous for the young child. They stayed at the Phugtak Cave and went to Doram Yangram where Mila gave the Tummo teaching, achieving the psychic heat yoga. Thereafter, he wore only a cotton cloth.

The young boy stayed at Chogkar Cave, and everyone was amazed by the Elder and Younger Cotton Cloths, as they were known. While there, Mila gave Mahayana yoga and other teachings and everyone developed deep devotion. One lady patron thought, "Although this Great Saint knows all the teachings, his post-meditation practice of body and speech are merely torma offerings." And she was disappointed in him. But one day when she went to Milarepa's room with the idea of doing prostrations, she found a blazing fire on the couch where the master normally sat. Addressing Shengong Repa, she asked, "Where is Mila?" He replied, "I don't think he has gone anywhere. Let us go together and see." When they went in, they found the Lama in his accustomed place on the couch. "Where have you been?" they asked. "I have been nowhere," he replied. So the woman developed deep confidence in the Lama and determined to ask his pardon for harboring doubts. But the next morning they found that the Lama had disappeared without a trace.

One day Mila went to Tshonga Drechu where many disciples came to pay their respects. Among them, five young women wearing festive clothes and ornaments sang a song called "The White Mountain Tise [Mt. Kailash]" to test him. At the end, one of the women developed deep devotion, and offering Mila her clothing and turquoise headdress, requested the teachings. From him she received the Tummo practice, and within three days achieved the psychic heat realization. Later, Rechungpa gave the woman further teachings. In Chaksedo at Nam Tsho Chukmo she practiced meditation in silence for eight years. Later she went directly to a heaven realm.

From Tshonga Drechu Mila and his young disciple went to Chimlung Khurbu where they saw Ngandzong Jangchub plowing the field. They said to him, "We two yogins ask that you give us something to eat." He replied, "If you are true yogins, you are used to singing a song inspired by whatever appears around you. So please, sing a song inspired by my plowing the field." Mila then sang a song about farming. Seeing that Mila carried a cane walking stick, the man asked Mila to sing a song about the stick. When Mila sang about his white cane stick, Ngandzong Repa became his disciple.

Once a man came to fetch Rechungpa with a message from King Tsede. Together, he and Mila went to Lo, where they gave teachings that inspired all with profound faith. Before Mila went away, everyone bid him farewell and requested a song. He sang:

I am a person, I am one,
I am the yogi, I am the repa yogin of
Tibet . . .

Once, Mila said to Likhor Charuwa, who had asked permission to go see his mother, "When you set out, do not delay. Go directly." But in Chebu Likhor was asked to read scriptures for a man who had died. Because of this delay, he found on arriving at his old home that his mother had died several days before.

Thus he realized that if he had obeyed the Lama, he could have seen his mother while she was yet alive. Thereafter he developed profound faith in Milarepa.

Great Saint went to Tsarma in Nyanam where there lived a lady known as Ngak Dormo who worked in the fields. Also, working there were Ghomma Shene and his father. The three started talking among themselves and one of the men said, "Nowadays, who is the greatest master alive?" The other man replied, "Perhaps it is Sangkar Lotsawa." And the first man said, "I believe it is Jomo Shama of Nyanam." But Ngak Dormo said, "Nowadays in our country Mila is the most famous." Just as she said this, a yogin wearing a cotton cloth appeared, saying, "I understand a person named Ngak Dormo lives here. Where is she?" In this way Ngak Dormo met him and invited him to her home, honoring him highly. That evening before Mila retired, Ngak Dormo prepared a comfortable bed with wool coverings. Mila said, "I have no need of these," but she insisted. While Mila stayed there, Ngak provided for all his needs.

At a place a short distance away called Kharna, Mila also meditated for a time. In the Nyanam area a female saint and her daughter provided for his needs. Meanwhile, Ngak Dormo offered Milarepa twelve pints of tsampa, a whole carcass of dried meat, and a ball of butter. Thus he had all that he needed.

Later, Mila decided to go to Lachi Snow Mountain. On the way snow fell for nine days and nine nights. All the people were distressed and two elderly people wept unceasingly. Everyone made special prayers at various intervals, thinking that Mila had died in the snow. Later, Driban Tashi, Gomchen Tshedrak, Kyaba Khamsum, Kyiton Shakwang, Nying Khung Yära and the patron Dormo went in search of the Lama. They suffered frostbite and when they arrived at Dukmo, all they saw was a giant snow leopard stretching on the ground. They thought: "The Lama's body has been eaten by the snow leopard." Then they saw the footprints of the snow leopard turning into the footprints of a man. "This is impossible," they said. But when they followed the footprints, they heard the Lama singing. Entering the cave, they found Mila finishing his meal. Four pints of tsampa, a portion of the dried meat, and a third of the butter remained. Everyone strongly requested that Mila visit the town. The villagers, believing that the Lama had died in the snow, came to see with their own eyes if it were truly he. When they saw him, they were overwhelmed and made prostrations. Then Mila sang a song of the Lachi Mountain, and word of his fame spread throughout the country like the light of the sun and the moon.

Arriving at Lachi on the evening of the fourteenth day of the middle summer month, Mila witnessed many obstacles arising, including a battle between gods and demons. But he sang a song and all those hearing it became subdued and developed profound devotion. Even the hardest to tame, Mutek Thangtrin, supplied Mila's needs for a month.

Later, Milarepa resided on the left side of Lachi Mountain, attended by Dampa Gyak Chung. Milarepa gave him teachings and meditated under a tree, saying, "You will not have time to meditate here when you are older." He also said, "Do not build a temple or make offerings to demons, and do not destroy ants' nests in the countryside." At the time, Dampa did not understand the meaning of Mila's words but later, events came to pass exactly as Mila predicted. When Dampa returned from twenty years of study in Central Tibet, he tried to build a temple at Nashuk, but because of a lack of wood he had to cut down trees from the right side of Lachi Mountain. He also had to ask guidance because of jealous rock spirits, and was forced to scatter ants' nests when he laid the temple's foundations. Then he realized that Mila had foretold the future.

Once, while Mila was meditating in Western Tibet, an important person of the region died, and the people all around performed ritual prayers on his behalf. When they learned that Mila was nearby, they invited him to come to their village so that the people could receive blessings and make offerings. The head of the house in which the man had died made an offering of a fine horse, but Mila said, "Take your offerings back."

Then Mila went to Rangso Thang where he was highly honored. When he left that place, Drangton Phagpa, Geshe Ngadungwa and Jo Se Chöpa sought him out and invited him to the city where they honored him. As the Lama prepared to leave that place, the men refused to let him go. But when Mila promised to return later, they allowed him to leave.

At his next meditation place the wind energy travelled up Mila's body and through his crown chakra. He stopped breathing, meditated, and experienced bliss. At midnight many women appeared before him, folded their hands and said, "Be mindful." With that the Lama brought his mind back to the earthly plane and meditated, allowing the wind energy to return to its normal place. At the moment of the sun's setting, the energy again rose up and through the crown chakra, causing him to stop breathing, but he meditated as before and his energy returned to his body. He thought: "The fact that my wind energy has returned to its own place is due to the promise I made to the people that I would return."

Then Mila went to Drin. A tantrika had a hidden consort who went to Mila, doing prostrations before him and offering rice. Mila accepted the rice in a cotton cloth. Suddenly, a small turquoise appeared on the cloth which he placed in front of the offering. "Go to Bodetse," he said. Then he went to Nyashing Phug. When the people of Drin heard that he had gone to that place, the devotees Lekse and Tashi Tsek agreed to supply his needs. Before this, the devotee Chöbar had asked Mila to accept his food offering. The Lama made this pronouncement: "First, I must accept Tashi Tsek's food, then you can make your offering." Chöbar went to Lekse and Tashi Tsek and said, "You make your food offering to the Lama first, and then I will make mine." "How did you know that we planned to make an offering?" they asked. He replied, "Mila told me." Thus, they realized that Mila possessed supernatural insight.

Mila was invited to Manlung where the people all made offerings on alternate days. When he stayed at Red Cliff Peak, he sang:

> High above, the southern cloud is floating.
> Below, the white vajra is floating . . .

Once, when the Lama was sitting above the forest, two devotees came to look for him, but not seeing him they set off again. As they moved away, Mila called after them, asking, "Where have you been?" They replied, "We went to see the Lama. Instead, we saw a stupa."

Once, a devotee appeared in the Lama's presence and looked straight ahead without doing prostrations. Mila called out to him to draw near and asked, "Why are you not doing prostrations?" He answered, "Because the Lama is not there." The Lama said, "I was in the samadhi of space." Another person asked, "What were you doing during that time?" He replied, "I have done nothing. People did not see Pandita Dipankara, either, when he was circumambulating the mountain peak, for he, too, was doing nothing. But because of interdependence, others received the impression of action. Therefore, the two form bodies of the Buddha appear according to others' mental attainments, but the Buddha actually did nothing."

Once, Tashi Tsering of Drin, who had not been in the

Lama's presence before, arrived in time to see the Lama falling off a cliff and arising without harm to himself. Everyone asked, "How could you fall from such a high cliff and arise again without loss of life?" Mila said, "If someone else had done this, his body would have been broken in many pieces."

Once Mila was seen floating in the sky in a crystal stupa. Another time, when he stayed at Rithong Tokli Tse on the Drongkha Shi mountain of Nepal, a man of the place who felt contempt for the Lama came to see him. Addressing Mila, he said, "The fame of the yogi Milarepa is baseless. The true spiritual friend is Bari Lotsawa. He possesses parasols and trumpets, and gives heaps of gold to those who approach him." A few nights later, he saw three visions of the Lama riding on a lion in the sky. He and others seeing this vision developed profound devotion to Milarepa and honored him. The Lama's attendants said to the man, "Previously you had no faith. Why are you honoring Mila now?" The disciple replied, "We are devoted to the Lama because we have three times seen him riding snow lions in the sky." Gampopa said that these events came to pass a year before he met Mila.

Once, at a ceremonial gathering, a lady asked a disciple of Mila's to name certain of the Lama's qualities. He said, "The Lama possesses the ability to see the future, as well as samadhi, freedom from concepts and other qualities." She replied disdainfully, "You cannot describe your Lama's qualities." He said, "If you know his qualities, please tell me." She went and brought forth a stupa and said, "When I make supplications each night Mila appears in this stupa three times and I make offerings." Thus it was clear that the lady was a Dakini.

Once, when Mila and his devotees were going to Chakdranglung in Drin there was a great snowfall and Mila flew overhead beyond his disciples' reach. Concerning nourishment, he said, "All I need is four handfuls of rice each month." Gampopa agreed to provide this for him, but when there were no humans to serve him, the Dakinis offered him various kinds of food and drink. Even so, he could go four, five and six days at a time without food. "I never think about food," said he. "When I enter into samadhi I have no need of it."

One year, as the seventh month of the Tibetan calendar was drawing to a close, he was staying in solitude at Chuwar at Drok Menlung when a plague befell the people, killing many humans and animals. On the eleventh day of the following month, as the sun set, a young woman wearing pearl and turquoise ornaments and silken robes appeared, radiating light. In her hands were a pair of white silken cloths decorated in scarlet with designs resembling flames, surrounded by the five jewels. Touching her head to Mila's feet, she circumambulated him seven times and prostrated nine times, saying, "Oh great Jetsün, our leader is gravely ill. Please come to that snow mountain." And she pointed in a far direction. Great Jetsün replied, "The day is now well advanced, so I can't leave. I will come when the sun rises." The woman said, "A miraculous path of light will appear that will allow Jetsün to proceed to the snow mountain without obstacles. Therefore, please come today." Great Jetsün said, "Let me see that path. I am an old man, but I have never heard of such a thing. In what direction does it lie? Point it out to me." The woman pulled a bolt of white wool from her body and threw it across the sky to make a bridge, saying, "Please use this path." No sooner had Jetsün set foot on the cloth than he arrived, like a flash of lightning, on the right side of the peak of the High Floating Queen of Snow Mountains [Gawishankar]. On that spot stood a white silk tent in which hung a piece of gold cotton cloth held up by a sapphire-like jewel. A standing shell served as the tent post, and the pegs were made of coral. On a couch lay a lady fine in every respect, her hair falling to her feet. Lifting her head and looking at Great Jetsün from blood-shot eyes, she said, "I am gravely ill; please heal me." Jetsün asked, "What has caused your sickness and when did it start? How serious is it?" In this way he learned what had happened. "My illness was caused by unhealthful smoke that rose up when humans burned impure objects during these last summer months," she replied. "It became especially severe from the twenty-sixth day of the eighth month. Therefore, I requested that you come here. My infected breath has afflicted all the people of that country and they have now fallen prey to various plagues." Great Jetsün thought: "This is how so many people and animals died in that country. I must make this being enter into a commitment." Aloud he said, "Beautiful lady, I previously gave you the Bodhisattva vow and the recitation mantra of the yidam. I have also given you the teachings on cause and effect. But you have not remained true to your samaya vows, for you have no patience even with a small sickness. You have caused much harm to many lives—even to beings who are blameless. Now, it is hard for me to trust you when I see what you have done. If you promise to stop bringing disease on other beings, I will see if I can help you. But if you do not promise, I will immediately leave, and you will continue to experience suffering because of your broken vows." The woman became fearful and clung to the feet of the Jetsün, saying, "It is the nature of us ignorant beings to commit errors, so please do not be angry with us. In general, the higher gods will not harm others if others do not harm them. In particular, I have not harmed anyone because of my vows to you, Jetsün. This sickness arose naturally because I became ill. Just as the swelling of the streams in summer causes the ground all around to become damp, so the attendants who surrounded me—meat eaters and rakshas—harmed others. If I should become well, all those around me will also keep their word to you. By this action, the diseases will disappear of themselves. This once, please show your compassion." Mila said, "Perform the purification of the hundred-syllable mantra, invoke the Triple Gem repeatedly, and perform the Ushnishavijaya practice to extend life." Next day the woman was able to arise from her bed and do prostrations; after eight days she returned to a fully normal state, and her complexion became more radiant than before. Great Jetsün said, "Beautiful lady, since you have recovered your health, I will return to the people below to benefit them. Tell me which are the right materials for beings to burn so you do not fall ill again. What kind of prayers should they say?" She replied, "According to the samaya of the Loka Dakinis, if one among us is ill, all will fall ill. In addition, the gods and demons in samsara will also be affected. This is because of interdependent origination. In the same way, when I am well so are the others. But that they might return to health more quickly, they should recite the mantra of the essence of Tathagata's ushnisha, read the profound Mahayana sutras, and bathe in the vase water. They should also create a boundary around the city and make torma and tshok offerings mixed with butter, cheese and sugar, with adornments of other foods. This will stop the various sicknesses."

Great Jetsün returned to the White Cliff of Drin and told the people, "I had a dream in which the leader of the Dakinis became displeased because of the smoke and steam from dirty cooking fires. For this reason, many gods and demons became angered. To pacify them, collect the materials to perform a tshok offering with many tormas. Invoke the Triple Gem, offer tormas to the Dharma protectors, share what you have assembled with the gods and demons of samsara, and pronounce the word of truth. In this way, the great plague will cease."

On the twenty-ninth day of that month, Tashi Tseringma, along with five Dakinis of her retinue and other followers, approached Jetsün with many kinds of magnificent foods and drink placed in vessels made of four kinds of precious jewels. They also did prostrations, circumambulated him many times and sang songs to repay his kindness. They also requested the profound teachings which Great Jetsün offered in a song.

Once, while Mila was at Drin, Darmatak, one of his disciples, became lost, causing his relatives to mourn him. When the Lama asked about the cause of their lament, they replied, "Darmatak is surely dead." The Lama replied, "He is not dead." The relatives stopped crying and asked if the Lama could bring him back to them. Later, Darmatak reappeared, so proving that the Lama had perfect supernatural insight. In this way he possessed limitless qualities.

Milarepa was never separate from the samadhi state, experienced no duality between meditation and post meditation, and achieved the absolute truth of Dharmata, the manifestation of Dharmakaya.

On the eighth day of the fourth month in the Year of the Bird Mila entered Mahasamadhi at the age of eighty-two. His cremation took place both in Tise and Drin. At that time he appeared in three different places; in one form he became the object of offerings of Tashi Tseringma, and in another he went to India.

IV. THE RIPENING OF THE PROPER VESSELS

In general, Great Saint had many disciples, among them four heart-sons, eight close disciples, six disciples who appeared just before he passed away, and one peerless son who holds the Lineage.

The four heart-sons are: Nyenchung Repa of Gungthang; Seban Repa of Dobse; Mandzong Repa of Chimlung; and Drigom Repa of Tamo. The eight close disciples were Repa Shiwa Öd; Repa Sangye Kyab; Repa Sang-yuwa; Repa Dorje Wang; Shengom Repa; Rongchung Repa; Kharchung Repa; and Langom Repa. The six disciples who appeared just before he passed away are: Nyamme Rinpoche; Likhor Charuwa; Wurton Gedün; Kyiton Shakgu; Dampa Gyakbuwa; and Drephen Trashi. Among them his only Dharma heir and foremost unparalleled heart-son, he who holds the lineage, is the Dharma Lord Gampopa Nyamme Rinpoche. The Lord Gampopa was prophesied by the Buddha in many of his teachings. Glorious Phagmodrupa also said:

I prostrate to the precious Lama
Who in an earlier time was Metok Dadze,

Who at the time of the Buddha appeared as Dawö Zhonnu,
And who in this degenerate time is a great being.

The Sutras say, "Earlier he achieved enlightenment in the name of Buddha Padma Lama; at the time of the Buddha he appeared as Dawö Zhonnu; in this time he came bearing the name of physician and had as disciples not less than seven hundred monks who all achieved the quality of samadhi, the complete realization of Dharmata." The Hidden Treasure Text by the King of Tibet, Songtsen Gampo, who was the emanation of Chenrezig, said:

In the Land of Snow,
In the degenerate time,
The teaching of great compassion
Will arise.
At that time the image of the Buddha
Will be no different than the Buddha himself,
And the image of Chenrezig
Will be no different from the true Chenrezig.
All the teachers will honor them.
Through the great meditator who is the essence of the teaching
And a precious Bodhisattva
There will appear many great beings
Who possess limitless qualities.

This great, unparalleled being (Gampopa) combined two streams of the teachings: that of Atisha, and that of Great Saint. The Dharma Lord Drikungpa said, "This precious Kagyu lineage brings the two lines together: From Atisha come the precious true Bodhicitta, the pure moral discipline, the assembly of teachings, the cultivation of the mind, the method of consecration, and others; from the teachings of Great Saint come the Mahamudra of the co-emergent wisdom, the Six Dharmas of Naropa and many others.

Atisha (982-1055)

One of the great ornaments of the world is the pandita Jowoje, an emanation of Buddha Maitreya. Glorious Phagmodrupa said: "The Bodhisattva of the tenth level and master of the five knowledges knowingly emanated in Bengal for the benefit of sentient beings, and came to the Land of Snow by the power of his aspiration. I prostrate to him who causes the harvest of devoted sentient beings to ripen like the waxing moon."

From the *Revealed Hidden Treasure of the Dharma King Songtsen Gampo:* "There will come a bird-faced bhikshu born in the north. His translator, the learned Bodhisattva Rinchen Sangpo, will honor this Buddha's image, circumambulate him, show him many signs of respect, and serve him. At this time there will appear a King called Jangchub Öd, who will be a learned Bodhisattva. He will invite to Tibet a Bodhisattva pandita who has the quality of the three trainings and three vows,[1] and who is master of scholarship and meditation. He will make offerings and prostrations, and paying homage to the statue of Buddha Shakyamuni will cause the teachings to flourish. One of his disciples, a precious

[1] three trainings: the ethics of morality, samadhi, wisdom; three vows: Vinaya, Bodhisattva, Vajrayana

spiritual master and lord of teachings possessing Bodhicitta, will be known by the name of Jambudvipa. He will be surrounded by more than five hundred disciples who will also pay honor to the Shakyamuni image and will cherish the teachings of compassion."

In the *Revealed Hidden Treasure of Padmasambhava* it is said: "This Tsogyal, the combination of the Four Mothers, without departing from the natural state of abiding, will emanate sixty years from now as Lambu Dronme, and will reveal the meaning of the essence of perfection. She will cut all Dharma in the mind expanse and will perform the action free from conceptualization. She will be confused with Gyachamma, who will be influenced by the non-virtuous Pekar. At the time of Machik at Dengri Langkor in Latö there will appear an Indian, one of my supreme disciples, known as a glorious naked one. He will bring teachings from India called Pacifying the Suffering. At that time in central Tibet, a son of the virtuous King Dipankara (Atisha), who is the emanation of my speech, will cause Dharma to pervade throughout Tibet."

Thus was prophesied the coming of the Lord of Beings, Atisha, whose life has three major aspects:

I. possessing the teachings of the lineage lamas;
II. mastering the five aspects of knowledge and the three trainings while keeping the three vows purely; and
III. receiving the vision and teachings of the yidams while seeing the absolute truth of the Dharma-as-Such and causing the teachings of the Buddha to flourish.

I. POSSESSING THE TEACHINGS OF THE LINEAGE LAMAS

This section has three aspects: (A) the lineage of the profound action, (B) the lineage of the profound view, and (C) the lineage of the profound experience.

A. The Profound Action Lineage

The teachings which Lord Maitreya gave to Asanga were in turn given by him to Vasubandhu in the following manner: in general, the Abhidharma has been destroyed three times, first by the Tartar tribe, then by heretics, and finally by a beggar with the attainment of the sun's energy. This is how it came to pass: once, the Indian King sent a cloth to the King of the Tartars, at the center of which was a child's footprint. The King of the Tartars thought: "In general, the people of the central country are expert in magic spells. This must be such a spell." Thus, he sent an army to destroy the Abhidharma teachings. Those who did not perish continued their practice.

Among the heretics was an old lady possessing the knowledge of the science of sound. She therefore understood the meaning of the sound made by the gong when it was beaten in the monasteries. Once, hearing such a gong, she said, "We should learn something from that sound."

By beating the gong of the Triple Gem
The objects of offering of gods, nagas and yakshas
Destroy the brain of the heretics.

The people therefore felt that the gong was harmful to the heretics, and so sent soldiers to destroy the Abhidharma teachings. After this, those who did not perish continued to practice the teachings.

Finally, two beggars came to a Buddhist monastery to demand food. When the monastery attendant threw water at them and chased them from the place, the beggars became intensely angry and agreed that one of them would dig a shallow ditch near a sunny place, while the other would search for food. After some time, the beggar bringing the food asked the one sitting in the ditch, "Have you realized the achievement of the power of the sun?" The other replied: "I have not; perhaps I should cease my efforts." The first man rejoined, "I have worked hard to provide you with food, even during times of famine. If you are not going to realize the sun, I will kill you right where you are sitting." So for three years the beggar practiced realizing the sun, and in the end achieved his goal. The other beggar helped his friend out of the ditch, and together they pretended to be a blind man and his attendant. The two then went toward the monastery where they had begged unsuccessfully, and the meditator shot sparks of fire from his eyes which burned the entire building. When the fire was at last put out, some said the water had issued from a sacred text. When they later opened this text, it turned out to be the Guhyasamaja.

Around this time a Brahmin lady named Salwai Tsultrim, who was devoted to the Buddha's teaching, said, "The Abhidharma, the light of all teachings, has declined. Sentient beings are now plunged into the obscuration of darkness, with no great pandita to cause the teachings to flourish. As I am but a woman, I stand no chance of seeing the noble ones. Therefore I must give birth to a child who will cause the teachings to flourish." From the woman's union with the King there came forth Asanga, and from her union with a Brahmin came Vasubandhu. In order to foster the intelligence of both children, she made them sleep under a shade tree, fed them three kinds of milk products, and annointed their tongues with sandalwood paste. She also taught Asanga to recite the mantra of Trinyensale, and Vasubandhu the mantra of Machachenmo, telling both to meditate on the yidam deities. When the two young men had grown up, they asked their mother which of them should maintain the family home. She replied, "You are not born to maintain a house. The Abhidharma has been destroyed three times and the teachings have declined. You are born to cause the teachings to flourish, so direct your efforts toward this end." Thus, Vasubandhu went to Western India, met the master Sanghabadra, studied the Low Vehicle Abhidharma, and became a great master in the study of the Sutras, while Asanga went to Southern India and meditated for three years in the Asura cave known as Bird Feet. When no signs of the practice appeared, he determined to abandon the cave. However, seeing drops of water falling from one rock to another and creating a depression thereon, he thought, "There is nothing gentler than water and nothing harder than rock. Yet with time water can wear away rock. I have put but little time into the practice of the Noble One, so I shall return to the cave for another three years." Nonetheless, he did not attain the signs. But on coming out again, he saw a pigeon's nest lodged in a rock and thought, "Because the pigeon comes out in the morning and returns in the evening, the rock has become smooth. Now there is nothing softer than a bird's feather and nothing harder than rock, but with time even a feather can wear rock away. Perhaps if I spend more time, I can realize the Noble One. So I shall return to the cave for another three years." Still, he did not attain the signs, so he came out again and this time saw an old man whittling down an iron slab by rubbing it with a pigeon feather and sand. Asanga asked him: "Why are you doing this?" and the man replied, "I am turning this iron into a sharp needle." Asanga asked, "Is it possible?" and the man replied, "With time it is indeed possible." Asanga thought, "There is nothing softer than a bird's feather and sand, and there is nothing harder than iron. But if it is possible by taking time to create a needle thus, then I must put more time into the practice of the Noble One. Therefore I shall return to the cave for another three years." Nevertheless, he still did not attain the signs. So he came out again and in the valley below saw a dog whose body was covered with maggots. When he saw this, Asanga felt strong compassion, and went to a city called Atsinda to pawn his mendicant's staff and begging bowl in exchange for a sharp blade. With this he cut a piece of flesh from his own body in order to attract to it all the maggots from the dog's body. Then he took the dog on his lap, closed his eyes and licked the maggots off. The dog disappeared and Buddha Maitreya appeared in his place, surrounded by a rainbow halo. Asanga said, "You don't have much compassion for me, for it took you so long to appear." Buddha Maitreya replied, "I was there from the beginning, but you didn't see me because of your obscurations. I was in the drops of water and all the other manifestations that you saw. If you doubt me, hoist me onto your shoulder and show me to the people of the town." Asanga hoisted Maitreya onto his shoulder, went to the town and told the people, "Maitreya is here, so do prostrations." They replied, "What is that monk saying? No one is with him." But a lady meditator of pure karma saw a white dog on Asanga's shoulder. In the samadhi of Dharma continuity Asanga saw the emanation body of Buddha Maitreya and received the teaching called "The Clarification of the Center and Boundary." Then he saw the sambhogakaya form of Buddha Maitreya and received the *Sutra Alankara* and other Mahayana teachings. Within three years he recorded these five teachings[1] in a text and also wrote the *Teachings of Yoga Charya.*

Asanga saw that Vasubandhu had mastered the Low Vehicle and was abusing the Mahayana teachings. Vasubandhu said, "Alas, Asanga has meditated for twelve years in the forest, yet he has not achieved samadhi. Now all he does is write elephant-loads of texts." To alter Vasubandhu's wrong view, Asanga sent two of his highly realized disciples towards him, instructing them, "One of you recite the *Dasha Bhumi Sutra* at dusk, and the other recite the *Lodrö Misäpa Sutra* at dawn. If Vasubandhu has a sharp knife, hide it. And if he wants to cut his tongue out, tell him, 'Do not cut your tongue. Your brother has a method for purifying your obscurations, so go to him.' Then bring him here."

Thus, the two went to Vasubandhu, and while his disciples were asleep, Asanga's disciples recited the sutras. When Vasubandhu heard the *Dasha Bhumi Sutra,* he thought, "The Mahayana teaching is good cause and good result. I see I have been abusing this teaching; this is a fault of my tongue,

---

[1] *Center and Boundary; The Clarifying of the Dharma Expanse; the Clarification of the Sutra Alankara; Abisamaya Alankara; Uttaratantra*

so I should cut it out." And he went to look for a knife, but could find none. Asanga's disciples then did as he instructed and brought him to their teacher.

While Vasubandhu was listening to the teachings, he asked many penetrating questions, for his co-emergent wisdom was sharper than Asanga's. Asanga then went into profound meditation, and with his body of mental emanation went to the Tushita Heaven to see Maitreya and clarify Vasubandhu's questions. He also received there many other Mahayana teachings, all of which took some time. Growing impatient, Vasubandhu pushed Asanga, saying, "Answer my questions." Asanga's body fell over, whereupon Vasubandhu became frightened. At once, consciousness returned to Asanga and he said, "I will give you the answers." Vasubandhu interjected, "Before you do, tell me why you just now appeared as one dead?" Asanga replied, "For five hundred successive lifetimes you have been a pandita, so you have great co-emergent wisdom and limitless confidence. I have less wisdom, so I must depend on good yidam deities. I therefore went to them to seek the answers. At the same time, I received many other Mahayana teachings and this took some time." Vasubandhu said, "Please show me your yidam deity." But Asanga replied, "This would cause my samaya to decline, so I cannot do it." Vasubandhu said, "Then please lead me to Maitreya." Asanga said, "Catch hold of my cloth and I will take you to Tushita." There, Asanga abided in samadhi, achieving perfect communion with Maitreya. But Vasubandhu could not see Maitreya; instead, he only saw Asanga as a hollow body filled with light. When Asanga awoke from samadhi, he asked Vasubandhu if he had seen Maitreya and been inspired by the Mahayana teaching. Vasubandhu replied, "Even you I saw as a hollow body of light, so how could I see Maitreya or hear the teachings?" Asanga said, "So you did not have the fortune enough to see Maitreya. Let us go back." Vasubandhu insisted that Asanga tell Maitreya of his wish to see him. When Asanga did so, Maitreya said, "Because he is an ordinary person and has abused the Mahayana teachings, he cannot see me in this lifetime. He must make aspiration prayers to see me in the next life. In addition, to purify his obscurations of speech, he should write the Eight Prakaranas, develop devotion to the Mahayana teachings, and write commentaries on them. As you, Asanga, are realized in the Abhidharma, you should write a commentary on two of my texts for the benefit of all beings in general, and for the benefit of Vasubandhu in particular." At this moment Asanga showed Vasubandhu his face and gave him the teachings on the five texts of Maitreya. The teachings were thus given through Maitreya as master, Asanga as translator, and Vasubandhu as supplicant. Vasubandhu was greatly pleased and praised his elder brother thus:

My elder brother is like a Naga,
And I like a fish desiring rain.
Though the Nagas cause rain in the sky,
It is rare for it to fall in the fish's mouth.

Asanga was prophesied by the Buddha. It is said in the *Manjushrimula Tantra* text:

A bhikshu called Asanga
Who sees the meaning of the texts,
Reveals the various ultimate meanings of the Sutras,
And is master of virtuous action,
Will become a noble commentator.
By the power of the Tantras
His wisdom will increase:
He will see the meaning of suchness,
Compile the Sutras,
Cause the teachings to be maintained for a long time
to come,
Live one hundred fifty years,
Be reborn in higher realms after leaving the body,
Experience lasting peace,

Remain in samsara for a long time,
And ultimately achieve enlightenment.

Asanga gave teachings to Vasubandhu, who gave them to Arya Namdrolde, who gave them to the commoner Namdrol De, who gave them to Chok-gi De, who gave them to Dulwai De, who gave them to Khenpo Yangdak Namnangze, who gave them to Seng-ha Badra, who gave them to Rinchen Zangpo, who gave them to Rata Prajnapala, who gave them to Gunamaitra, who gave them to Atisha.

B. The Profound View Lineage

The coming of the Lord of Sentient Beings, Arya Nagarjuna, is prophesied in many Sutras and Tantras. In the *Mahamega Sutra* the Buddha said, "Ananda, four hundred years after I have passed away, Lichavi Zhonnu Semchen Thamchekyi Thonga Gawa will appear as a bhikshu called Naga, who will cause my teachings to flourish greatly. Finally, Tathagata Jnanakara Prabhava will appear in a world called Rabtudangpai Öd." And in the same Sutra it is said, "In this fortunate world there will appear one thousand Buddhas. Thereafter, for sixty-two kalpas there will appear no Buddha, but one hundred thousand million Pratyeka Buddhas. Later, seven Buddhas will arise. Yet later, this world will be called Ngonpar Dangwa (Fully Clear) and in it a Buddha called Jnanakara will appear." And in the *Ngawoche (Great Drum) Sutra* it is stated:

O All-Seeing Happy World Teacher
Manifested in the form of a monk,
Maintain the teachings for a long period
And beat the great drum of the teachings.

In the same text it says:

After passing away
He will be reborn in the world called Dewachen.
At that time by miraculous powers

He will manifest in many forms.
One emanation body will remain
In Dewachen at the eighth Bodhisattva level,
And one will go to Tushita
And will proclaim this Sutra from Maitreya.

And in the *Manjushrimula Tantra* it is written, "After entering Parinirvana I, Tathagata, will appear after four hundred years as a bhikshu called Nagarjuna, who will benefit from this teaching, achieve the joyous level of a Bodhisattva, and live for six hundred years. This great Lord will practice the Knowledge of Macha, will write many commentaries, will realize the suchness of the non-observation meaning, will go to Dewachen after leaving that body, and will definitely achieve Enlightenment after that time." The *Lankavatara Sutra* states, "In the future, who will hold this tradition? Listen, Great Wise One, in the Bheta country in the South a Bhikshu named Palden, who will be called Naga, will cause the division between nihilists and eternalists to disappear. This ultimate great vehicle will flourish throughout the world, will achieve the joyous bhumi state, and will go to Dewachen."

Thus was this great being prophesied. Nagarjuna was born a Brahmin in the city known as Great Rosary, near another city known as Resistance-by-Battle, near the banks of the river Murum in the South. His father was a revered physician known as Nampar Gyalwai Dawa and his mother was known as Rigdenma. The family had two sons: the first was Lodrö Phak, and the second was Sonam Phak. The younger son vanquished the pride of the elder, and to destroy his father's pride in his accomplishments as a physician he composed medicine texts known as the Four Branches of Benefit, Equalizing the Four Elements, Correct Diet, and others.

One day, the son prostrated before his father and set out for the great university of Nalanda where he was ordained a bhikshu by the Abbot Rahula Badra, and given the name Lodrö Sangpo. For three years he practiced the teaching on the *Knowledge of Machya (Peacock) Sutra* and achieved the signs. He then went to Likhara Shingphel to beg alms. Entering the house of a goldsmith, he saw that he was practicing the alchemic art of transmuting base metal to gold. Merely by observing he immediately grasped the technique.

The Abbot appointed him as overseer of his monastery while he went into retreat in a solitary place in the forest. When a famine occurred in the area, Nagarjuna used the alchemic technique, supporting all the monks through the gold he created. When the Abbot returned to the monastery after six months, he struck a rock with his walking stick and transformed it into gold. The Abbot said, "If you had informed me of a famine, I would have caused a rain of barley to fall and a clay representation of a cow to give milk. But instead you maintained the monks through impure action. You must leave this place." Nagarjuna prostrated before the Abbot and planned to go to Palkyiri Mountain in Southern India.

On an island in the ocean lived a man known as Zwayapala who was able to transform rock into gold, cause a rain of jewels to fall, and a drawing of a cow to give milk. So Nagarjuna proceeded there and learned those arts. He then went to Palkyiri and through the art of extracting nourishment from inanimate objects remained there six hundred years. Causing a rain of jewels to fall on the poor of the city, he became known as Bhikshu Shiri. He also transformed the Belt Mountain into gold, and caused milk from a drawing of a cow to flow in such profusion that travelers were able to drink for a year.

Nagarjuna became an object of worship for King Thardro Zhonnu. Once, while the King was at war, his wife became enamoured of Nagarjuna and suggested that they live together. When Nagarjuna refused, the Queen became so angry that upon the King's return she told him that Nagarjuna had made the suggestion, but that she had refused. In this way, the King and his retinue lost confidence in Nagarjuna, who felt obliged to depart the kingdom. But before doing so, he wrote the following verse:

The nature of woman
Is not recognized by the ignorant
Because of their obscurations.
When a woman loves a man
She will stay with him as long as it suits her.
But she will discard him in a moment
When she is no longer interested.
This is her nature.
Women are not stable of mind;
Skillful men should beware.

He left this verse at the house of a goldsmith who became abusive of him. To show the smith his powers, Nagarjuna transformed a rock into gold and gave it to him. Thereafter, he proceeded South.

Meanwhile, King Thardro Zhonnu discovered Nagarjuna's poem and realized that it was his wife who had been at fault. So he asked that Nagarjuna return, but the latter refused. However, he sent the formula for his technique of extracting food from inanimate objects, and promised the King a life-span of six hundred years. The King was overjoyed and ruled the kingdom according to the Dharma.

There was no branch of knowledge unknown to Nagarjuna, and he composed myriad different texts, thus benefitting many sentient beings and causing the teachings to flourish widely.

In the *Manjushrimula Tantra* it is written, "At the end of time a powerful one will appear who refutes all argument, and the scandalous mantras of heretics." It is also said in the same text:

At that time there will come my bhikshu,
The learned one who will be known as Servant of the
  Mother.
Through completely pure qualities
He will compose songs of praise to me,
And record my qualities.
His mind is completely clear.

He will enjoy the teachings of the Buddhas
And will practice the Tantra.
Manjushri himself will cause his qualities and
morality to grow.
He will give teachings and become learned in many
areas.
He has the karma to be born in animal form,
But because of complete devotion to me
He will live in the Milk Garden
In a pleasant city known as Main Lord.
He will stay with my disciples contentedly,
And will think only of me.
Because of the purity of his devotion,
He will later dwell for a time in the god realm.
Thereafter he will be reborn in the human realm,
And will become a monk adhering to my teachings.
By offering me his total devotion,
He will become known as Servant of the Mother
And will observe pure discipline.
He will compose various commentaries according
to the Tantras
To benefit all sentient beings.
He will reveal many elegant sayings,
And will be superior in devotion and in resolving
disputes.
During that time beneficial causes
Will arise to help all sentient beings.
Through this virtuous karma
This wise person will be reborn in higher realms,
Will gradually experience various forms of bliss,
And will achieve the omniscience of enlightenment
And the inconceivable ultimate state.

Thus he said.

Chandrakirti was a disciple of Nagarjuna, who was adorned with many samadhi and realization qualities. He lived four hundred years in the human realm, spending about one hundred of them at the feet of Nagarjuna. His disciple, the great master Rigpe Khuchuk, attained the Bodhisattva's bhumis and lived three hundred years. In turn, his disciple, the elder Kusali, achieved bhumis as an upasaka (householder keeping the precepts). His disciple, the younger Kusali, lived two hundred years during which he attained bhumis, became a bhikshu and achieved the realization of Mahamudra. His disciple was Atisha, who attained avadhuti in seven years.

C. *The Profound Blessing Meditation Experience Lineage*

The great Vajradhara gave teachings to the Master Tilopa, who was an emanation of Vajradhara. He, in turn, gave teachings to glorious Panchen Naropa, who gave them to the great saint Dombhiwa, who gave them to Atisha. Atisha directly realized Naropa, who placed his hand on Atisha's head and said, "All the Buddha's teaching is given to you."

II. POSSESSING THE THREE TRAININGS AND KEEPING THE THREE VOWS PURELY

Atisha was born as a Prince. His father, who was known as Gewai Pal (Glorious Virtue), was King of Bangala in the East in the city of Vikrama Puri in the region of Lahore. His influence was as great as that of Tongkun, King of China, for he controlled an area equal to two million, seven hundred thousand courtyards. His mother was Queen Palmo Öserchen (Glorious Radiating Light). They had three sons: the eldest was known as Padma Nyingpo (Essence of the Lotus), the middle son was Soma Svara or Dawa Nyingpo (Essence of the Moon), and the youngest was Palgyi Nyingpo (Essence of Glory). Padma Nyingpo had three consorts and nine sons, the eldest of them being Sonam Pal who later became a great scholar and monk. He was known as Dhana Shri Pandita, and wrote a commentary known as *The Wisdom Path of the Bodhicharya Avatara.* The middle son was Atisha, and the youngest was a monk who became known as Bhikshu Virya Chandra. Until he was twenty-one, Atisha studied the sixty-four arts, all the arts of sound and logic. He also received complete empowerments from Rahula Gupta Vajra and Lord Yonden Sangpo (Gunabadra), who was a great master of realization. In addition, he received the vision of Hevajra and instructions from the Vajra Dakinis.

At the temple known as Rinak (Black Hill), Atisha was given the name of Jnanaguya Vajra. When he was staying at Vikramalashila University, he received the empowerment of the completion stage from Avadhuti, a disciple of Naropa who was born in Bangala, and who possessed the quality of foresight. He remained seven years with Avadhuti performing the Avadhuti action in the upasaka precepts. He also received many Tantra teachings, especially the stabilization meditation. Once he came to the central country, where in a dream he saw a temple filled with monks, which he greatly desired to enter. But one of the monks said, "This place is only for monks. As you are a lay person, you are not allowed here." When Atisha awoke, he thought, "Perhaps I should become a monk. This dream appears to have been a sign from Maitreya." When he asked Upasaka, who had a good knowledge of Dharma, Upasaka told him he should be ordained by the master Sangye Yeshe (Buddha Jnana) of the Mahasangika School, which more readily offers the Tantra teachings. Atisha preferred to be ordained in the Ame School which used Sanskrit, but they refused the Mahayana as the Buddha's teachings. Upasaka again urged that he be ordained in the Mahasangika School. Thus, at the age of twenty-eight, Atisha was ordained by the Abbot Shila Rakshita, who achieved higher realization and possessed the quality of samadhi. The Mahasangika School arose from the master Yeshe Sangye.

At Bodh'gaya Mativihara, Atisha was given the name Dipankara Shri Jnana (Glorious Wisdom Source of Light). From then until he was thirty-five years old, he studied the three yanas from many masters and attained omniscience.

Atisha studied the text called *Tsana Akyi*, concerning customs and manners, written by the Brahmin Tsana Akya. He also studied the non-Buddhist teachings of Vishnu, Siva and Rishi Kapila, along with other views and tenets, and

Hindu Tantras and texts on the analysis of signs and omens, both Buddhist and non-Buddhist. When he studied the art of sound, he memorized a chapter of the text each morning and evening, but feeling that this was not sufficient he meditated on Saraswati [the embodiment of wisdom in female form] until one day at dawn he actualized the art of sound. Saraswati appeared to him and said, "You are realized." He also studied a non-Buddhist text on sound called the *Light of the Word* by the Brahmin Norlha, and others. Among Buddhist texts composed by Tsandra Gomi [contemporary with Chandrakirti] he studied the *Tsandra Byakarana* and the *Mani Byakarana*, the *Pani Byakarana*, the *Indra Byakarana*, the *Radza Byakarana*, and many others. These are the sciences of sound and language. In logic, Atisha's non-Buddhist studies included texts by Rishi Akshipada and many others. His Buddhist studies included texts by Acharya Diknak called *Pramana Samuccaya* and *Pramana Vartika*, six texts by Acharya Dharmakirti, and one text by Acharya Shanti Rakshita. In this way Atisha studied widely. He also investigated the science of healing, studying texts written by rishis such as Rishi Lekthong, writings by the Buddha, and medicine texts including the *Four Branches* composed by Arya Nagarjuna, and the *Eight Branches* composed by Ashvaghosha. In addition, Atisha mastered the arts of wood cutting, sewing, image-casting, drawing and others. Among the non-Buddhist texts he studied the *Great God Shankara*, and among Buddhist texts one by Arya Nagarjuna. He also studied the science of the inner meaning, including the Tripitaka of the Mahasanghika, the Sarvastivadi, the Abhidharma, and the Sutras of this tradition. He studied the four categories of Vinaya and the Great Abhidharma Treasure Teachings of Vesheshika in eight hundred chapters compiled by Arhat Upa Gupta, which are common to all four lower vehicle schools. These studies, which he accomplished under master Dharma Rakshita at Otantapuri, generally take twelve years, but because of Atisha's great perseverance he completed them within seven years. He would go into seclusion for periods of six days, coming out on the seventh day, but even then continuing his studies.

Atisha studied the Brief Abhidharma common to both low and high vehicles, and the commentary by Master Sarva Rakshita and many others.

His Study in Mahayana

1. The perfection vehicle
2. The secret mantra vehicle

1. The Perfection Vehicle

Atisha studied the Bodhisattvayana, including the four noble truths, the *Sutra Alankara* composed by Acharya Ashvaghosha, and many *Prajnaparamita* sutras and other perfection vehicle texts. He realized many commentaries on the Sutras and studied the five commentaries on the Mahayana by Lord Maitreya. He studied and accomplished many commentaries written by Arya Nagarjuna.

At Solnak Thang Atisha gave the Uttaratantra teachings to Khutön, and at Yerpa he gave the *Sutra Alankara*. He was invited to Samye Kharchung where he taught the six different types of Mahayana teachings to Ngok. He also studied many Yogacharya texts written by Acharya Asanga and Vasubandhu, as well as the instruction of the Tantra of Yogacharya translated by Gya Tsondru Sangye, a tradition of Acharya Ratna Akara Shanti, a commentary of the *Prajnaparamita* in the Mind-Only school and the tradition of Acharya Singhabhadra, and the commentary of the *Prajnaparamita* in the Madhyamika school. In Trulnang, Atisha translated the commentary on the *Prajnaparamita* composed by Acharya Lekden Namnang, and in Yerpa for ten months and nineteen days he gave the teachings on the *Samuccaya Sutra* of Bodhisattva Labtu, the *Bodhicharya Avatara*, and others.

2. The Secret Mantra Vehicle

His secret mantra studies included: the four Tantras of the Secret Mantra Vajrayana; the *Tantra of the Origin of Tara*; the *Tantra of Tsundana*; and the *Tantra of Manjushri*. Within the Charya Tantra he studied the *Tantra of the King of the Three Samayas* and the *Tantra of Complete Enlightenment*; within the Yoga Tantra the *Tantra of the Collection of Realizations*, the *Tantra of the Female Vajra*, and the *Tantra of the First Glorious Supreme*; within the Supreme Yogacharya Tantra the *Tantra of the Union of All Buddhas*; and within the Anuttara Tantra division the *Guhyasamaja*, the Tantra of Method in the traditions of Arya Nagarjuna, King Indrabodhi, and Acharya Buddhajnana, along with the commentaries of the three texts and their instruction.

Atisha also studied the *Dasang Thigle*, the *Tantra of the Nonduality of Method and Wisdom*, and many others. Within the category of the Tantra of Wisdom he studied the *Tantra of Namka Dang Nyampa*, the *Tantra of the Original Buddha*, the *Tantra of the Illusory Vajra*, and others.

In a dream, Atisha offered a handful of pure gold to Pandita Wakishvara Kirti, the Western Gatekeeper at Nalanda, prostrated twelve times, and received from him four hundred fifty-two Tantras. When he awoke, the meaning of these Tantras had taken permanent root in his mind. Within these instructions were six Tantras explaining the ultimate meaning of the teachings.

Atisha then related to Geshe Tonpa that his pride had been broken by Jomo (a nun) in the following way: In one of his dreams there appeared a monastery containing a mountain-heap of texts. A blue lady appeared and picked up a small text at the top of the heap, saying, "This small text represents the sum of your knowledge of Tantra." She then told him the name of many Sutra texts of which he had never heard, asking if he knew of them. In this way he had to alter his proud view that he knew all the Tantric teachings.

Geshe Nyakrumpa told the following story: "In India, even if one is greatly skilled in the knowledge of the five aspects, if one does not keep the three trainings, he is considered of no importance, and the texts which he composed will be destroyed. On the other hand, texts composed by a scholar who keeps the three disciplines are placed atop the victory banner where their teaching flourishes widely." Thus, Atisha was fully trained in the three disciplines and completely mindful of even the smallest moral rules of the Vinaya. He was the complete holder of the Vinaya discipline.

In the perfection path of the Mahayana, Atisha cultivated Bodhicitta, steeping his mind in the waters of loving-kindness and compassion toward all sentient beings. With altruistic thought and perfect ethics he directly and indirectly benefitted all. He was a great Bodhisattva who practiced all the trainings in the Path of the Secret Mantra Vajrayana Diamond Vehicle, in meditation remaining continually united with all the Buddhas. He possessed the vajra mind of realization, thus keeping the morality of the different vehicles, and surpassing everyone in adherence to the discipline.

III. SEEING THE VISION OF THE ENLIGHTENED YIDAMS AND RECEIVING THEIR TEACHINGS; REALIZING THE MEANING OF THE SUCHNESS; SPREADING THE TEACHINGS OF THE BUDDHA.

Atisha received the visions of the outer Yidam, Jo Meyuwa, Arya Avalokiteshvara, Tara, Damtsiksumköpa, and others. He also had visions of the inner Yidam, Shri Hevajra, and others. Through their blessings he received many teachings both in the waking and dream states. At times when he meditated one-pointedly to transform events, he would see clearly in his dreams what would transpire. He possessed the wisdom of the three times.

Reciting the hundred-syllable mantra of the Tathagata in Tibet during the new moon, Atisha received the visions of the Buddhas of the ten directions. He remained continually in the presence of these Buddhas, making offerings to them and benefitting all sentient beings.

Atisha was a great Bodhisattva free from all controversy. Even ordinary beings perceived him as a second Buddha, and his fame pervaded the world, causing him to become the master of all other teachers. Thus, during the reign of the King Dewa Belpo, the great master Dipankara Shri Jnana invited him to Vikramalashila from Bodh'gaya, and he became the crown ornament of the kingdom.

The Building of Vikramalashila

A yogi from Central India, wishing to obtain the powers of a King, practiced the meditation of Lhamo Öser Chenma. Accomplishing the meditation, he received a prediction to go to Bangala in Eastern India. Journeying there, he found that every inhabitant took his turn being King for one day, after which he inevitably died. That particular day it was the turn of a son of a shepherdess, who was very distressed about the situation. When the yogi asked the cause of her woe, she told him the story and he said, "May I then take his place?" The woman was overjoyed.

When the yogi was enthroned, he discovered that the Queen was an evil Naga. She advanced with the intention of eating him, but being armed with confidence in his meditations, he managed to subjugate her. Everyone present was amazed and he was empowered as King of that region under the name of Gopala, which means "He who looks after cows." Thus, he ruled all of Bangala and enjoyed the company of five hundred queens, each of whom had a fully-ordained resident nun.

As the youngest queen had never attracted the attention of the yogi King, she had her attendant nun perform a special meditation to help her win his favor. The nun then gave the Queen a bowl of cooked meat to offer the King, but when she went to him to make the offering, she couldn't find him. She then threw the meat in the sea, thereby gaining control over the ocean god, who arose in the form of the king. By him she conceived a child, but when the real King heard of this, he asked who the child's father was. The young Queen replied, "It was you who appeared to me one night," thus causing the

King to realize that the Queen had been tricked by a false manifestation of himself. He therefore hid, waiting for the ocean god to reappear, and when the creature manifested, the King grabbed hold of him, asking the reason for his presence. The god then told him the story of the Queen's meat offering, and said that he had no control over all that had resulted. He asked to be released, offering the King the son whom the Queen had conceived by him. Thus, when the child was born, he was known as Dharmapala, and he caused the kingdom to increase greatly.

At that time a yogi who had accomplished the Tara meditation engaged in a war to destroy the heretics in Bhalentara. On the way, he met a black man who said, "Do not immediately destroy the temple of the heretics; first, dig in this mound of sand and you will find a temple of the Buddha Khashapa. Then, when you enter the battle, make a sound which includes all the harmonies of the universe together, and the heretics' temple will disappear of itself." This black being was an emanation of Mahakala. The yogi uncovered the temple, which was known variously as the temple of Trikaruka, and the temple of Chosomangpuri, and the Hidden Ocean. Then he entered into battle, causing all musical instruments to sound at once. Hearing this, all the heretics were instantaneously subjugated, and the whole of Bhalentara was placed under the yogi's authority.

At that time in the mind of a master called Palgampala, who had gained the realization of Mahamudra, there arose the thought, "If I were to build a monastery on a rock near the Ganges, the teachings of the Buddha would be greatly benefitted. But the temple would be better built if the construction were undertaken by the King rather than by a mere monk." So he thought he should cause himself to be born as the son of King Dharmapala.

One night the Queen had a dream that a monk wearing the saffron-colored Dharma robes and holding a bowl and staff was saying, "I seek lodging here." Thus, she conceived a child who, under the name of Devapala, was to become a powerful ruler of the Mangata country, and was to build the monastery he had foreseen on a rock near the Ganges. Its northern gate was named Vikramalashila (The Scent of Morality). The King supplied the needs of twenty-seven monks from each of the four lineages of the Vinaya (one hundred eight monks in all), and the monastery furnished the needs of twelve monks from Tibet, Oddiyana, and other places, as well as seven monks studying the sciences of sound, logic and torma-making. Generally, there were five thousand monks in the monastery, one hundred eight scholars, twenty-one great scholars, twelve excellent scholars, seven supreme scholars, and four ultimate scholars. Among these were two great sthaviras, Shrimitra the great Vinaya holder, the great Acharya Naropa, the great writer Wakishawarikirti, the great debater Ratna Akara Shanti, and Atisha, who was one of the seven supreme scholars.

Atisha fully kept the discipline of the four Vinaya lineages. Within the monastery Nagarjuna's image was erected on the right and Atisha's on the left, in consequence of which Atisha was recognized as the second Nagarjuna. On one side were depicted all the great yogis and on the other all the great scholars, with Atisha appearing among both groups.

To fulfill the wishes of the King, Atisha gathered all four Vinaya lineages in the monastery. Generally, his disciples spread throughout India, Nepal, Pakistan and Oddiyana, but there were five special disciples who were like his heart, head, eyes, right and left hands. These were the great panditas Bodhiwa, Ratna Akara, Mati Umasingha, Shenyen Sangwa, and Sai Nyenpo. Although they were not equal to the master in their blessings and other qualities, they were equal in understanding. Atisha also had many realized disciples in India, as well as Bhikshus and Bhikshunis realized in Mahamudra. Because his fame pervaded the ten directions, he was invited to Tibet by the Bodhisattva King.

In the Western part of Tibet, the King Trashigon had two sons, Trong Nge and Khore. Of these, Trong Nge had two sons, Nagarandza and Devarandza. As Trong Nge renounced the kingdom to become a monk, his rule passed to Khore. Meanwhile, Trong Nge worked hard to re-establish the teachings of the Buddha, becoming known as Lha Lama Yeshe Öd. He was considered an emanation of Manjushri, and was prophesied in the *Manjushrimula Tantra*.

Khore's son Ngadak Lhade in turn had four sons: Öd De, Lhatsun Jangchub Öd, Shiwa Öd, and Tangchung. At the time of the Tibetan King Lhate and the Central Indian King Devapala, Atisha was residing at Vikramalashila. In Tibet Lhatsun Jangchub Öd was greatly saddened by the decline of the teachings of the Buddha. Further, because Acharya Marpo was translating texts about *sang ngak thigle* (the secret Tantric drop practice), all the monks were marrying and all the householders were abandoning the Nye-ne discipline, thus causing the teachings to decline. So Lhatsun Jangchub Öd twice sent messengers to India to invite Atisha, but as he could not come, Lhatsun thought of inviting a master second in rank. Meanwhile, he sent for a Tibetan geshe, Gungthangpa, who was twenty-seven years old, well versed in the knowledge and practice of the Vinaya, and eager to journey to India for study. When the geshe appeared before him, the King related how the teachings had been corrupted, and how following the tradition of his forefathers who for the benefit of beings had invited thirteen great masters, he had tried unsuccessfully to bring Atisha to Tibet. It remained his hope that Atisha would eventually come to Tibet, but if not, he would accept a master second to him, and for this purpose he proposed to send Geshe Gungthangpa to India. But Gungthangpa said, "Please do not ask me to do this. I am going to India to study, and this mission would be an obstacle to my work." The King said, "You are not supposed to defy the King's orders, as this is so important a matter. This is my only request. Give me this happiness and I will do something good for you in return. Indeed, I will supply your needs either for your study in India or Tibet, or simply for your upkeep should you decide not to study." Strongly requesting the Geshe's help, he left the monk no choice.

When the geshe set off to India, the King gave him a large bar of gold and fourteen additional ounces of gold to take to Atisha as an offering. To the monk he gave seven ounces of gold for his own use, and seven more ounces of gold to pay for the expenses of the journey. To a man with a slight knowledge of Sanskrit he gave five ounces of gold, and to three others he gave three ounces each. The five together went to India to seek Atisha.

One night after arriving, they stayed in a bamboo hut when a man named Atsara, seeing the gold that they were carrying, planned to rob them. Realizing this, the group fled the hut and went on to Bodh'gaya in central India, from whence, because of the level terrain, they saw the roof of Vikramalashila, three days' journey away. A law in the land forbade them to cross the Ganges in daylight, but they persuaded a sailor to take them across in the evening. When they reached the monastery early the next morning, they heard someone reading a Sutra in Tibetan. It was the translator Gya Tsondru Senge from whom Gungthangpa had earlier on studied the Abhidharma. When Gya asked if the Geshe was coming to study with the master or carry him away, Gungthangpa replied, "The King of Tibet sent us to bring the teacher back with us." The translator said, "Just pretend that you have come here to study. There are thirty great scholars after Atisha, such as Tathagata Krita, Sunmate Kirti, Vairocana Krita, the Nepali Kankapi and others. But I will tell Atisha your wish and we will see what will happen.

One day the translator called the Geshe to Atisha's cell, and the Geshe placed before him all the King's gold as a mandala offering, explaining that the Tibetan King was a bodhisattva who requested that he come to Tibet. Atisha said, "Indeed, the Tibetan King is a bodhisattva, and one should not disobey a bodhisattva's orders. Earlier, when they sent messengers to invite me, one of them died. I felt such regret that I did not care to come. This time I will ask Arya Tara whether or not I can benefit sentient beings in Tibet.

Take back your gold." So Atisha performed an offering before Tara's shrine, as well as mandala offerings and aspiration prayers. Later, Tara appeared in his dreams saying, "There is a city of heretics known as Chukhyer (Water Carrying) near the Vikramalashila monastery. In the middle of that city is a small old temple where you will find a yogini. Ask her whether you should go to Tibet."

The next morning, Atisha took a handful of cowrie shells, went to the temple he had seen in his dreams, and made a mandala offering. After a time a yogini appeared with hair flowing nearly to the ground. Making mandala offerings before her, Atisha said, "The King of Tibet has invited me to his land. If I grant his request, will I benefit beings there?" The Yogini replied, "You will benefit many beings, especially one upasaka, but your life will be shortened by twenty years." Atisha thought, "If I can benefit beings, what do I care if my life is shortened?" And he prepared for the journey, telling the messenger from Tibet, "I will not undertake any new activities, but just to complete what I have started will take eighteen months. Can you wait that long?" Geshe Gungthangpa replied, "For you I would wait even three years." Atisha said, "Then, until I am ready to depart, use your time to study." Because he was near the master Atisha and the translator Gya Tsondru Senge, the monk was able to accomplish much during his time in India.

After completing his work at the monastery and before leaving for Tibet, Atisha made a series of brief journeys to accustom the monks to his absence. At last, the day arrived when Atisha was able to tell the Geshe, "We must now go to Bodh'gaya to make offerings individually." He then sent all his texts ahead to Tibet in the care of Gya Tsondru Senge, but the translator died on the way. Gungthangpa worried over the fate of the texts, but Atisha calmed his mind.

Atisha came to Nepal where one of his friends provided for his needs for one month. At the request of the people there he composed the text known as *Chödü Dronme (The*

Lamp of Brief Action). From there he proceeded to Mang-yul in Western Tibet where he stayed for one year. He then went to Lake Manasarovar near Mt. Kailash through Purang.

One day, they stopped for a noon break. Meanwhile, Atisha was performing a water offering ceremony. Gungthangpa asked if he might record it. This became known as the water offering of Khasarpani, which is a special offering on the visualization of Chenrezig. Atisha then went to Tulung where the King welcomed him. There he met the great translator Rinchen Tsangpo who, though a great scholar, lacked a profound understanding of actual practice. Rinchen Tsangpo therefore requested that Atisha give meditation practice teachings. Thereafter, when he practiced the Guhyasamaja, he received the vision of the enlightened deities. He and others translated many texts and refined those translations which had been done before. Together with Atisha, they gave teachings to many people.

Gungthangpa said, "Now the great master has only one year to remain in Tibet. Then he must return to India according to the agreement he made with his Indian disciples." Knowing that Atisha's time in Tibet was limited, many people flocked to him to receive teachings while they could. The King, Jangchub Öd, made an offering of three hundred ounces of gold and asked Atisha five questions: (1) "Atisha," said he, "you are a great master. Here in Tibet some masters say that the Hinayana and Mahayana have existed from the beginning, while others say that they have existed indefinitely, and that Hinayana can cultivate Mahayana thought. Which view is correct?" Atisha replied, "As Tibetan scholars are meditating on the Dharma I will answer you in time." (2) In like manner the King asked his second question: "In Tibet some masters say that the different stages of realization arise from meditation practice, whereas others say realization arises spontaneously, thus eliminating the need for meditation. Which is true?" (3) The King's third question was, "In Tibet some scholars say that skillful means, or method and wisdom, should be united.

But others say they should be kept separate. Which is true?" (4) His fourth question was, "In Tibet some masters say we need the Pratimoksha vows as a basis for the Bodhisattva vow, but some say not. Which is true?" (5) The fifth question was, "In Tibet some say that monks should be given the secret wisdom empowerment and some say they should not. Which is true?" To answer these questions Atisha composed a text known as the *Lamp for the Path to Enlightenment*. To the first question he replied:

> The final vehicle is one,
> But relatively there are three categories of beings;
> Those of inferior, middling and superior capabilities.

To show that it is necessary to do meditation practice for higher realization, he replied to the second question this way:

> Meditation practice is needed.
> Through this practice
> One will gradually achieve wisdom heat and so forth,
> As well as the supreme joy and others.
> Thereafter, full enlightenment is not far off.

To show that it is necessary to unify method and wisdom, he replied to the third question thus:

> Wisdom without method
> And method without wisdom
> Remain in bondage.
> Therefore, one should abandon neither.

To show that it is necessary to have any one of the Pratimoksha vows to cultivate bodhicitta, he replied to the fourth question in this way:

> Having any of the seven Pratimoksha vows
> Establishes the basis for the Bodhisattva's vow.
> Without these there is no Bodhisattva vow.

To show that the secret empowerment should not be given to celibates he replied to the fifth question thus:

Celibates should not be given
The secret wisdom empowerment.

This text Atisha composed from his personal meditation experience.

Atisha was then asked to compose a meditation practice on the principal mandala deity as Chenrezig, based on the Guhyasamaja Tantra. In reply, he composed the sadhana of Chenrezig which, when the King Jangchub Öd practiced it, enabled him to receive the vision of Chenrezig directly.

In Shangshung where he stayed for one year, Atisha produced many realized disciples. Then he returned to Purang where the elder monk Serso achieved clairvoyance merely by attending him. He could see mines beneath the ground.

The Story of Geshe Tonpa's Meeting with Atisha

At Gyashing in Purang he met Geshe Tonpa who had been born in the North Central part of Tibet to the Drin clan. As his mother died young, Geshe Tonpa was reared by a stepmother. One day he threw a stone at a dri which his step-mother was milking, thus causing her to spill the milk. In anger the woman beat him, and he decided to leave home. At this point he met the master Setsun Wangchu Zhonnu, who was a disciple of Pandita Jnanakirti, and had studied in Tibet and Nepal. From Nepal Setsun planned to go to India, but meanwhile he met with an Indian magician. As Setsun, for his part, was learned in astrology, the two men were known as the two clairvoyants.

One day, as they sat next to each other on neighboring thrones, the magician placed a vase on empty space, challenging Setsun to equal his power. By doing astrological calculations, Setsun was able to see that the magician's father's head was lying under a stupa. "If you continue to practice magic," he told the magician, "your father's head will be buried beneath a stupa." Thenceforth the magician regarded Setsun as an enemy, so the latter returned.

At this point Geshe Tonpa, who was seventeen years old, met Setsun and received teachings from him. Setsun went to

Kham where his intelligence and way of teaching resembled Atisha's. Later, Geshe Tonpa wished to go to Kham and followed Setsun, but he travelled too far and instead met Dru Namkha from whom he studied the Abhidharma. Later, he met Setsun again and served him devotedly. Because he was wearing skin garments, the clothes stuck to him when the rains came, so that to remove them he had to tear his own flesh. He learned the teachings so well that when anyone made mistakes about them he was able to correct them. Thus his fame grew.

Jowo Setsun told Geshe Tonpa, "As you understand the teachings so well, you must give up all ordinary occupations and study the Dharma." So he continued to serve the Lama and to study. Whenever he received offerings he accepted them out of compassion, but as he was little concerned with this life, he never kept more than the little he needed to survive. He was also offered many domestic animals, and at night he wove a protection circle to keep them from harm, all the while contemplating the teachings. In this way he tried to please Setsun, hoping to receive special teachings from him. "No matter what happens," he thought, "I should please the master. There is no finer occupation than this." The many people who came to see Jowo Setsun and receive his blessings remarked on Geshe Tonpa's devotion and service.

Around this time, a young monk from Kham who was well versed in the lore of India told Geshe Tonpa the story of Naropa, Shantipa and others, and of their realizations. Geshe Tonpa asked, "Nowadays, does anyone exist as great as they?" In reply, the monk spoke of Atisha's wisdom and realizations. The moment Geshe Tonpa heard Atisha's name, the hair of his body stood on end, and he asked himself, "How can I meet this being?" In all, he served Jowo Setsun for twenty years, from the age of eighteen until thirty-eight. At the end of that time, he told Setsun that he had heard of Atisha and formed a plan to see him. Setsun replied, "As your father is still alive, you should see him one more time. Further, I have no need of all my texts, so you can take as many of them as you like." Geshe Tonpa loaded a pack horse with texts and after seven days' journey he and the friend who had accompanied him, Yeshe Gyal, arrived at the latter's birthplace. Geshe Tonpa asked Yeshe if he wished to visit, but Yeshe wanted only to reach his master.

At Sokchukha the two met Patsab Berchung who had been studying since his seventeenth year and had a good understanding of the Tantras and other teachings. When Patsab asked Geshe Tonpa to give him teachings, the latter said, "I have no time to give teachings because there is a great master in Western Tibet who has come from India, and I wish to see him. Next year around this time my friend Ngok Lekpe Sherab will come, and you can receive teachings from him. Master Kuchung from Yonru is also very intelligent; he, too, can give you teachings." Patsab then asked if, in the future, Geshe Tonpa would promise to be his teacher. Geshe Tonpa replied that this might happen if no obstacles prevented it. He then said, "As you have much wealth, build a monastery in an isolated place where the monks can study." This the man did some time later, in addition offering Geshe Tonpa seven horses loaded with valuable packs.

Geshe Tonpa took the northern road, but for a time lost his way. While wandering, he made prayers to the Triple Gem and invoked the Dharma protectors by offering tormas. Next morning he saw from afar a wild horse running down a road. Taking this as an auspicious sign he said, "Let us follow that animal." When the horse rested at night, the men, too, rested nearby.

One night Geshe Tonpa had a dream in which a man dressed in rich clothing appeared, saying, "Lately I bade you farewell; now you will soon meet the pandita." When he awoke, he realized that this was an omen from a Dharma protector. At the same time, Atisha had a dream that in three days his new great disciple would come to him.

After three days it indeed came to pass that Geshe Tonpa met Atisha, who immediately recognized him and inquired after his health. Geshe Tonpa prostrated three times and made an offering to Atisha of a bolt of silk cloth. He also made offerings to the translators. Atisha placed his hand on

Geshe Tonpa's head, made the sign of the protection mudra, and recited auspicious prayers. Geshe Tonpa offered Atisha a butter lamp which glowed throughout the night. Thereafter, he remained at the master's feet, studying the teachings. Later, when the two journeyed to Mang-yul, Geshe Tonpa led Atisha's horse the whole way, himself leaning on his walking stick.

One day Naktso Lotsawa discovered texts belonging to Atisha, one on exorcism composed by the Indian rishi Nyami, and one a Tantra on the history of Tara. Seeing that Naktso was poring over them, Atisha said, "Only if I give you permission are you allowed to look at these," and he took the texts back. When Geshe Tonpa arrived, Atisha gave him those texts as well as the great Manjushri Yamantaka text.

When the two came to Mustang, Geshe Tonpa received the vision of Tara. Then they journeyed to Mang-yul Sone Chenmo, where they stayed one year. There, the great meditators Zhonnu Tsultrim and Shangtsun Trime received teachings from Atisha, in particular the practice of Tara which immediately enabled them to receive a vision of Tara. Thereafter, the meditators supplied all Atisha's needs for some time, translated many Tantra teachings, and taught many Prajnaparamita and Tantra teachings.

From India the King and others sent messengers to bring Atisha back, and Atisha made preparations to return since his three years were completed. But on the way to Nepal they encountered wars and upheaval, so they were unable to proceed. They therefore stayed two years in Mang-yul, building there the Keru temple. As the Tibetan King had asked, Geshe Tonpa also told Atisha about Samye and other monasteries, and about the number of monks who inhabited Central Tibet, asking if Atisha might not go to those places. But Atisha said, "It is too far." Later, as they were talking together, Geshe Tonpa again brought up the topic of the monasteries. Atisha was gratified at the motivation that existed in Tibet and did prostrations toward that land. "All the Tibetans are part of the Mahayana family," he said, "and though it may be difficult for them to achieve the arhat state, some surely will achieve the level of stream winner. So great a number of monks does not exist even in India." Encouraged by his words, Geshe Tonpa renewed his plea that Atisha might come to Central Tibet. Atisha replied:

> I have promised to achieve the benefit of the sanghas
> And not betray their request.
> Therefore I will go
> If the sanghas wish to invite me.

So Geshe Tonpa sent the following message to powerful persons in central Tibet:

> In Jambudvipa, shaped like the wheel of a
> horse-drawn cart,
> In a place in the north near Loti (Tsangpo River)
> In the glorious Himalayas
> Lies the source of many precious jewels.
> It is known as the Land of Snow.
> There reside the Tibetans,
> Great of mind, strong and healthy.
> The King, a great Bodhisattva,
> Attended by retinues of great warriors,
> Translated the teachings for the benefit of others
> And built monasteries like Samye and so forth
> With the richest materials
> And noble proportions.
> To fulfill the wishes of these great beings
> Who cause the nectar of the teachings to flourish,
> I, the upasaka Gyalwa Jungne,
> With deepest respect address:
> The followers of Shakya, that Lord of Beings [Buddha],
> Who is a great Bodhisattva worthy of devotion;
> Lhatsun Bodhi Ranza, Gelong Longchen Pön,
> And the great saint Sumpa Yeshe Lodrö—
> The three Mahayana pillars
> Who keep firm the Mahayana lineage;
> The two spiritual masters who open the eyes;
> The twelve glorious masters and two great masters
> of conduct

Who maintain the discipline according to the
Dharma;
The two brothers, masters of the Dharma college;
Wangchuk Gyaltsen, who fulfills the wishes of
spiritual friends;
The two sons of Shakya Zhonnu Gyalwa;
Lekpe Sherab, scholar and saint and so forth;
The noble bhikshu sanghas;
And all disciples and patrons.
I pray that you are all well
And encountering no obstacles
To the enlightenment path.
Now, in a brief way, I will say this:
As you know, there has come here
A great scholar whose name is Shri Jnana [Atisha],
The most highly respected master in India,
Who possesses limitless qualities.
When he spoke with the King
He was told of the land of Central Tibet,
But refused to journey there saying, "It is too far."
Later, in Shulka in Nepal,
I told him again of the monks in Central Tibet.
Pleased was he, and with devotion did prostrations
Saying, "So great a number of monks does not
exist even in India."

By his speaking thus, I was encouraged
And hoping that you, too, desired to see him,
I requested again and again
That he come to Central Tibet.
Atisha said that as he promised to benefit the sangha
And not betray their wishes
He would come
If the sangha asked it.
Should there be a helpful translator,
A young monk of capacity,
Have him in readiness for the master.
If you agree to his visit,
Those who prepare for it

Should come here in the autumn.
Many monks on horses
Should make the event known to all the people,
And all the monks should return to their discipline
If they have departed from the morality in any way.
Atisha does not like the clash of views,
So please do not dispute,
But be peaceful of mind.
Please meditate on this virtuous letter
Which is written for the benefit of all
To the monks of Shakya,
For it is filled with many meaningful and useful qualities.
Try to achieve virtue and meaning in your conduct.

Myriad monks of Central Tibet arrived in a procession to invite Atisha to their land. They stayed three months and five days. In Shultsang during that time Atisha gave many teachings and established multitudes in virtue through the cultivation of Bodhicitta and so forth. He expounded the meaning of the Tantra teachings, established the monks in the proper discipline, and cut doubts at their root.

At Nyangro Atisha met with Great Yogin and Gonpawa. Through Atisha's teachings Geshe Yulsang received the vision of the eleven-faced Chenrezig. Then Atisha went to Rong where he gave teachings to Garge, who received visions of Chakrasamvara and Vajrayogini.

Atisha then went to Samye and translated the *Five-skandha Madhyamika*. At the request of Ngok he also translated the six Madhyamika texts of Nagarjuna. From there he was invited to Garchung by Kutön. Then he went to Sölnak Thang and translated the *Uttaratantra* and others. When Kutön invited him to Yarlung, he offered Atisha one hundred ounces of gold. Kutön stayed in Lhading and Atisha stayed in Sölnak Thang.

Because of Kutön's great wealth, Atisha announced to an assemblage of followers, "This Kutön Tsundu is a Chakravartin King, whereas I am just an ordinary person." Great Yogin was not pleased with Kutön, so he asked Atisha if he might leave. Geshe Tonpa said, "If Great Yogin is not pleased, he can surely leave." But Atisha said, "Even if a messenger went seeking throughout the world, he could not find such a one as Great Yogin; I will therefore not let him leave."

Great Yogin spoke with Atisha, who removed his hat and said, "You were born in Eastern Tibet, and I was born in Eastern India. Due to the power of our karmic connection, we met here. Therefore, you must not leave. If you are determined to go at all costs, I will go in your place. And if you have the daring to escape, then so be it." Then tears came to Great Yogin's eyes, and he promised to serve Atisha for the rest of his life. Atisha was pleased at this.

Then Geshe Tonpa said, "If Kutön is unhappy, I will leave." And Atisha said, "If you go, I will do likewise." Geshe Tonpa said, "He will not accept your leaving." Atisha said, "We have many ways for making this happen."

Atisha gathered his belongings and returned to a place near Samye. Several monks and Tokton Jangchub Jungne invited him to Chamtsig. There he translated the *Tungwa Chishag* (The Confession of the General Downfall) and so forth. At the request of Chag Trichag and others he translated the *Seven Dharmas of Chenrezig*, the *Sadhana of the Cultivation of Bodhicitta, Pleasing the Sentient Beings*, and a chapter of shila composed by Acharya Gunapravada.

In the Mouse Year Geshe Tonpa invited Atisha to the North for a month, offering him eight hundred ounces of gold and one each of one hundred different kinds of rich goods.

In the Ox Year Atisha went to Nyethang and lived in a tent until a house was made ready for him. Atisha ordered Geshe Tonpa to build a monastery for monks, but the Geshe replied, "I already have a monastery, and as long as it stands I will build no other. That monastery is Atisha." After Atisha passed away, Geshe Tonpa did indeed build a monastery in Nyethang.

In Nyethang Atisha experienced hesitation about one of the teachings. But in a dream he saw Lord Maitreya and

Manjushri surrounded by many Bodhisattvas, discussing the teachings. In this way his questions were resolved.

Later Atisha sent gold to India and ordered the panditas there to build eight stupas as protection against the eight fears. He also commanded them to make a representation of the vision he beheld in his dream. All the Indian panditas assembled, and to please Atisha, whom they acknowledged as a great scholar, they invited the most highly skilled artisans of Eastern India to do the work and send the drawing back to him.

One day, as Atisha prepared to leave Nyethang, he entered into samadhi, gazing into the sky. Great Yogin offered him water, saying, "It is time to drink." But the water fell to the ground. Geshe Tonpa said, "Wait a moment, Ame," and Atisha at that same instant received a vision of Maitreya. Geshe Tonpa's face grew dark and he said, "Ame, the two of us don't have the fortune to share this vision."

In Nyethang a herdsman separated a yak and dri who had been bound together by a rope. After the dri wandered off, Atisha at some distance away said, "The yak is still in difficulties." When they investigated, they found that the yak's feet were indeed entangled in the rope and that he was unable to move. This was proof of Atisha's clairvoyance.

Once in Yerpa, Atisha passed unobstructed through the walls of a house. A nun also saw him circumambulating a stupa in the sky.

When Atisha crossed the pass called Sapkyi-la, he received an offering from a sick lady in Yerpa. By the time he reached the top of the mountain, he said, "The woman has died." Ngok said, "Perhaps we should do prayers for her." But Atisha replied "Because of her offerings, she has been reborn in the god realms."

At Nyethang Atisha became ill and told Geshe Tonpa, "Perhaps now I will die." Geshe Tonpa with tears in his eyes repeatedly asked about his health. Atisha said, "This sickness represents my co-emergent deities. Please obtain the essences of herbs and flowers which prolong life. I will not use them out of attachment to this life, but to practice the essence of Bodhicitta."

Atisha wanted to send Great Yogin to India with gold, assisted by an Indian Atsara to whom he addressed his words in Sanskrit. As Great Yogin understood Sanskrit, he realized the nature of Atisha's plan. Going to Geshe Tonpa, he told him of what he heard, and asked him to persuade Atisha to allow him to remain. Geshe Tonpa said, "I will do what you say, but not just now because Atisha has a profound wisdom mind and would guess our plans. But I will address him later, as if by chance." Some time later, when speaking to Atisha of other matters, Geshe Tonpa requested that Great Yogin be allowed to remain. Atisha said, "Great Yogin is a gentle spirit; no one else can accomplish this mission as he can." And he sang this song:

> Supreme generosity is the giving of joy;
> Supreme friendship is reliability;
> Supreme achievement is the absence of sickness;
> Supreme bliss is nirvana.

Geshe Tonpa said, "Rejoice, Ame; this verse is composed for you."

Atisha blessed a mound of gold, as well as thirty ounces of gold dust placed in a leather pouch. When Geshe Tonpa touched it, Atisha said, "Give that back to me." And again he blessed it. "You may meet a robber on the way," he said to Great Yogin, "but he cannot harm you." Then Great Yogin wept at the thought that he would not see Atisha again. On the way he indeed met a robber, but he was unharmed and soon managed to free himself. When he arrived in Nepal, he learned of Atisha's parinirvana. Before this, however, he had the vision of Lord Maitreya.

Atisha gave gold to Geshe Tonpa and said, "Tell Great Yogin that he should not be proud about his caste or status as a monk, but should only practice the meditation of loving kindness, compassion and Bodhicitta. He should concentrate one-pointedly on achieving omniscient Buddhahood by dispelling obstacles and developing all the positive conditions."

Geshe Tonpa said, "I am an upasaka and know little about how to deal in the world of men, so I cannot take your place." Atisha replied, "I have blessed you, so simply obey me." Geshe Tonpa then asked, "When you die, how should I care for your body?" Atisha replied, "Act according to the *Sutra of Parinirvana*."

On the eighteenth day in the Horse Year, Atisha entered Mahasamadhi at the age of seventy. His body was cremated. Having stayed two years in Western Tibet, two years in Mang-yul Gungthang, three months and five days in Tsang, and nine years in Central Tibet, Atisha spent a total of thirteen years in Tibet.

Geshe Tonpa took Atisha's relics and went to Taklung through Kyichu and from there to Nam. In Nam, he stayed at Chemalung at the invitation of the sons of Patsab Berchung. They offered him the areas known as Charma in Tre, Chemalung in Nam, and Radreng. As Great Yogin was staying at Mang-yul, Geshe Tonpa wrote him a letter asking him to come to Chemalung. In the Monkey Year Geshe Tonpa built a monastery in Radreng. He also built a retreat house for Great Yogin, and houses for the yogin Sherab Dorje Gonpawa and the great meditator Jampa Lodrö of Chime. He also added a kitchen and storehouse for their use, and appointed a novice monk to serve them. Yogin Trichog and Chagthar were sent to Nepal to fetch silver which, along with all the offerings Geshe Tonpa received, was used in building a silver stupa in memory of Atisha. Many mantras were placed inside the stupa, which was decorated by the artist Tsekse. During Atisha's lifetime and after, the butter lamps remained lit.

All Atisha's disciples gathered in Radreng, and Geshe Tonpa supplied their needs for nine years. On the eighteenth day of the fifth month of the Dragon Year Geshe Tonpa entered Mahasamadhi at the age of sixty. Afterward, the monastery was maintained by Great Yogin.

Great Yogin was born in Eastern Tibet in the Tiger Year. He was one of seven brothers. In that country it was a tradition that families who did not have sons would borrow one from families where sons were plentiful. Great Yogin was therefore given to another family, but soon after, a son was born to them. He then went to yet another family where the same event occurred, causing him to say, "I am auspicious." His mother told him to become a monk, and he took vows with an Abbot wearing a blue *shamthab* (lower garment). He labored a whole day and night, making tea for the Khenpo. When he became sleepy, the Khenpo would kick him in the head. Once, when his mother visited him, she said, "Now go to Central Tibet for further study," and she supplied him with the necessities, as well as much silk cloth. For three days she remained with him, and when she left him, her parting words were, "When you get to Central Tibet, may you meet a spiritual master who will choose you for a disciple. May you receive all the teachings and achieve the realization so that you and I both may perfect the path of complete enlightenment."

Later, Great Yogin thought, "Perhaps my mother was a Dakini."

Hearing of the fame of Phamthing in Nepal, he journeyed with the intention to meet him. Instead, he met Atisha in Nyangtso, who inquired where he was going. "I am going to Nepal," said he. Atisha, whose clairvoyant powers enabled him to see that this was a proper vessel, said, "Do not go; I will give you the teachings." Then Great Yogin became a bhikshu and Gonpawa became a novice monk, with Great Yogin supplying the necessities for them both. Great Yogin offered all his silk to Atisha and became one of his attendants. Gonpawa began doing meditation and Great Yogin took care of the Radreng monastery for twelve years. He was known as Jangchub and died at the age of sixty-three in Radreng.

Geshe Gonpawa thought, "The time has come for me to take care of Radreng Monastery." And this he did for seven years. His two principal disciples were Nesurwa and Kamawa, and his own name was Wangchuk Gyaltsen. He was born in the Dragon Year and passed away in Radreng when he was sixty-six years of age.

After the three principal disciples of Geshe Tonpa had maintained Radreng, Geshe Potawa assumed control of the monastery. His family lineage was known as Nyö and his father was called Tripo. His name as Abbot was Dorje Wangchuk, and his personal name was Rinchen Sal. From Lantsul he studied the Vinaya discipline and attended Geshe Tonpa, studying with him for seven years. After Geshe Tonpa's passing, he studied with Great Yogin and Gonpawa, and then went into retreat. After Gonpawa's passing, he governed Radreng Monastery and gathered sixty great disciples such as Geshe Langri Thangpa, Shang Nyukrumpa and others. One night he had a clear dream in which he was plowing the ground with utmost difficulty. When he awoke, he interpreted the dream to mean that his teachings were of no use to others. Another night he dreamed he was holding a sword, and he interpreted this to mean that his wisdom was sharp. Then he dreamed that he was blowing a conch shell, which he took as a sign that he would gain fame.

Geshe Potawa stayed in the mountain called Phenpo and gained such wisdom that in one verse he could read ten different meanings. Knowing that constant meditation is difficult, he gave teachings in one session. Geshe Potawa was born in the Hare Year and passed away at the age of seventy-nine.

The next in succession was Geshe Phuchungwa, expert on the Abhidharma, Vinaya, and Prajnaparamita, who studied with Geshe Tonpa for seven years. After the latter's passing, he entered a retreat, staying in Phenyul. His principal disciples were Phabong Khawa of Lhasa and Geshe Yangdagpa. His name was Zhonnu Gyaltsen and he was born in the Sheep Year. He passed away at the age of seventy-six.

The next in succession was Geshe Chen-ngawa who was born in Nyen to a wealthy family. By hearing of impermanence and samsara from his father, Zhonnu, his mind was moved. Geshe Chen-ngawa went to a monastery at Lushö Rugpa where a woman gave him a four-line verse to memorize. When he was eighteen years old he ran away to Tholung Tsadok. That night he dreamed of blowing a conch shell trumpet whose sound pervaded the whole of Tibet. Around the same time a nun dreamt of a foot-high crystal stupa growing out of her own head. In the morning the two discussed their dreams and said, "Perhaps we should search for someone to tell us the meaning of these dreams." But the nun said, "Possibly someone will come here who can do this for us." A Khenpo called Sherab Senpa arrived, and from him Geshe Chen-ngawa took monk's vows, also learning to stabilize the mind.

Later, Geshe Chen-ngawa stayed with a family at Lusho Rugpa for one year. When his mother visited him, she asked, "Why are you staying here? Better to go to Radreng." He followed her advice and studied with Geshe Tonpa for seven years, receiving the vision of Jowo Jamphel Dorje [Manjushri].

Geshe Chen-ngawa was born in the Bird Year and passed away at the age of seventy-three. At the time of his death, flowers fell from the sky so thickly that they reached people's knees. His principal disciples were: Tölungpa, Shawagangpa and Chya-yulwa.

Geshe Chya-yulwa met Tölungpa when he was thirteen years of age, and studied with him for five years. When he reached the age of eighteen, he attended Geshe Chen-ngawa with whom he studied for nine years. Thereafter, he went into retreat for three years, following which he gave teachings to the disciples.

His principal disciples were Geshe Naljorpa and Gonpa-tsundru Bar. Geshe Nyukrumpa passed away at the age of sixty-nine.

Gampopa (1079–1153)

Gampopa was a disciple of Geshe Chya-yulwa. He was born in Nyal, Southern Tibet, to the clan known as Nyi. His father, Nyiwa Lhaje, had four sons of whom Gampopa was the third. He was named Nyiwa Gunga. Even as a child he was of gentle and compassionate mind, without a trace of anger, enjoying a robust constitution and becoming expert in the arts and all games. By the time he was sixteen years old he was an acknowledged scholar in the study of the Tantra teachings and a great physician. He married and had one child, but because of a plague both wife and child died. For this reason he completely renounced samsara.

At the age of twenty-five, Gampopa went to Dakpo Ronkar where he took full monk's vows from Khenpo Lodan Sherab of Maryul. Master Sherab Nyingpo of Shangshung, and Jangchub Sempa of Mite who gave him the name Matikirti or Sonam Rinchen. From Geshe Lodan Sherab he studied the Chakrasamvara teachings of the Sagkar tradition. He also studied the Vinaya and other teachings from Cha Druwa Zinpa, and received many oral instructions of the meditation lineage. In all the teachings he understood the importance of meditation practice.

Gampopa went to Central Tibet where he studied the complete teachings of Atisha with Geshe Nyukrumpa, Gya

Chakri Gangkawa, Geshe Chya-yulwa and others. He became a well-known scholar and master. At this time he felt the need of doing a meditation retreat, and so built a small house for himself close to the monastery known as Sarka which had been built by his parents. His needs were provided from farm land that he owned. Practicing meditation diligently, Gampopa could remain in samadhi for thirteen days at a time, putting at rest within himself the seeds of desire and hatred, and all gross and subtle negative emotions. He had little need of sleep, but when he did dream, he received the sign of the ten bhumi levels of the Bodhisattva path which are explained in the *Golden Light Sutra*. Not only did lice and other insects and germs keep their distance, but he could go for five days at a time without taking nourishment. Through meditation Gampopa experienced great bliss.

Once, during the spring, Gampopa came out of retreat and went for a walk around the monastery. While in a meditative state, he came upon three beggars talking among themselves. As he made the mudra of offering water to the hungry ghosts, one of the beggars said. "We are the poorest people around. I wish we could obtain food and drink without working. How wonderful that would be!" The second beggar said, "While you're at wishing, don't leave it at mere food. Make a wish to become a King like Tsede of Tibet." The third beggar said, "Even Tsede will one day die, so his happiness is not lasting. As long as you are going to wish, wish to become a great yogi like Milarepa who needs no clothing or human food. He is fed nectar by the Dakinis, rides atop a white snow lion, and flies in the sky. Now that would be truly wondrous."

Merely by hearing the name of Milarepa the hair of Gampopa's body stood on end, tears came to his eyes and a special devotion, unlike any he had felt before, emerged in his mind. For a moment he could not even move, but in time he returned to his retreat hut and determined to make the seven-branch prayer his main practice. As he tried to do this, however, he found his mind so distracted that he began to ask himself, "What is happening to me?" He then sat upon his meditation cushion for a long time until all outer phenomena dissolved into emptiness. The entire universe was experienced as but an aspect of the mind. Then, there arose the thought, "Perhaps I can now see into the minds of all sentient beings." After his evening meditation session he returned to the spot where he had come across the three beggars and asked them, "Where is that great yogi you spoke of?" "He is in Mang-yul Gungthang," they said, "and he is called Milarepa. His teacher was Marpa Lotsawa, whose teacher was the glorious Naropa." "What kind of teaching does he offer?" asked Gampopa. They replied, "He teaches the Six Yogas of Naropa, and we haven't seen him, but many people go to him to receive teachings." Gampopa said, "What qualities does he possess?" and they replied, "Though many people go to see him, sometimes they do not find him. Some perceive him as a white chörten, and some as Buddha Shakyamuni, so clearly he can manifest in many different forms." "And where does he reside?" asked Gampopa. They replied, "He stays in the mountains of Nyanam and Drin." Gampopa asked, "If I wish to go there, can you lead the way?" They said, "You look young. We cannot keep up with you, so go in that direction and when you arrive in Lato you will find him, for he is well known there." Gampopa then offered them a great supply of vegetables and other food. That night he invoked the Triple Gem before sleeping, and in his dreams saw himself blowing an enormous trumpet whose sound pervaded the whole of the earth. Indeed, people were remarking that there was no larger trumpet in Central Tibet. Then an enormous drum appeared in the sky unsupported, and when he beat upon it, it made a perfect sound. Many wild animals heard the noise, and many people gathered around. A lady dressed in the fashion of Southern Tibetans appeared, saying, "Beat the drum so that all may hear." And she handed him a skullcup filled with milk, saying, "Give this to the animals." Gampopa remarked "This milk is surely not enough for so many animals," and she replied, "Drink this, and not only these animals but all sentient beings of the six realms will be benefitted. I am going in the western direction."

In explaining this dream later, Gampopa said, "Those who are not proper vessels should be trained in the stages of the path. The people who appeared in my dream were symbols of such beings, while the wild animals were symbols of practitioners in retreat. They will be sustained by the teachings of Mahamudra and the methods of Milarepa." These events indeed came to pass exactly as Gampopa foresaw in his dream.

Gampopa then sold his farm for four ounces of gold, and set out to find Milarepa in Western Tibet. Mila was surrounded by his attendants Nyishang Repa, Loro Rechung, Gomthak Jodor, Seban Tonchung, Mekong, and Konggur. Nyishang Repa said, "Milarepa knew that you were coming, and he will accept you as a disciple. Just wait here for a few days, and do not become impatient. You will see him in time," and he told Gampopa to settle at a spot under a rock. At last Gampopa was summoned and found Milarepa sitting on a boulder, surrounded by disciples. Performing many prostrations, he offered Milarepa gold and tea. Milarepa said, "This gold and I do not agree. Use it for your needs while you are in retreat," and he returned it. He then asked, "What is your name?" and Gampopa replied, "My name is Sonam Rinchen [Precious Merit]." Milarepa repeated the name Sonam three times and said, "The merit comes from great accumulations, and the preciousness refers to your value to all sentient beings." Then he sang a song, saying, "This is my greeting to you, master from Central Tibet."

Gampopa collected firewood and stored it in his cave, and gave one ounce of gold to his patrons Könchog Bar and Barye with the request that they supply him with food during his retreat. He then requested the teachings from Milarepa, who asked if he had already received teachings and empowerments. Gampopa replied that he had received the four empowerments of Guhyasamaja, the Hevajra, the magnificent blessings of Dagmema, the teachings of Luipa, the magnificent blessings of the Six-Ornament Vajra Varahi from Lama Lodrö of Maryul, and many empowerments from other Lamas. He recounted his thirteen-day experience of samadhi, at which Milarepa laughed. "Ha," said he, "You won't obtain oil by squeezing sand, but only from mustard seed. So practice my tummo teachings and you will see the true nature of the mind. The Tibetans did not allow Atisha to teach the Tantras." Gampopa said, "There are many Tantric teachings in Kadampa," to which Milarepa replied, "Yes, there are Tantric teachings, but no quintessence instruction there. Although there is a complete arising and completion process in a single meditation practice, this is merely the samadhi of analysis. Meditating on the selflessness of the stages of the path has only a relative value. Practice meditation on the method path." Gampopa then received the tummo teachings, experienced heat, and after seven days received the vision of the Five Dhyani Buddhas. When he recounted this to Milarepa, the latter said, "This is like seeing two moons by applying pressure to your eyes, and it occurs through the control of the wind element. It is neither good nor bad. Continue with your meditation."

Gampopa thought, "Though the Lama has not said that this is a good quality, I feel joy nonetheless." And he exerted yet more effort in meditation.

After three months, Gampopa one day saw the entire universe turning like a wheel. He began to run, but fell down and for a time lost consciousness. Upon returning to his senses, he told Milarepa, "The wind in my right and left channels entered the central channel." Milarepa said, "This is neither good nor bad. Go on with your meditation."

Another time in early morning Gampopa saw myriad Chenrezig forms seated on moon discs, filling all of space. When he told Milarepa, the latter said, "This is due to the increase of the *thigle* [vital energy] at the crown chakra, the wheel of great bliss. This is neither good nor bad. Go on with your meditation."

At dusk he saw the Hell Realm of Black Lines, and felt as if his heart were crumbling. His wind energy increased. When he told Milarepa, the latter said, "This is due to the tightness of your meditation belt. Loosen it and hold the upward wind. This is neither good nor bad. Go on with the meditation."

Gampopa next saw the celestial beings from the six desire realms, the upper ones showering rains of nectar onto the lower. He also saw his mother dying of thirst. Milarepa said, "The rain of nectar comes from increasing the vital energy in the right and left channels of the throat chakra. The thirst of your mother comes from the opening of the lower end of the central channel. Do the following yoga exercises and meditate for one month," and he indicated a special yogic technique.

Doing this practice, Gampopa began crying and trembling all over uncontrollably. It seemed to him that this was an obstacle of the Maras, but Milarepa told him, "The heart chakra is filled with *thigle*. Do the yoga exercises I gave you regularly. These signs are neither good nor bad." Thereafter, Gampopa had little need of food.

One day Gampopa saw the moon in eclipse, as fine as a horse's hair. The wind in the right and left wind channels merged in the central channel. "This is neither good nor bad," said Milarepa.

Gampopa continued practicing the meditation diligently and saw the face of the Red Hevajra. When he told Milarepa, the latter said, "The red seed essence received from your mother has increased at the navel. This is neither good nor bad."

Thereafter Gampopa practiced strenuously, and one day saw the skeleton mandala of Chakrasamvara in the Luipa tradition. Milarepa said, "The navel chakra is filled with *thigle*. This is neither good nor bad."

For eleven days Gampopa practiced diligently and one night his body pervaded space. From his crown chakra to his toes were gathered sentient beings of the six realms, many of them drinking milk, and some drinking from a star. A great sound was heard, but no one could tell from whence it came. In the morning when he loosened his meditation belt, the vision disappeared. On telling Milarepa, the latter said, "The wind is directing the *thigle* into the body's inconceivable number of channels. And this wind is close to becoming transformed into the wind of wisdom." Milarepa then gave him the supermundane teachings [the realization of the Vajradhara state].

Gampopa practiced diligently and one day saw the entire country of Drin filled with smoke. In the afternoon the area around him was completely dark. He could not even see the road to the Lama, and had to feel his way along the path like a blind man. Milarepa said, "Sit by me, meditate, and be at peace." And he gave Gampopa the blessings which dispel obstacles. In this way the darkness dispersed.

One night in a vision Gampopa saw his own waist without flesh, and his bones covered by the joined channels of his body. Milarepa said, "Your channels are rough, so you should do a meditation to make them smooth."

Gampopa practiced for a month and saw the faces of the Seven Medicine Buddhas. At this time he needed to breathe in and out only once a day. When he stopped the meditation on the winds, his visions disappeared. In the early evening, when Gampopa meditated on holding the wind, he saw the limitless sambhogakaya Buddhafield, and experienced its enjoyments. When he released the wind energy, twilight fell. Thinking that he might have created obstacles in the meditation, he began making mandala offerings and saying prayers.

At dawn, as he retained his wind energy, he saw the faces of the thousand Buddhas surrounding Shakyamuni. When he went to Milarepa at daybreak to recount his experience, the latter said, "Now you have seen the Yidam deity and the sambhogakaya and nirmanakaya spheres. Soon you will see the dharmakaya sphere. Journey to Central Tibet and do meditation practice. I have dispelled all your previous dangerous obstacles. Now you will face the dangerous path of clairvoyance, also filled with obstacles. When you achieve this state, you will experience the dangerous mara of the son of the gods.[1] It is important to keep this and all siddhis you obtain secret. Generally, this Mara cannot penetrate superior beings, and as you are a superior being you must keep your tantra practice secret. You will benefit many beings, so sustain the assembly of disciples."

Gampopa asked, "When will it be the right moment to gather disciples?" and Mila replied, "When you see the true nature of the mind and stabilize it. Test if you can send the wind through the fingertips. When you can do this, you are free from the dangerous narrow path of the wind."

That night Gampopa piled a heap of dust on a rock, placed his fingertips upon it, and practiced retaining the wind. At midnight the dust began blowing around in a circle like a whirlwind. In the morning he told Milarepa, who said, "You have become master of the wind practice; it is now channelled properly, so you have no further need to stay with me here. You will receive miraculous powers and manifestations and the ordinary and extraordinary attainments, and will be called Bhikshu Vajradhrik Jambudvipa Kirti [World-Renowned Vajradhara].

Milarepa then gave him all the empowerments, teachings and blessings which he possessed, and said, "Now return to your own country and practice. Do not befriend those having an increase of the three poisons, for you can be influenced by them. There are beings full of anger, who heap abuse on others and on the Dharma. In such beings' minds, hatred blazes like fire. For example, a snake, although without wings and feet, is nonetheless an object of fright to many because of its strong anger. When one has strong anger in the mind, one perceives everyone as the enemy. And a person who is greedy, even to gathering small pebbles, and who

---

[1] the sense of pride.

gathers everything lest he should one day be in need, is as filled with burning desire as boiling water is with heat. Likewise, beings who do not feel it is time to meditate on the practice of the perfect meaning, who believe it is impossible to achieve Buddhahood within one lifetime, and who take no care to develop Bodhicitta will fall into the shravaka path. And those who reject the special method fall into the state of nihilism which is bound by ignorance. So don't deal with such persons. If you speak with them, they will first ask about your teacher and the kind of teaching you are studying. If you tell them, they will become angry, hate the teachings and the teacher, give up all attempts to practice, and be reborn in the hell realms. In that way you would be the cause of others' accumulating negative karma. Therefore, do not keep company with persons having the three poisons.

In the samaya, one should not remain with shravakas more than seven days. In general, one should be full of mindfulness, like a bird or a wounded forest animal. Be clean, peaceful, compassionate, kindly to all beings, and devoid of conceptual thoughts. Pass your time in silent retreat, not leaving your meditation seat. And do not abandon your vajra master, even if you realize the Buddha state. Progress as much as possible in purification and accumulation. Work at avoiding even the smallest negative action, even if you perfect the understanding of cause and result. Do not cease practicing the four-session Guru Yoga, even though you have the experience of the inseparability of the meditation and post-meditation states. Do not slander the Dharma or persons even when you have achieved the equalization of self and others."

Gampopa then went to Central Tibet, and by meditating in Sewalung and Gelung realized the basic nature of the mind, and the full meaning of his Lama's words. He thought, "This is like returning to one's own home, free from effort." He realized that this was his last birth in samsara. Meditation brought about the view, like an object returning to its owner.

He fully realized the Lama's great kindness and thereafter had no increase or decrease in realization, nor any acceptance, rejection, or doubt.

When Gampopa meditated in the place called Sup, he had a dream in which a lady was cutting the throat of her son and crying out, "Cut the cycle of births." The body of the boy then rolled down the mountain. Thereafter, he had no further dreams, and so his sleep was always an experience of the clear light.

Later, Gampopa said, "It took me a long time to stabilize the mind, and I had to work hard, but for you it will be less difficult to meditate because you possess the instruction of the profound method path. This Kagyupa lineage has a blessing unlike others. If they meditate diligently, many will reach the path. To dispel obstacles, experience the teachings, and increase meditation practice, it is enough to follow the profound guru yoga, Mahamudra practice, and Tummo."

Gampopa then meditated for seven years in Rölka. Many people gathered there, presenting heaps of offerings which he divided among the area's inhabitants. In the summer he went to Öde Kunggyal mountain. One day around dawn, he heard a voice in the sky saying, "Neglecting to benefit beings is the downfall of the Bodhisattva." He thought that he should leave because of an expected downfall, but a person appeared in the guise of a king wearing a crown and a giant turquoise around his neck. He promised Gampopa to care for his needs if he would but stay on the mountain, and advised him if he chose not to stay to proceed to Dagla Gampo where his own son would care for Gampopa's needs. "I am a sky-flying hungry ghost," he said. "Though I do not mean to harm others, many suffer because of me. I confess my evil deeds and ask that you grant me the refuge ordination and Bodhisattva vow." Gampopa gave him the purification method of the four powers,[1] teachings on compassion,

---

[1] the power of refuge, the power of repentance, the power of making a vow, the power of the antidote.

refuge, ordination, the Bodhisattva vow, and instructions on Mahamudra. Then, the figure disappeared into space like a rainbow.

From there Gampopa went to Dagpo, hoping to do a twelve-year retreat there. For this purpose he built a retreat house in Sanglung, hoping to achieve that state in which one can acquire all necessary nourishment by transforming the elements. However, a lady smeared with ashes and holding three peacock feathers appeared before him, saying, "It is more important to cause the teachings to flourish than to enter upon a long retreat."

A few days later, Geshe Gyalwa Chungtsang Chen came to see Gampopa, as did Geshe Nyaknak Marpo. Soon, around sixty disciples gathered about him. After he gave teachings to these disciples, Gampopa again planned to enter a strict retreat, but so many proper vessels arrived from Ü, Tsang and Kham that he was obliged to remain and give teachings. Within a short time a great number of disciples arrived who achieved the realization of the teachings, mastery over the channels and winds, and the six clairvoyances. These disciples would not accept any form of support without first checking whether they came from one of the eight impure sources [whether the gifts had been stolen, etc]. They meditated continuously, not even pausing to lie down, and adopted the twelve ascetic disciplines.

Gampopa manifested in limitless forms. People from Dagpo claimed that on the thirteenth day of the twelfth month he went to Lhasa, that on the fourteenth day he prepared a ceremony, that on the fifteenth day he made flower offerings, and that on the sixteenth he did the concluding prayer offerings, making many offerings to other monks. On the seventeenth day he returned to Dagla Gampo Monastery, bringing with him many sacred texts, as well as barley, butter and wool cloth. There, he made dedication prayers. However his patron Gebum, with his retinues, requested that he come to him at the same time. Thus, on the fourteenth he made preparations, on the fifteenth he made flower offerings and on the sixteenth he recited the concluding prayers. Then, along with seven monks, he flew up into the air, which was found by all to be a great wonder. Many offerings were made to the monastery, for which Gampopa did the dedication.

At the same time, the monks in retreat declared that on the thirteenth day Gampopa came out of his retreat, that on the fourteenth he gave instructions to the monks from Tsang, that on the fifteenth he gave teachings to the monks from Kham, and that on the sixteenth he gave teachings to the monks from Ü. Thus, the group declared that the precious Lama had never left the area at all! However, three of Gampopa's attendants, Selchang, Shegom Changseng and Gompa Lengtse said that during this same time the Lama gave no teachings, neither did he leave the area, nor eat the offerings, but instead sat in solitary retreat.

Once, Gampopa's attendant, Gompa Lengtse, remarked to Gampopa, "In the past, the shravakas achieved great states of samadhi like the overpowering contemplative manifestation, the all-encompassing contemplative manifestation, and others. How did they attain this?" Gampopa replied, "If one practices, there is no reason why one cannot achieve these states."

One morning when Gompa Lengtse went to the Lama's room to make an offering of yogurt mixed with sugar, he saw a great fire blazing up to the ceiling. So frightened was he that he ran from the room calling another attendant, Selchang. When they returned together, the Lama had transformed the fire into the all-encompassing contemplative manifestation, and in this state was simply sitting on his meditation seat.

Once, the same attendant went to the shrine to make a butter lamp offering and found the place filled with water. "What is happening here?" he thought. The voice of the Lama called out, "Come here." And with that he transformed the water into the all-encompassing contemplative manifestation.

Again, when the Lama was seated in a room high up in the monastery, the patron Gyalson arrived and asked the attendant if he might see Gampopa and make offerings. When the attendant entered the room to check, he saw a golden stupa radiating light. He then went back to Gyalson with the hope of showing him this marvel, but when the two returned to Gampopa's room, they only found the Lama seated there.

Once, Gompa Lengtse, bearing a torma, went to Gampopa's room to receive the Chöd teaching which cuts the four maras. Not seeing the Lama there, he went outside, but there was no sign of him there either. Then he heard Gampopa's voice calling out, "What do you want? Come here." And all at once he was seated in his usual place of meditation.

Once, Lord Phagmodrupa said to Lopon Gompa, "Gampopa casts no shadow. Have you noticed that?" So at night, when Gampopa was standing before a butter lamp, Lopon looked and saw that this was indeed so. Again during the day he noted that the Lama cast no shadow.

Once, when Gompa Lodrö arrived to make an offering of one hundred thousand leaves of paper, he received permission to enter Gampopa's room. There, he saw the form of the thousand-armed Chenrezig. Returning to Gampopa's attendants, he asked who had built so marvelous a statue, and also where he might find Gampopa. Lengtse led him to the Lama's room, where they found him seated in the spot just occupied by the Chenrezig form.

Once, when all the monks in retreat decided to make a great offering to the Lama, they built a giant throne and made tea for all. When Gompa Sheshön went to find the Lama and escort him to the feast, Gampopa gave him his body-touching robe and told him to go on while he himself closed the door to his room. Waiting nearby, Gompa Sheshön looked toward the shrine and saw that the Lama was already seated on the throne. And when he entered the shrine room, the monks asked him why he had not preceded the Lama, taking his robe.

On another occasion, Lama Gompa remarked to Gampopa, "A Bodhisattva who has achieved the first bhumi can demonstrate miraculous powers by placing the three thousand universes into the smallest dust particle. The dust particle does not grow bigger, neither do the three thousand universes grow smaller, yet the one fits into the other. How wonderful this is!" Gampopa replied, "This is the nature of phenomena. Anything may be achieved. The small eyes of human beings can see the whole of a face; four inches of a mirror can take in horses and elephants; a small bowl of water can reflect the entire moon. Now look at me." When Lama Gompa looked, he saw that the Lama had transformed into a Buddha as large as the entire mountain of Dagla Gampo, yet he fit into a room which normally held only five people. His room had not grown larger, neither had his body grown smaller.

Once, when the sun was in eclipse, the thousand monks in the monastery saw the Lama flying in the sky and sprinkling water from a vase.

Another time, Gargom Karpo requested that the Lama give the transmission of the thirteen Yidam deities. Gampopa agreed, and as he was reciting the mala mantra of the thirteen deities, a red light issued from his mouth and dissolved into Gargom. Gargom felt great devotion, and as he began doing prostrations, the Lama manifested as the four-faced, twelve-armed Demchog (Chakrasamvara).

Once Kyogom, on behalf of his mother, constructed a thangka showing the five Buddha families. He requested that the Lama consecrate it quickly. Gampopa agreed, saying, "Burn this stick of incense and make a mandala offering." He then transformed into the Buddha and from his ushnisha radiated a glorious light which dissolved into the thangka. The air resounded with the tinkle of bells and the beat of the damaru, and the sky was filled with parasols, auspicious banners and canopies. The sound of cymbals was heard, and a rain of flowers fell. When Kyogom saw this, the Lama said, "This is the way to do a rapid consecration."

Once, Geshe Gyalwa Chungtsang Chen thought, "The precious Lama does not permit the novice monks to do anything but meditation, so how can they acquire knowledge?" That night he dreamed that the entire mountain of Dagla Gampo was transformed into caves, in each of which was a precious stupa beautifully carved and radiating light. Some were fully finished and some were still being painted. Many people were doing prostrations before them, saying that they were the refuge of all beings in samsara, including the gods.

Next morning he went to Gampopa's room to tell him of the dream. Before he had time to recount it, the Lama said, "Generally, those who rely on intellect hate me and have contempt for me, but my novice monks are exactly like the stupas you saw in your dream. These beggar children are the refuge of all the sentient beings in the six realms of samsara, including the gods. I can encompass the needs of all, both high and low. Some say I cause the teachings to decline, but if you watch closely, those who benefit from the Buddha's teachings will be well known in the years to come."

Radzi Gomkye became adept at meditation merely by hearing the Lama's name. Although Gyasom Dorseng did not see the Lama, he nonetheless mastered meditation through his devotion and mandala offerings. Limitless beings like Nampa Phenne and others achieved meditation merely by seeing the Lama's face.

Once, Rukom asked, "When one achieves the one-taste state, do body, mind and appearance become one?" Gampopa demonstrated by waving his hand through a pillar. Just as there are no obstructions when one moves one's hand in space, so can body, mind and appearance become one."

Once, on the way to Drabkyi Tsali, Gampopa crossed the river on his meditation mat while fingering the mala in his left hand, and doing the water mudra with the right.

When Gampopa was staying at the mountain of Dregu, the

King Lhagom requested that he consecrate a temple there. When Gampopa threw a flower into the sky, it dissolved into the shrine. At the same time his ritual vase remained in space and his robe hung on a sunbeam. King Lhagom and the others gathered there saw Gampopa in the form of Chenrezig Khasarpani.

When he was staying at the Yenphug cave, Gampopa told his attendant Lekse to keep silent for seven days. During this time, he repeatedly passed through cave walls without obstruction. He also manifested as a gigantic skeleton riding a tiger in the sky, a sword in his right hand, a skullcup in his left, and a khatvanga staff by his left shoulder.

Once Gampopa remained for three days standing with his heels together and making the mudra of the joined nectar thumbs over the crown of his head. On the first night he appeared in seven forms; on the second night he appeared in fourteen forms; and on the third night his many forms filled the entire cave. Then all the forms disappeared.

Gampopa could remain an entire night breathing in and out only once. Those of his disciples who were weak in realization, those who needed to dispel obstacles, those who needed the teachings to increase their realization, and those who needed the instruction teachings all had their wishes fulfilled merely by performing the torma and mandala offerings and doing yoga exercises. Thus, Gampopa possessed inconceivable and inexpressible qualities, such as the six clairvoyances and others.

To demonstrate impermanence to others, this great being, though free from birth and death, left his body on the fifteenth day of the sixth month of the Bird Year at the age of seventy-seven. At that time there appeared in the sky many parasols, banners and canopies, while different kinds of music were heard and a smell of incense pervaded the region. On the eighteenth day of the month, when Gampopa's body was cremated, the earth shook and five-colored smoke appeared along with different colored lights and the sound of offering music. These phenomena occurred throughout the entire area of Dagpo.

When people from the four directions of Dagpo gathered for the ceremony, they saw a rain of blue flowers falling from the sky. The Lama's heart and tongue, as well as many precious relics, emerged unharmed from the fire. For three days all the people gathered there felt no need of food or sleep, being dissolved in the samadhi of great devotion.

The Glorious Phagmodrupa 1110–1170

The precious Lama Dagpo Lharje, whose coming was prophesied by the Buddha, was a great being who had many highly realized disciples. Among them were four supreme disciples—Dharma Lord Phagmodrupa, Lopon Gomzul, Lopon Gomchung, and Lama Tsurphupa (the first Karmapa); four great disciples—Lama Shri Phagpa, Sergom Yeshe Nyingpo, Yogi Chöjung, and Somching Yeshe Nyingpo; and the close disciples Dampa Kyelpo, Gyatsa Repa, Josey Layakpa, Dagpo Dulzin, Gargom Karpo, and so forth. His close attendants were Joden Lekse, Chang-ye Salchang, and Badrompa, among others. Of all these, his only heart son, the unsurpassed lineage holder, was the glorious Lord Phagmodrupa.

In a previous life Lord Phagmodrupa was the King Pawajin, who achieved enlightenment in the form of the Buddha Shakyamuni.

The *Samadhi Rajasutra* states, "At one time I was the King Pawajin. My sons from that life, Metok Dadze and Padma Lama, will in the future protect the Dharma. Gaje will attain Buddhahood under the name of Shive Gyalwa."

The praise known as the *Wisdom Rosary* states:

> Although the Lord achieved supreme Buddhahood,
> Because of previous aspirations to protect the
> Buddha's teachings,

And to attend to the Lamas,
He caused other disciples to achieve realization
Through the profound instructions.
I prostrate to the skillful and great compassionate
one.

The *Praise of His Lives* says:

> Raise the discussion
> Of the profound and vast vehicle teachings
> With the Lord of Shakya,
> The Lord of the World.
> Hold the secrecy
> Of the body-speech wisdom.
> Homage to the feet of the Lama,
> The three kinds of King.

This last means that three different beings arose at different times known as King Indrabuddhi. This is related in the *Namchak Barwa Tantra*, which describes the Buddha's emanations. The *Letter Hidden by King Songtsen Gampo Who is the Emanation of the Noble Chenrezig* also states:

> The Bhikshu practicing the fully Tantric teachings
> Will be shown homage and devotion
> By many great beings.

The Life and Liberation of the Glorious Phagmodrupa Recorded by the Great Lord Drikungpa proclaims: "The glorious Dharma Lord Phagmodrupa, the Lord of the Three Worlds, attained Buddhahood in the pure, natural Dharmakaya. Through the complete perfection of the two accumulations, the great activities of body, speech and wisdom mind manifest solely that all sentient beings might achieve peace and happiness, might be separated from suffering, and might attain the fully perfected state of Buddhahood."

Thus, I have heard that the great Buddha, the compassionate teacher whose teachings flourished in the northern hemisphere, appeared in the southern of the four continents in the center of the great three thousand universes. As prophesied in the *Prajnaparamita Sutra*, the Dharma was promoted in the North through the activity of the Kings and Ministers who are the emanations of Bodhisattvas, and through all the great spiritual masters, particularly the Dharma Lord Phagmodrupa, who emanated in Kham (Eastern Tibet) where the people are strong, brave, dependable, and highly skilled.

Generally it is auspicious to be born into a noble family, but in the Buddha's teaching, caste and ancestry are not important. For this reason, Phagmodrupa was born into a poor family. He himself said, "My father was a cruel man who cultivated non-virtue and misbehavior." The family earned their livelihood through impure means, but Phagmodrupa, like a lotus in the mud, remained unstained. When he was four years old, he took the novice monk's vows from the great Khenpo Phagpa Trulpe, the emanation of the noble Arya, and Yanthub Tsultrim. To give proof of his progress in the understanding and realization of the virtuous Dharma, and to show his own interest, effort, and joyous perseverance, he perfected his training in reading and writing without relying on others' advice. He also studied and learned the Dharma unceasingly, especially concentrating on the responsibilities of monks. He progressed greatly. Realizing, at the age of eighteen, that one should train in the precious knowledge and wisdom while still young, he proceeded to Central Tibet (Ü-Tsang) where there are many great masters.

The source of the precious wisdoms resides in the seats of the three great families of Bodhisattvas (Manjushri, Vajrapani, and Chenrezig) from whom one may obtain the wisdom that is like the wish-fulfilling gem. Phagmodrupa was blessed by beings endowed with noble, keen minds, who had earned the wisdoms through study and practice, and who, possessing the merit and power to promote the Buddha's teaching, demonstrated that only by hard work can one achieve the great quality of study, contemplation and meditation practice.

Phagmodrupa offered all his belongings to his Lama and other monks, as well as to friends, hosts and other beings generally in upper and lower Kham. In order to understand the general and particular meaning of all Dharma, and to demonstrate the wisdom realization of all the great Buddha like Panditas, he attended to the great spiritual master Tölungpa Chenpo and many other scholars in central Tibet. From them he received all the knowledge and transmissions. Thus, he became the great master of all the teachings and reasoning of the Buddha and the great scholars. Seeing that the secret Vajrayana is the essence of the Mahayana teachings, he studied and practiced all the tantras from the great master of the Four Tantras, so becoming the Lord of the Vajrayana teachings. From the ocean of teachings of the Sugatas he recognized that the quintessential teaching is only achieved by realized and experienced great yogis. To show that teaching to others, he attended the realized great yogi Galo, the Bodhisattva Dawa Gyaltsen, Jomo Lhajema and many others, and from them received the complete instructions. As the Bodhisattva Norsang he received teachings and instructions from different Lamas without distinction. Thus, he became the master of all the different aspects of knowledge. He also demonstrated that morality and ethics are the foundation of the Buddha's teaching, the basis of the three trainings, and the only thought of the Buddhas of the Three Times. Without morality and ethics one can no more attain qualities of realization than one can obtain juice from a plant by beating its husk. Thus, for example, Phagmodrupa refused to partake of alcohol even at ganachakra feasts, and though conditions were difficult in Central Tibet, he would not eat even the smallest piece of meat. Whatever he did eat or drink he first blessed.

Because of Phagmodrupa's confidence in the understanding and realization of the teachings, he became like a vajra mountain and maintained the training of the morality even at the risk of his life, thereby accomplishing all the Buddha's teachings. He never loosened the belt of his robes [to sleep] except when changing his clothes, and if he made even a minor mistake, he immediately purified it in front of the monks. Nor did he collect possessions, such as horses and other animals. In brief, his qualities were inconceivable and inexpressible. From the moment he achieved enlightenment until he passed into parinirvana he served all beings without exception. He paid homage to all his teachers, and received from them the instructions and qualities of a Buddha, like one vase being filled by another. He felt grateful to be a servant of all, taking their hardship upon himself. In the same way he assumed responsibility for all the monks, and concerned himself so little with his own welfare that the only nourishment he took was the remnants of others' food. In his studies he was without pride or jealousy, treating high and low equally. For these reasons he was honored as the crest ornament of all beings.

According to the Buddha's teachings, practitioners should study, contemplate and do meditation practice only. Those without proper training, who rob or profit from business, farming or herding, will not achieve these qualities. Phagmodrupa demonstrated the practitioner's life fully. And though he was unequalled in his wisdom and qualities, he continued to search for the qualified Lama, as it is from him that there is the opportunity to obtain the Dharma eye which sees unerringly. But to demonstrate that one can achieve ultimate realization with the transmission of the Lama's blessing, but without dependence on his relative words, he went to Dagla Gampo Monastery as the attendant of Khenpo Rinpoche Shangsumtokpa. By seeing Dharma Lord Gampopa, and engaging in a discussion of three questions, he recognized the nature of the self-awareness wisdom mind, and fully realized the definition and meaning of the general and particular whole Dharma. The inner meaning of all the teachings and instructions was laid bare, all afflicting elaborations of the mind ceased, all hopes and fears were purified, and he saw the Lama directly as a Buddha. He also achieved the meaning of effortlessness, free of all activity. Thus he said:

> If there is no attachment to experiences,
> There is therefore no attachment to the text;
> If there is no end to siddhis,
> There is therefore no limit to food
> And no fear of hunger.
> I am free of the fear of death,
> And free from the mind's projections.

When there is a connection between master and disciple one can, even in a short time, receive all the qualities like one vase being filled by another. To demonstrate this, Phagmodrupa showed the highest respect and ultimate devotion to Lord Gampopa during his two-year stay at Dagla Gampo Monastery; and even the master's attendants and senior monks he respected as the precious Lama himself. Generally, he saw all the monks as Buddhas, and did prostrations to those among them who were senior, as well as to those fully-ordained monks junior to him. He stood up whenever the four noble monks appeared, and paid respect and devotion to even a single word of the Dharma teachings. He was never separated from the Lamas and images of the Buddha.

As all rivers converge in the ocean of the Buddha's qualities, and as geese are attracted to the lotus lake, countless disciples gathered about Phagmodrupa. Yet to show that one must never break even a single minor precept of the refuge, he kept his life simple in every aspect, for he was indifferent to such things as clothing and food. He made offerings of food and drink to the Triple Gem, and repeated the refuge and Bodhisattva prayers. Indeed, he lived exactly like any ordinary monk. Once, when he was wearing an old shirt which was faded from washing, one of his very close disciples requested that he put on a new one, since the monastery possessed enough material. Phagmodrupa replied, "Whatever cloth you have, use it for the monastic community." The little wealth Phagmodrupa accumulated was never given to those already rich, but became the comfort of the poor. Free of the five wrong means of obtaining livelihood,[1] Phagmodrupa never wasted the offerings he received, but dedicated their merit.

Though Phagmodrupa received all the qualities of hearing, contemplation and meditation practice, to serve as an example to others he continued his meditation unceasingly. Once, the spiritual master Lang Senge Gyaltsen, who had received many teachings from Phagmodrupa, requested that the master recount his life story. Phagmodrupa replied, "I don't have any special qualities to speak of, and I have never thought about this life. Even when I was studying I never interrupted the four sessions of meditation." When the spiritual master Mar Tönjam, who was the teacher of Chungpo Drok, remarked to Phagmodrupa, "You have the qualities of a Buddha," he replied, "Even ordinary beings with this kind of effort and perseverance will definitely achieve these qualities." When he travelled a long distance, the rest of his party slept, but Phagmodrupa sat up straight and meditated. He said, "I fully concentrate on the essence of the meditation practice for the benefit of all sentient beings, and as my practice progresses my five afflicting emotions are self-purified. I have achieved confidence in the practice of loving-kindness, compassion and Bodhicitta without self-cherishing, and full skill to ripen all sentient beings with many different methods. I am free from grasping and fixation concerning myself and everything related to me. I am fully realized in the Mahamudra state of non-duality of self and all sentient beings without exception." Thus, he pacified the fire of the dangerous path, and through the vajra wisdom of emptiness

---

[1] flattery, hinting, seeking reward for favors granted, pretentious behavior, and contrived means.

annihilated all the different activities related to the duality of self and the eight worldly Dharmas of the mountain. Because of his full achievement of the Dharmakaya, he accomplished his own benefit and that of all others, received the prophecies of the glorious Lama, the blessings of the Dakas and Dakinis, and the empowerments of the root and lineage Lamas. Phagmodrupa once said:

> An auspicious environment is important.
> May I receive free environments
> Such as forests and solitary places.
> All the Buddhas of the Three Times
> Achieve full enlightenment,
> The state of Buddhahood,
> In the forest
> In front of the Bodhi tree.
>
> All great beings,
> Like Metok Dadze and others,
> Achieve the great meaning
> In the solitary forest.
>
> Like glorious mountains and forests,
> All the previous great Mahasiddhas
> Achieved siddhis in the solitary forest.
> It is in solitary places
> That followers achieve and perfect their qualities
> And dispel the errors
> Of the five afflicting emotions.

This theme he repeated again and again.

Having accomplished his solitary aspiration, Phagmodrupa gathered an ocean of disciples, ripened their mind stream, and developed their precious qualities until they became like the full moon. In order to cultivate their prosperity, happiness, and glorious insight, he depended on and emphasized meditation practice and retreat. Even we, looking with ordinary eyes, can see that many sentient beings benefitted. During the waxing moon all the teachings were experienced through hearing, understanding and meditation practice, and all negative karma and obscurations were dispelled. To be freed of the fault of idle talk, the disciples concentrated on the equipoise of the mind in samadhi, and in calm abiding. During the waning moon Phagmodrupa, who was himself in seclusion, sent his monks into retreat, later asking them to recount the realizations they had during the fifteen-day period. Thus, all the disciples gained great experience, had their obscurations dispelled, and achieved insight into the different mind-states of other beings. Even during the waxing moon Phagmodrupa meditated strictly in the mornings, teaching his disciples to do likewise. Dawn, he said, was the best time to gain all the precious qualities, for all the Buddhas achieved liberation at that hour, as well as all the other qualities of the path. So he placed great importance on the meditation practice accomplished in the morning.

One text states, "The Buddha and all his retinues meditated in the absorption state until the noonday meal. Then, they donned their Dharma robes and partook of food offerings, while devotees did prostrations. After eating, they gave teachings to all who came, including those difficult to tame. In the afternoon, when the mind is clear and the wind cools the heat of the day, they built a lion throne under the shade of the tree while the ocean of the sangha gathered. Seated motionless on the precious throne, the Buddha fearlessly gave the teachings."

Likewise, Phagmodrupa sat as fearlessly as a lion amidst the ocean of the sangha, gazing on all his disciples and moving his wisdom tongue between his shell-like teeth. The voice of his profound teachings resounded like the song of the nightingale, the roar of thunder, or the melody of Brahma. These teachings were neither too long nor too short, and included verses from the Buddha, along with the explanations and pith instructions empowered by his own profound experience. All that he said was presented according to the disciples' level of understanding, predispositions, and karmic connections. The root of the hearers' doubts was cut, enabling them fully to understand and rejoice. To those who gathered solely for the purpose of Dharma, Phagmodrupa unhesitatingly gave the teachings, meanwhile himself maintaining a pure Dharma way of life that led other beings away from worldliness.

Fully peaceful
And freed of desired objects
Is the Bodhisattva
Abandoning the four types of farming,
Or the mendicant living through right livelihood.
Since you do not tarry long in one place
You, great being, have no need of ambition.

As the wish-fulfilling gem grants all wishes
To the Dharma King, the source of all peace,
You protect the gods, nagas, and dharmapalas
With an auspicious environment in all directions.
Through your endless shower of compassionate
blessings
You bring whole nations peace and happiness.
So what need have they of ambition?

Even if one hasn't the clairvoyance
Of seeing the past, present, and future,
If one follows the teachings of the Omniscient One
And practices them without faults,
There is no need of ambition.

In whatever direction the Bodhisattvas travel,
Even in the abodes of the gods, yakshas, nagas,
and gandharvas,
If they do not conflict with the teachings of the Sage,
They will be honored, served, and respected by all.
Thus, there is no need for attachment to ambition.

Thus he taught all his disciples, each according to his ability, that there is no need for ambition.

Generally, when their circumstances are positive, happy and peaceful, beings are respected and sought after even if they don't want it. But when they are passing through difficulties, they are abused and hated. In contrast, the great being Phagmodrupa

> Treated all compassionately as if each was his
> own son,
> Never abandoning the destitute,
> And acting peacefully toward even those who
> harmed him.
> Free from the three spheres he was,
> For he annihilated the self.

Thus, he exchanged his peace and happiness for others' sufferings. Through the profound interdependent arisings and the four great activities, he gave blessings and empowerments and benefitted all sentient beings. Even in one session many among the great assembly gathering had errors dispelled and achieved great qualities. Numbers of disciples coming from far places underwent great hardship and wished to remain longer. "I have great hope for you," Phagmodrupa said, "as I have gone through much hardship for you." Thus all sentient beings are under the protection of his wheel of nonduality wisdom, the perfection of precious Bodhicitta.

When Phagmodrupa was close to Parinirvana, an evildoer placed poison in his food, so that he experienced pain throughout his body. With great devotion his precious disciple said, "Because of this negative action, will your enemy go to hell?" Phagmodrupa replied, "I have accepted the responsibility so that this person not only will not go to hell, but will not even go to one of the lower realms." He then requested that four fully ordained bhikshus say the mantra of Akshobya and other purification practices so as generally to neutralize the negative karma of those having evil thoughts, and particularly to neutralize that of the being who poisoned him. When this had been done, he himself began to feel well, happy and peaceful.

At the beginning of Phagmodrupa's illness several of his major disciples suggested that they do powerful healing mantras, which are strong and cooling. With these mantras one was supposed to partake of some alcohol. But Phagmodrupa said, "Even though my life is at risk, I will not permit anyone to drink chang because it will cause a great amount of negative karma." He then explained the benefits of abstaining from alcohol, and the error involved in drinking, warning all his great disciples, whom he cherished more than himself, not to drink.

The glorious Dharma Lord,
Who actualizes the Three Times,
Achieved the wisdom of understanding
Of all the subtle points of cause and effect.

To all the sentient beings
Whom he regarded as his own son,
And the followers of his great disciples
Whom he cherished above himself,
He gave his essence profound teachings
Of cause and effect.
Sustaining oneself on the falsity of desire and hatred
Is like being nourished by alcohol and meat.

According to the testimony teachings
Of the King of knowers of the three times
Who himself realized this truth
And taught it to others,
He did not accept such ways for himself
Nor allow them to be adopted by others.

Through properly keeping the samaya,
The essential point of the Vinaya precepts,
Bodhisattva vows and Vajrayana,
He conveyed all the qualities of the Tantra
As if he were filling a vase,
And asked disciples to keep these teachings
In their heart center.
He explained repeatedly

That there are three hundred sixty kinds of sexual activity,
But these teachings of the channels, winds, and drops
Are by themselves not profound.
The essential point of profound Tantra,
Buddha taught,
Is to purify them within the clear expanse.
Otherwise, they only create
The suffering of samsara.

The complete life and liberation of this great being cannot be expressed by others, including gods. One lifetime is not enough to tell even a single aspect of his life story, so what I have recounted here is but a tiny part. I have exerted myself day and night, and continue still. If I have made errors I confess them before the Dharma Lord and all his great disciples. In the future may his followers benefit others and achieve peace by acting according to the example set by the precious Lama.

All the sons of this great sage, the Lord of the World,
Are born of his clan,
Just as Kings, Brahmins, horses and elephants
Belong to a line of direct descent.
If one does not hold the life story
Of the wisdom body, speech and mind,
How can one be a Bodhisattva?
Otherwise, the clan is not important.
Among the castes,
The followers of the great sage
Are his sons.

If one does not follow and study
The story of the wisdom body, speech and mind
Of the precious Lama, supreme sage,
How, then, can one become
Inseparable from his body, speech and mind?

Even if one absorbs just a part of his life story,
By following it with body, speech and mind
One pleases the great being,
Planting the seed of the Dharmakaya,
And the seed of the form body
Which will manifest in the two rupakayas.[1]
In order to realize
The inseparability of the peerless precious Lama
Whose reality of body, speech and mind
Is all the Buddhas of the three times,
One should emphasize the training
According to the story of the wisdom body, speech and mind.

As the sun's rays shine even on dirt,
So does the sun of the qualities
Of the Lama, Lord of the World,
Shine on me.
Though dirt is negative,
The light shines on it without discrimination.
Just so, the light of Buddhahood
Coming from the protector, the Lord precious Lama,
Is limitless, thought beyond conception.

According to our ordinary mind his life story—
Birth, renunciation, mastery of knowledge,
Practice, attaining to the solitary forest
And gathering an assembly of disciples,
Roaring with the thunder of emptiness
At the suns of the lion King,
Leaving behind myriad testaments
Concerning cause and effect,
And the teachings of the Buddha
Offered through the wisdom of varieties [omniscience]—

[1] nirmanakaya and sambhogakaya.

I felt to be essential and profound
For the followers, and sentient beings of the three realms.

If one realizes the all-pervading emptiness,
There is no teaching to be taught
Beside dependent arising,
Inseparable from emptiness.
The precious Lama also
Taught nothing other than this.
Even the Buddha, who fully perfected the two accumulations,
Could say no more.
So one should emphasize the teachings
And follow the example of this life story.

The Dharma Lord, glorious Phagmodrupa, who led the life I have described, was born in the Takpa Korkor in Dro Ne, Kham. His father was Athar and his mother was Za Achak. His clan was Dung Üe. He established his monastery in Phagmodru at Thatsa in Central Tibet. On the twenty-fifth day of the eighth month, at the age of sixty-one, he passed away with numerous auspicious signs. The four great disciples among his vast assembly of students were Khetsun Nyang Ro Rintor, Togden Menyak Gomring, Kalden Yeshe Senghe, and Tsangpa Kundan Rechung. His attendants were the glorious Taklung Thangpa and so forth.

The Twenty Verses of Praise to the Great Drikungpa, Lord Jigten Sumgön

by Lingje Repa

NAMO GURU

The wisdom-minds of all Buddhas and that of the Supreme Yogin are as pure as space.
By that, may all beings be victorious!
I pay homage at the feet of that glorious one and will praise you, Supreme Being.

From beginningless time, you achieved full Buddhahood.
Your nonconceptual compassion pervaded space.
Through that, you were not satisfied with your benefit of beings.
I prostrate to you who have the power of glorious compassion.

In order to bring all beings to the Supreme Path,
You properly attended glorious lamas.
You gradually travelled the Stages of the Path.
I prostrate to you who have the power of skillful means.

You are the heart-son of the Dharma Lord, the Precious Lama, and compiler of his teachings.

You are the Dharma-heir who comes from blessings.
I prostrate to you who have the power of unshakeable devotion.

In the past, you were not attached to your kingdoms, sons, wives, or others.
You had limitless renunciation.
You became special through the patience of morality.
I prostrate to you who have the power of glorious merit.

You have limitless effort in performing virtuous deeds.
You are constantly absorbed in the nature of Dharmakaya.
You have the completely pure primordial wisdom of the Two Knowledges.[1]
I prostrate to you who have the power of perfect primordial wisdom.

Like water mixed with water, you are one with all the Buddhas.
From within the state of inseparable union, you perform all their activities.
I prostrate to you who have the power of the Dignity of the Seven Horses.[2]

You possess the treasury of the good qualities of all the Buddhas.
You have perfected the Ten Paramitas[3] and the Ten Strengths.[4]

---

[1] The wisdom that perceives the full range of things to be known, and the wisdom that perceives their true nature.

[2] A poetic synonym for the Sun of the Buddha's Activities.

[3] Generosity, morality, patience, perseverance, meditation, wisdom, skillful means, aspiration, power, primordial wisdom.

[4] According to the *Tibetan-English Dictionary of Buddhist Terminology* by Tsepak Rigzin (Library of Tibetan Works and Archives, 1986), pp.

You have accomplished the Ten Bhumis and possess the merit of the Ten Abilities.[1]
I prostrate to you who have the power of the Victorious Sage.

In limitless, immeasurable realms,
You completely fulfill the wishes
Of limitless beings without exception.
I prostrate to you who have the power of the Wish-Fulfilling Gem.

Sometimes you abide in Tushita and (from there) enter a womb, take birth, and so forth.[2]
From the Dharmakaya, you perform limitless activities.
I prostrate to you who have the power of various miracles.

Sometimes, for the benefit of others, you manifest as a Shravaka, a Pratyekabuddha, a lion, an elephant, and so forth.
Sometimes you appear as a craftsman.
Your limitless manifestations benefit beings.

194-95, the ten strengths are: the power of knowing right from wrong, of knowing the consequences of actions, of knowing various mental inclinations, of knowing various mental faculties, of knowing various degrees of intelligence, of knowing the paths to all goals, of knowing the ever-afflcted and purified phenomena, of knowing past lives, of knowing deaths and births, of knowing the exhaustion of contaminations.

[1] Life, mind, necessities, activities, birth, wish, aspiration, miracle power, wisdom, Dharma. (Special thanks to the Ven. Lama Kalsang Gyaltsen, who provided this list of the Ten Abilities from Sakya Pandita's *Illumination of the Sage's Intent.*)

[2] Here, "and so forth" refers to the rest of the Twelve Deeds of a Buddha: Descending from Tushita, Entering the Womb, Taking Birth, Developing Proficiency in the Arts, Enjoying the Kingdom, Renouncing the Kingdom, Undergoing Austerities, Going to Bodh'gaya, Subjugating the Maras, Attaining Enlightenment, Turning the Wheel of Dharma, attaining Parinirvana.

I prostrate to you who have the power of various
emanations.

In the ten directions of limitless space,
You give limitless teachings in various languages
Through the power of your wisdom-speech.
I prostrate to you who have the power of
inexpressible speech.[1]

You have the manner of The Accomplished One,
The Lion, and so forth.[2]
The synonyms of your ultimate names
Are mentioned in the Sutras and Tantras.
I prostrate to you who have the power of the
union of No More Learning.

You came at this time in the Land of Snows and
quickly established in the state of the Noble Ones
Many of those who were difficult to tame.
You perform the activities of teaching.
I prostrate to you who have the power of the alchemy
of gold.

I offer all enjoyments, equal to the limits of space,
And an ocean of offering clouds of Samantabhadra.
Seeing the bad deeds collected by beings since
beginningless time,
I reveal them all, one by one.
Please accept us.

I rejoice in you whose wisdom-mind is as pure as
space
And who perform limitless benefit for beings.

---

[1] Here, "inexpressible" means that the true meaning of Mahamudra is beyond words. It can only be experienced through the practice of meditation.

[2] These are the names of two of the Thousand Buddhas of the Fortunate Kalpa.

By the fearless sound of your Lion's Roar in the ten directions,
Please turn the Wheel of Stainless Ambrosia.

By the power of your compassion and aspiration,
Please remain until the end of samsara and do not pass into nirvana.
By this virtue, may all beings, as limitless as space,
Become your equal, Supreme Victorious One.

In this world, Supreme Being,
Your glory and fame pervade the Three Worlds.
You fully ripen limitless beings.
May your life be limitless and firm.

Whoever holds, reads, or memorizes and repeats
Even one verse (of this prayer)
Will dispel the samsara of many kalpas
And be reborn at the feet of that Victorious One.

Your qualities, Supreme Being, could never be fully expressed,
Even if one were to describe them for kalpas.
By the virtue of this joyful, respectful praise,
May all beings achieve supreme bliss.

Thus, the Lord of Yogins plants the Victory Banner of the Three Vows and causes the Buddha's teachings to flourish. From within his mountain-like realization, he proclaims the Lion's Roar of Shunyata and subjugates those with conceptual views. He directly points out the meaning of Mahamudra. By showing the inconceivable highway of Interdependent Origination, he dispels the inner and outer obstacles of disciples. He never tires of gathering sentient beings by way of the Four Kinds of Training.[1] By the limitless, unobstructed power of his loving-kindness and compassion, he defeats all

[1] These are the four ways of gathering disciples: giving the necessities of life, using pleasant words, giving teachings according to Sutra and Shastra, and following the teachings oneself.

classes of demons. In this way, from within the pure Dharmakaya, he possesses the vast, direct perception of all appearances as reflections in a mirror. That Great Being, possessing limitless wisdom, is renowned as Kyura (Lord Jigten Sumgön). I, the mendicant yogin Lingje Repa,[1] from within the Perfect Meaning,[2] have completed this Praise of Twenty Verses.

---

[1] Lingje Repa was a chief disciple of Phagmodrupa and was the principal teacher of Tsangpa Gyare, who founded the Drukpa Kagyu lineage.

[2] This means that Lingje Repa directly perceived the truth of Lord Jigten Sumgön's attainments and that his praise is not exaggerated.

(Translated from the Tibetan by the Ven. Khenpo Könchog Gyaltsen with the assistance of Rick Finney.)

Dharma Lord Jigten Sumgön (1143–1217)

Unparalleled among all the great disciples of Phagmodrupa is he who holds the lineage, the Dharma Lord Jigten Sumgön, the glorious Drikungpa, a Buddha of the Three Times. The *Rinchen Chagya Metok* (Flowered Precious Seal) states:

> I am the Buddha of the Three Times
> And the Buddhas of the Three Times are I.
> I and the Buddha of the Three Times
> Are one activity.
> If a being is unceasing in devotion to me,
> He will meet with the endless treasure qualities.

Lord Jigten Sumgön had earlier attained the state of a Tathagata in the name of Lurigdrönma. *The Successive Lives of the Dharma Lord Drikungpa* says:

> For limitless kalpas in the past
> He attained Buddhahood, or omniscience, as
> Lurigdrönma
> In order to benefit sentient beings.
> He lived many millions of years,
> And turned the wheel of stainless Dharma.
> Millions of kalpas after his passing
> There appeared a Buddha
> By the name of Gyalwa Drakpe Gyalpo
> (King of Fame),

At the time of this Buddha's teaching
There appeared a Bodhisattva emanation
Who was called Tenpa Sangche (Glorifier of Teachings).
The chief patron then
Was a member of a wealthy family
Who in a later incarnation
Was known as Palchen.
Tenpa Sangche gathered
Hundreds of thousands of disciples
Who were adorned with the ornament of pure morality,
And achieved the realization
Of stainless, co-emergent wisdom.
After a thousand years had passed
That Bodhisattva emanation reappeared
As the Buddha Marme Dze (Dipankara),
While the Bodhisattva emanation of the time
Was known as Tsukphuchen,
And the patron Palchen
Emanated as Shri Phukpa.
From then until now
That Bodhisattva Tsukphuchen
Continuously performed many virtuous deeds,
While thousands of sincere disciples appeared
Who realized the unborn nature of the mind.
Limitless kalpas after the passing
Of that great, brilliant-minded being
There appeared in this world called Mije
The Buddha Shakyamuni, the Lion of Men.
Among his disciples
His excellent, unparalleled heart-son
Was Lichavi (Vimalakirti)
Who has ultimate confidence.
This youth creates joy in all who see him.

Other texts explain the many different names by which he was known in this world:

In Oddiyana, I was known as energetic and discriminating;

In the central forest, as black and virtuous;
In Ha Ha Gö, as the true expression of wrath;
In Sosaling, as the light of the sun;
In the glorious mountain, as Dzinna Bodhi;
In the Simu Island, as Deje Gawa;
In Ame Tsundi, as the Sun and Moon;
In Nagara, as Melodious Fool;
In the Snow Land, as Ratnashri;
And everywhere, as the great patron.
At times I am known as the trainer of heretics,
At times as a great writer.

From the same text:

All you yogins! Do not differentiate
Between me and the Three Great Kings [of Tibet].
They and their activities
Are the manifestation of the wind and mind energies.

From the *Hidden Treasure of Songtsen Gampo, the Emanation of the Great Compassionate Lord*:

A bhikshu Bodhisattva born in the East,
The great yogi who holds the Tantra teachings,
The precious being who keeps the morality purely,
Will change the face of the Buddha[1] and serve devotedly.

Those who serve greatly are arya nobles
Who will be respected by all.
Why are they aryas?
They served the Buddha greatly,
Having no other activity.
Therefore this Buddha's image
Will be benefitted by various activities,
And there will be many aryas
Producing the four gathering disciples,[2]

---

[1] meaning: he will develop the Buddha's teaching so fully as virtually to transform it

[2] upasaka, upasika, bhikshu and bhikshuni

The Buddha's teachings,
And statues of the Buddha
Which will seem as if endowed with life.
In this snowy land, the kingdom of Tibet,
There are many holy mountains,
Such as sacred Tsari, self-arisen Chakrasamvara,
Along with precious stones and waters.
Many arhats live on snow mountain Tise [Kailash],
While a stream of nectars flows there.
The self-arisen six syllables
Appear on the Gere rock,
As well as the mountain mudras of the Dakinis.
Naga Bodhisattvas live on the lake
Known as Nam Tso,
And benefit all the rivers.
Many great practitioners live in the Thanglha mountain;
Naga Bodhisattvas live

In the lake of Nub Tso;
And there are many rishis on the snow mountains.

From the *Hidden Treasure of Padmasambhava*:

In Tso-Ngu,
On the lake of the upper Dan,
Ratnashri will appear
As a son of the great yogin Dorje.

Although this is Lord Jigten Sumgön's reality state, he took form as an ordinary being. His father was the yogin Naljorpa Dorje, and his mother the Hidden Yogini Tsuma. He was born in the Water Pig Year at Tso-Ngu in the upper part of Tsar Tod in Eastern Tibet, a place which was rich in matters of Dharma. At the moment that he entered into his mother's womb, she had a dream in which the essence of Vajrapani dissolved into her body in the form of a white wisdom text known as Dorje Chu. From that moment she was filled with bliss and experienced many samadhi states unknown to her before. The environment was filled with peace, prosperity and happiness.

Lord Jigten Sumgön was given the birth name Pal Thar (Glorious Liberation) by Leguwa Palshen Lön. He could read and write perfectly by the time he had reached the age of six, and fully absorbed the Manjushri Nama Sangiti text by merely reading it once. From his uncle Khenpo Dharma, who had gathered five hundred Brahmacharya [celibate] disciples, he received teachings and the meditation practice of Vajrakilaya and others. When he reached the age of nine, he was already giving meditation instruction, and so began gathering disciples. From his teacher, and from Jetsun Khorwa Lungkhyer, he received teaching and instruction on Mahamudra which he practiced diligently until he was able to achieve the quality of meditation for three days together, not even stopping to partake of food. During the evenings, while in the forest tending animals, he would transform his sleeping state into the clear light. Because he mastered the illusion-like samadhi and other meditation practices, he was able in his dreams to travel to the Buddhafield of Tathagata Arakta Padmasyachakyu, and achieve many great qualities. He received the teachings of Lamrim [progressive stages on the path of study and practice] and all the instructions of Atisha from Master Kyebu Tampa and Master Radeng Gomchen of Kadampa.

As Lord Jigten Sumgön's father passed away when he was fifteen years old, he thereafter cared for his mother's needs, both practical and spiritual, but she, too, passed away quickly. When he was seventeen his master Radeng likewise passed away, but Lord Jigten Sumgön continued studying and practicing unceasingly.

When he attained the age of eighteen, Master Kyebu said: "You will be a great master like Geshe Langri Tangpa—and indeed even greater." At the age of nineteen Lord Jigten Sumgön journeyed South, and for three years benefitted and protected the people there by reading spiritual texts, meditating, and performing other Dharma activities. He also received the empowerments and teachings of Vajrayogini from Master Sangye Yeshe. At the age of twenty-two he was invited by the patron Agar to come to Lungmoche where he entered into retreat, sealing his door. During the day he dissolved his mind into the meditative Mahamudra state, and at night he practiced the generation of the enlightened deity Vajrayogini. He performed the rites of sindhura one hundred eight times, and in the middle of the night did torma offerings according to the text. In this way the days passed.

After one year the patron Nyasang returned from central Tibet and asked to see him, first offering an immense block of sugar and other things. Lord Jigten Sumgön refused to see her, but accepted the offerings through a tiny window. Looking at them he said, "These things have appeared neither through the merit of myself, nor of worldly actions, nor through the kindness of Nyasang. Rather, they have manifested through the kindness of the Lama and the Triple Gem." He thereupon worked even harder on his meditation practice. When Nyasang returned from further journeys one year later, she heard that the Lama's health had declined through unceasing practice. She therefore brought many further offerings such as tea, butter, and dried meat, and again requested to see him. He agreed to see her once, but later told his disciples, "The more one seeks to obtain the regard of others, the less one receives it. But if one simply practices Dharma meditation, all good things result. This is how it was with the patron Nyasang."

So Lord Jigten Sumgön continued practicing diligently and achieved the great magnificent blessings and signs of realization. Through his mental power he was able to cure dysentery. Once, a tantrika who was sick for twelve years set out to see him and receive blessings, but even before he arrived, he was healed. When the Lama was asked to visit a dying person, merely through giving the refuge and other blessings he cured that being. Earlier, the master Sing Sing, who was one of the wisest teachers around, had been his spiritual advisor.

Dhehuchepon Thung asked Jigten Sumgön to come and give teachings to his family and all the people in the surrounding area. At that time, a great leader known as Chökyi

Sherab, and another person known as Nagri Chotsun requested initiation, which he gave to them and many others, along with meditation instruction. Again the patron Agar requested that he come, but instead he entered into retreat. Agar's house and dzomo were stolen by the robber Khyisuk, who then went up to Lord Jigten Sumgön's hut and said, "Give me all your possessions." The Lama said, "I am an upasaka, a practitioner, so I have nothing to give." The robber said, "I will come inside and see for myself." Jigten Sumgön said, "Be careful, for my Dharma protector is very powerful." That night, as the robber sat among a group of revelers at a tavern, he died. Thus, word of the power of Lord Jigten Sumgön's spells spread far and wide, causing him to remark, "I received this power and many magnificent blessings. Now, whenever anyone dies after a conflict with one of my patrons it is said that this is due to my spells! That is not good, so refrain from concentrating on the ability to cast spells. And if someone dies, don't look upon it as happening through spells. Possessing strong power is my misfortune."

Once, when a drought appeared, the Lama went to the naga country and said, "I am a realized yogin. Please cause the rain to fall." At once there was a great shower. Another time, he was staying at Lhungmoche where people were hunting wild animals. When he gave them refuge and teachings, they ceased all their harmful activities. He actualized the power of the mantras, achieving the results attributed to them in the Sutras and Tantras.

At that time Goda Pandik, who came from Central Tibet, spoke of different masters, especially Lord Phagmodrupa. Merely by hearing Phagmodrupa's name the Lama's mind was stirred with devotion like the leaves of a tree in the wind. He thought, "I must see him." So, on the full moon of the first month he proceeded to Central Tibet, his entire journey being marked by a rainbow in the heavens. Just before leaving he went to Lopon Choshe who said, "There is another person going to Central Tibet; you can travel together." So he asked to accompany this person, but the man wished to delay the journey in order to collect certain provisions. In addition, a lady devotee who was also a patron strongly requested that Lord Jigten Sumgön not go, asking him to promise that he would remain awhile. Because of her devotion and insistence he felt he had no choice but to fulfill her request, but circumstances forced him to leave her sooner than he promised. Later, he told his disciples, "Don't agree to the request of anyone who asks you to delay. When I did, I ate the promise, and it was most delicious!"

Among his disciples at that time was a person called Mogami Gese, who acted as a patron for his travels. The master Sing Sing asked to accompany Jigten Sumgön, but the latter did not allow it. So he offered the master a horse, a cloth, and some bags of provisions for travelling, and the journey began.

At this time, Lord Jigten Sumgön was twenty-five years of age. On the way, he journeyed like the Bodhisattva Sadaprarudita, constantly meditating on the Lama. He thought, "Even if the Lama has five hundred disciples whose rank has earned them the white umbrella,[1] I will be chief among them." At night when he gazed up at the moon, he felt great devotion, and as tears streamed down his face, he said, "Even the moon above can see the Lama, but not I." Thus he proceeded like the Bodhisattva Norsang.

One night, after he came to Phenyul, he had a dream of Phagmodrupa, white of complexion, wearing white robes, and seated in a small hut. The next day he awoke and found that the walls of the house he was staying in were covered with the six syllables.

He next went to a monastery in Kyishö where the monks from Lhotöpa and Demawa were having an argument. The sight disappointed him and made him strongly feel that he should not become involved in such matters in the pursuit of his goal. Nevertheless, he acted respectfully toward the masters in that place.

---

[1] referring to the custom in which high disciples have a parasol held over their heads

He next proceeded to Nepo Dowa. On the way, he met a man who said that he was coming from the direction of Phagmodrupa Monastery. So great was Jigten Sumgön's devotion that he prostrated before him, and by journeying the entire night arrived at Phagdru before dawn.

As soon as he arrived, Jigten Sumgön called out to be received. A meditator from Kyishö came to meet him, and took him to a house where he rested. The next morning, on seeing a large bat he thought, "This is an emanation of Phagmodrupa." For three days thereafter he had to wait to see the Lama, though Phagmodrupa sent his attendants to welcome him and create a good connection. On the thirteenth of the month, he was at last allowed to meet the Lama, so he went forth, bearing offering bolts of brocade and silk, along with a horse. Phagmodrupa scolded him saying, "If I accept the horse, it means that I must either die or leave this place, so I cannot take it." Jigten Sumgön said, "Then, should I release him on the mountain?" When Phagmodrupa scolded him further, Jigten Sumgön wept with devotion and fervor until Phagmodrupa accepted him as a disciple. "I will give you special care," he said, "and will grant you whatever you wish. So there is no reason for unhappiness, is there?" Jigten Sumgön then offered the master tea, first circumambulating him eighty times. Lord Phagmodrupa accepted the offering with joy, and later that day gave his disciple the aspiration Bodhicitta and teachings. With this alone Lord Jigten Sumgön felt so satisfied that he seemed to need nothing more. But the next day he received the Bodhisattva vow, the Mahamudra instruction, and dedication teachings and meditation. Again he felt that he had no need of anything else. At one point Lord Phagmodrupa pointed a finger at Jigten Sumgön's heart center, and the mandala of his body was transformed into Heruka. That night in a dream he came upon a golden Vairocana with one face, after which he felt perfectly content. Phagmodrupa then said, "I have great hope for you. These signs are all due to the power of my magnificent blessings. For your sake I underwent great hardship." He

He then gave him the one-hundred syllable mantra meditation practice, and the instruction of Mahamudra. Lord Jigten Sumgön thought, "Now I have no need of receiving further teachings. I must simply do the practice." Three disciples from Lhotö remarked, "What manner of being are you? In the beginning you were so eager that you rushed in here in the middle of the night and now, having actually seen the Lama, you sit in a corner and don't attend the teachings." Lord Jigten Sumgön thought, "What they say is true," so he came into the assembly hall to receive the teachings. There, he made it a practice to recite the seven-branch prayer as many as ten times before Lord Phagmo-drupa even seated himself on the throne. Thus, when he received the teachings, he was able to absorb them all without missing a single word. The news therefore spread that an upasaka from Lhotö was receiving the teachings completely, without missing even one word.

Lord Jigten Sumgön had great devotion to the entire Sangha, but once, due to an error committed by Geshe Samyepa, his confidence was shaken. However, by meditating on all the monks as his Guru he rediscovered his sense of devotion.

While studying and practicing, Jigten Sumgön cared little for food and clothing. He never built a fire for his food, or visited others to partake of a meal, but instead remained silent, sometimes making a little soup. At other times he ate food remnants, or drank finely powdered ashes placed in water. At times of rest he went to a place where the monks did prostrations, and said the seven-limbed prayer twenty-one times. Each morning he did a long session of meditation, while at midnight he went outside and collected leaves from the birch tree for cooking. Many Khampas called him a disgrace to their tribe, but he answered, "The great lineage masters did not create an easy life for themselves. Like Jetsun Milarepa, I too do not have time for cooking, so perhaps I will not be a disgrace to the Khampas." They remarked, "He clearly has a lot of pride to speak in this way." But later they recognized the sincerity of his practice.

Lord Phagmodrupa gave the Great Pointing Out Instructions three times. Though his disciples could not understand them the first two times, they received the realizations at the third try. The master said, "I was not so clear as you are. You understand the instructions on the third repetition, but I took longer." Lord Jigten Sumgön achieved the realization that all practice is born in the mind, and later became renowned for achieving the yoga of the non-meditation state, the perfect fifth path. As all phenomenal appearances are actualized in the Mahamudra state, he thought, "It is enough to practice Mahamudra with great devotion to the precious Lama," so he entered Phagmodrupa's presence and recounted this realization. But Phagmodrupa scolded him, "What are you saying? Until you achieve Buddhahood, you need the five-fold profound path of Mahamudra. Therefore, do not separate yourself from it."

Hearing that a visitor was coming from afar, he made a large torma from his left-over food and offered it to the Lama, with the request that he might go ahead and meet the person in advance. In Radeng the patron Nyasang gave him two bricks of tea, and urged other patrons to make offerings. After they brought him sweets, hot cheese, tea and butter, he gave them teachings, but he did not have enough time to advise the many others who approached him. When he returned to Phagmodru Monastery, he was at first unable to see the Lama, so he meditated unceasingly in the clear light for three months. At last, he presented his own offerings and those he had been given by others. Phagmodrupa said, " Put those things in my bag," and Lord Jigten Sumgön thought, "Can it be that the Lama keeps anything for himself, even a bag?" Phagmodrupa told him, "So far, your karma has been to teach the Dharma only to my patrons. I will see if you can give the proper instructions or not." Then Jigten Sumgön received further teachings, and had a special insight that he was in fact free from all dogma. Like the meeting of two spaces, the two clear lights emerged in his mind. Phagmodrupa said, "With this kind of realization you must be born again. Though there have been many highly realized siddhas, all have been reborn because this kind of realization is still not complete," and he explained by using many examples and much logic.

Once, Jigten Sumgön acquired a brick of tea, and asked the monk Setön if he might make an offering of it to Phagmodrupa. Setön advised, "You will need this for yourself, so do not give it away." As he was not allowed to offer it, Jigten Sumgön later told his disciples, "If someone asks you whether he might make offerings, always allow him to do so. I was misled by the kindness of Setön." To the monks Jigten Sumgön twice made offerings of tea, and to Phagmodrupa hot, sweet cheese and other delicacies. All the Dharma instructions were spontaneously established in him. Whenever he saw Phagmodrupa and received teachings from him, he never went empty-handed, but offered whatever he had, great or small.

Near the monastery's central shrine was a mandala of four activities, which bore the auspicious signs. Since one was broken, he repaired and offered it. As a result, Phagmodrupa said, "The auspicious signs now belong to you." Later, after Jigten Sumgön improved the mandala yet further, he said, "I believe my ability to benefit sentient beings arose from this."

Phagmodrupa urged Lord Jigten Sumgön to become a monk, but he thought, "The life of a yogi is easier for practising the Dharma. Even as a yogi, one must observe social discipline, but a monk is subject to so many more restrictions that he is like an ox whose back is broken by its load of precepts." So he decided not to become a monk, but instead practiced the Method Path. When he asked if this practice was correct, Phagmodrupa replied, "It will be later, but for now do these: one hundred eight mandala offerings, one hundred eight hundred-syllable recitations, one hundred eight wind sessions, one hundred eight circumambulations, and one hundred eight prostrations. Do all of this in six sessions, day and night." So Lord Jigten Sumgön practiced in this way, enduring great hardships for some time. When he had completed these instructions, he went to the Lama, and smiling at him asked, "Now may I practice the Method Path?" Phagmodrupa replied, "You may do so, and indeed it is necessary." He then gave detailed teachings about winds, channels and drops. One day, as Lord Jigten Sumgön received the teaching, he developed profound devotion, due to which his winds were naturalized, and many qualities of the Method Path developed within him.

Once, when he was going to see Phagmodrupa, he saw important masters gathered there such as Lama Shang, Geshe Dan and others. Phagmodrupa dismissed them, saying that he had important work to do with Lord Jigten Sumgön. After they had gone, Phagmodrupa told him to sit in the meditation posture. Coming forward, he pointed to Jigten Sumgön's three chakras with his walking stick, and pronounced the sacred syllables OM, AH, HUNG. Then he said, "You will be a great meditator." Again he said, "Acting on the meditation, you will be a yet greater meditator." A third time he said, "I am happy that you will be a great meditator. Now go."

Once, when Jigten Sumgön went to see the Lama, he asked, "Through the meditation on Mahamudra, will the mind be fully pacified at the time of death, or will all this phenomenal world become more clear, enabling me to achieve the omniscient wisdom?" Phagmodrupa replied, "You will have the understanding." Jigten Sumgön thought, "To achieve this realization, either one should attain the rainbow body and the Dharmakaya mind, or one should have the knowledge of the three times. I may not have those." Phagmodrupa insisted, "Definitely you will achieve this." And raising his voice, he said, "I would not deceive you." (Later, when Jigten Sumgön did the meditations in Echung Cave, he achieved the omniscient wisdom, and felt content that he had asked the Lama the questions concerning it.) While still with his teacher, he, along with Lama Tonpa Sherab, received the three-fold Bodhisattva vow, and the Bodhisattva name Rinchen Pal Ratnashri.

At last, Phagmodrupa showed signs of becoming ill. Jigten Sumgön helped the Lama's attendant Tsangpa Chöchang, and offered a handful of medicinal roots. Phagmodrupa was pleased, and accepted them. Gazing on his many stacks of brick tea, he said, "Though these supplies are here in abundance, they cannot help me now." Jigten Sumgön performed great service with full devotion, and the Lama was very gratified. It was said that if there were three others like Jigten Sumgön making long-life requests of Phagmodrupa, the Lama would surely have accepted. All Jigten Sumgön's belongings he used for the benefit of the Lama and for offerings to the monks. Often, he went to the Lama's room, and at the time of Phagmodrupa's passing a golden vajra bearing a slight stain [signifying that Jigten Sumgön still had further purifi cation to accomplish on the path] was seen to emerge from the Lama's heart and enter that of Jigten Sumgön. From the body of the Lama many blessing relics emanated and his footprints appeared on rocks. Then Lord Jigten Sumgön was startled by the appearance of the horse which he had offered the Lama at their first meeting, and which had not been accepted. He sold the animal, but did not receive the money and sugar owed him until eighteen months later. With these he made offerings to the monks, and built a memorial to his Lama.

Before Jigten Sumgön had come to Phagdru Monastery, Phagmodrupa himself repeatedly predicted, "My lineage holder will come from Kham; he is an upasaka who will be on the tenth bhumi level." When Jigten Sumgön arrived, the Lama said, "Now my wish is fulfilled," and turning to Taklung Thangpa, his close attendant and disciple, he remarked, "Don't mistreat this upasaka. In ages past I was the Buddha Khorwajhik and he was Chenrezig."

Lord Jigten Sumgön had only one piece of cloth to cover

his lower body. When one of his friends offered him another, he sold it in exchange for powdered incense which he sprinkled on the memorial to his teacher.

From Master Tsilungpa he received further teachings given by his Lama.

At this time Sing Singwa and A-gon came to him with a request for teachings, but he would not accept, and sent them to someone else. Instead, he concentrated intensively on meditation, experiencing many obstacles such as seeing lions filling all space and penetrating his forehead, and many similar phenomena. With Master Tsilungpa he looked over the Lamdre text, but could find no instructions on dispelling the obstacles. And though he did everything possible according to the various texts, nothing helped him even slightly. For fifteen days he meditated on the statue of Jowo Shakyamuni in the temple in Lhasa as his own Lama, and circumambulated and supplicated him with one-pointed mind, but though this helped, it did not fully satisfy him. Later, all the obstacles were dispelled and he realized the teachings in the Echung Cave where he practiced the meditation unceasingly day and night. When he realized the meaning of dependent arising, his mind completely became attuned to the outer and inner world, and to the causes and conditions which determine whether phenomena act for benefit or for harm. He also fully realized the nature of virtue and non-virtue, and the meaning of the absolutely permitted and absolutely prohibited. One day he recollected that the Great Vehicle Tantra teachings state, "The cause of wandering in samsara from beginningless time is due to not gathering the winds in the central channel (avadhuti)." So he thought, "If the winds are not gathered in the central channel, what is the use of this life? If they are centralized, then even dying is acceptable." Thus, he practiced the exercise of the coarse winds as if his life depended on it. Through this effort he received the vision of the Seven Taras adorned with the blue utpala flowers, as well as many profound teachings. He also saw the faces of many Buddhas and Bodhisattvas, and received the opportunity to purify the six realms. Limitless Dakinis invited him to a ganachakra feast, and the worldly deities, creating obstacles in their wrath, were subjugated by him, though their unpleasant odor filled his cave.

In his meditation state Lord Jigten Sumgön became unaware of the passing of day and night. Once, when his eyes were bothering him, the King of the Nagas, Sokma Me, appeared before him and licked his eyes with his tongue, thus dispelling the disease.

After three years Jigten Sumgön returned to Phagdru Monastery and met Taklung Thangpa, with whom he entered into a dialogue on the profound teachings. He journeyed to several other places and then returned to Echung Cave where he meditated for two years. During that time he fell ill with leprosy. Sealing the cave and remaining within, he privately planned deliberately to transfer his consciousness. But sensing that others might believe he was hiding his sickness, he emerged from the cave and received auspicious signs. From there he went to the home of a patron and said, "I have suddenly contracted a disease." He then returned to the cave and did prostrations before an image of Chenrezig which had been consecrated more than one hundred times by Lord Phagmodrupa. Whenever he felt deep depression, he remembered the sufferings of the six realms and a great natural compassion arose in his mind. A stream of tears flowed from his eyes, so he said prayers again and again that he might become the protector, help and refuge of all sentient beings. During that time he noticed that whenever he meditated his sickness seemed to flow out from his legs like dust being carried away by a strong wind, or soft soil being raked by a plow, but whenever he ceased meditation, the sickness stagnated.

At last one day in mid-winter there was suddenly mighty thunder and a rainfall, and the Lama could feel a change in his winds. Experiencing great joy, he observed the departure of an enormous Naga which had filled the whole of the valley. That evening he fully recovered, like the sun coming out of eclipse. Doubting that the people could understand what was happening, he composed a song telling how within three nights and four days he was freed of all negative karma. In order to test whether these events were real, he found a leprosy patient and gave him the teachings. Within fifteen days the man fully recovered.

After three days Lama Legpa arrived and recounted a dream in which he saw the sun surrounded by golden syllables filling all of space. Lord Jigten Sumgön said, "You have had a significant dream." Thus, all obscurations were removed from him by the very root, and he was fully adorned with all the ornaments of the Buddha qualities. He realized the meaning of the outer, inner and secret interdependent arisings, and said, "I realize the cause for the different kinds of birth, except for those of the sky dragon and the conch shell." However, one day, due to the opening of the essential point in yogic exercises, he understood the birth of the dragon. Thus, he fully realized the truth of interdependent origination. Later he said, "I meditated for seven years; for the first five I did not know how to meditate; during the next two I achieved the present great realizations. If I meditated yet a few years more, I could go to the Buddhafields and take all of you with me."

To serve the limitlessly compassionate Lama and the Triple Gem, Lord Jigten Sumgön determined to benefit others unceasingly. Seven years previously a man had come to him, asking that he perform the upasaka vow ceremony, but he had declined. Regretting that he had not granted the man his wish, he asked him to return, whereupon he performed the rite.

Since even the ants in his cave were moving north, he departed and went to the peak of a mountain where a huge thunderclap was heard just above his head. At the same time a thunderclap was heard from the North, so he took these as signs that his renown would pervade the entire earth. He thought about proceeding North and remaining on the mountain between nomads and city-dwellers. Then Lama Yal came and requested that he perform rites for the anniversary of Lord Phagmodrupa's parinirvana. The first time he said, "I made a promise to do meditation practice, not to perform rites. So for now I must simply meditate." But the Lama became insistent, collecting a great amount of offerings for the ceremony, including meat and alcohol. During the rite Namka Gyen, the daughter of Lama Thöpa Drupa, appeared naked and in dancing posture. At that moment Lord Jigten Sumgön thought, "Is it virtuous to perform this ritual or not? Perhaps this appearance is due to the fact that I am not a monk. In order to benefit sentient beings, I must take the monk's vows. Besides, I will thereby be fulfilling the wish of Lord Phagmodrupa." So he took the monk's robes.

From Phagmodru he went to Wön in the company of the meditator Sherab Wöphul. There he made offerings of a bolt of silk, a turquoise, and so forth, and along with other monks received the full ordination from Khenpo Tselungpa. At that time he was thirty-five years of age. For the next two years he enjoyed the play of the different states of samadhi.

From Khenpo Tselungpa and other masters Jigten Sumgön studied the root Vinaya text and the Pratimoksha Sutra, making mandala offerings and seven-limbed prayers during each session, and realizing the inseparability of natural law and spiritual law. In Sangri, he meditated off and on in a hut for three months, attracting to that place about ten prominent Lamas, including Lama Sangriwa Drakkar. His renown extended far and wide. When Lama Tsariwa engaged in a dialogue with him on the teachings, strong devotion arose in his mind. When others asked him how he found Lord Jigten Sumgön, Lama Tsariwa replied, "He is indeed like a Buddha."

After this the monks invited him to return to Phagdru Monastery where he showed Lama Shang the means of meditating on the prana. Although this Lama was unwell at the time, he was totally cured within fifteen days after receiving the teachings. It was at Lama Shang's request that Jigten Sumgön composed the *Praise to the Life of Phagmodrupa*, which was the first text that he wrote. His attendants,

Gomshe and Palchen, requested that he stage a special blessing festival to bring about prosperity, so he placed flowers, tea and butter in an auspicious bag. Since that time the area has always been fruitful.

One night Jigten Sumgön had a dream that Lord Phagmodrupa had given him his own cushion. The next day all the monks gathered and made offerings, saying, "This entire seat [monastery] is offered to you." That night Lord Jigten Sumgön, accompanied by two other monks, departed the place and went to Tho. There many people made offerings and requested that he remain, but he did not accept. Nakshö Khenpo and Dorje Gyaltsen came to see him, mentioning that there was a place called Drikung, close to the Ti-dro White Rock Mountain. At once, Lord Jigten Sumgön felt he should go there for meditation practice. That night he had a dream that a local deity called Lha-pel, who wears a tiger skin and beats an enormous drum, came to visit him.

On the way to Kyishö Gangbu, a dark and obscure place, he performed mudras which caused the sun to shine brightly. He also gave meditation instruction to deer and antelope. His ability to give teachings to the animals caused his fame to extend throughout the land.

At Sangphu he bestowed the Bodhisattva's vow at the request of Lopon Jamseng and the other monks, who highly honored him. Instantly Palchenpo Choye, Gompa Sherab Yö, Nakshö Khenpo, Phajo Dorje Gyaltsen, and Lama Sangriwa arrived. When Nakshö Khenpo departed, Jigten Sumgön went with a retinue of four to Tselung. There, Nepo Mönlam Senge said, "Please take me to Drikung with you." Jigten Sumgön was pleased, and on the fourteenth day of the twelfth month they came to Chu-ngar. The following day they arrived in Drikung Thel, where the inhabitants of the plain gathered to welcome them. Lama Me-nyak told his disciples, "On that rock there is a master who knows how to meditate, so you should go to him to receive instruction." About ten monks including Gompa Könchog Pagan Tharpa, Gompa Bhande and others invited him, highly honoring him, and receiving the teachings. Thus, more than one hundred monks gathered around him, though he himself had only the intention to meditate. Gompa Könchog Gyaltsen, who acted as his patron, requested that he come to Kuthang, while Pön Marpa promised to make a clay image of Lord Phagmodrupa and offer it to him. But Lord Jigten Sumgön said, "It is not right to make an image from clay, but only from precious metal." So Drum Ton from lower Do and Lopon Gyalwa made silver offerings for that purpose.

Within three years monks who had finished their study came from Kyishö, made offerings of many texts, requested more instruction, and experienced the meditation. During this time Lord Jigten Sumgön was invited to Phatsen Nyar and Nyarpo. He wished to go to Mount Kailash, but as Jangchub Gyaltsen offered the monastery of Punda, he stayed there for a one-month retreat. Appointing Palchen Dorje Yeshe as head of that monastery, he departed in the night with a retinue of four. When they arrived at the bottom of Drongbu Pass, they saw many blackbirds in flight. Lord Jigten Sumgön stopped and meditated there, then built a *tho* (rock stupa). Some bandits were approaching the other side of the pass above and Lord Jigten Sumgön, knowing this, said, "Robbers will come, but if they get beyond the pass, then I am not a yogin." Lord Jigten Sumgön and his retinue changed their clothes so no one would recognize them and proceeded on their way.

When they arrived at Droktse Pass, many people recognized them and invited them to a place inhabited by nomads, where they were highly honored and respected. Then they went to Kyung Gom Monastery in Ko-Kyim where a large crowd gathered and performed a ceremony. Lord Jigten Sumgön gave many teachings and made tea for the assembly. People coming from Drikung made offerings, and he gave them the vast and profound Dedication teachings. A rainbow appeared above his throne and all those assembled felt strong devotion. Though the winter days were short, the sun remained high in the heavens all the time he sat upon his throne, but as soon as he descended night fell. Thus, everyone realized that he had the power to stay the sun. Many people afflicted with ailments were cured of their conditions.

Lord Jigten Sumgön next went to Drogkar. There Geshe Tsangpa took teachings from him. Whatever offerings he received in those places he gave back to the community. Then he stayed at Treukyab where, in the evening, some thought they saw a herd of yaks coming, while others saw robbers, and yet others said the mountain was on fire, or that a great fire was issuing from the mouth of Thanglha [the Dharma guardian who inhabits the mountain]. All moved to Chule. In the morning, as they were partaking of food, some said they saw a temple, but others said, "Since this is a barren plain, how can there be a temple? This must be a reception offered by Thanglha." Lord Jigten Sumgön took tea, placed his hat on his head, and set out for his journey.

For an entire day a line of non-humans formed to receive him. Some were as large as mountains, some as long as rivers, and one opened a large parasol. All performed the three prostrations and circumambulated him anti-clockwise in the fashion of non-humans. Then they disappeared. That night a huge umbrella opened over Thanglha mountain. On the plain the flames of an immense fire were moved back and forth by the wind like a red flag. In the middle of the night it dissolved within the mountain. These all represented a welcoming of Lord Jigten Sumgön by the Thanglha guardian, who was an eighth level Bodhisattva. This was seen by all but one of Lord Jigten Sumgön's retinue of twenty-five.

The Lama stayed at Theu-rang for one month, and there he received a vision of Ananda, who was as tall as a three-storied mansion. From him he received all the Buddha's teaching.

At this time Lopon Gyalwa, Khenpo Koltiwa, Geshe Godul and many other great beings came to him. He discussed the teachings with Lopon Gyalwa and the latter was fully satisfied. On the way, he saw the great Dharma protector, four-armed Mahakala. Then he went to Thanglha and stayed for eighteen days. He was invited by King Thang-de-Tse-de and others, and so from late winter until early summer he stayed there. At this time he was thirty-nine years old.

During the summer retreat he was surrounded by three hundred monks. One day, at the confession of faults (*posadha*) ritual, the monks arrived somewhat late. Lord Jigten Sumgön said, "From now on, we will no longer perform this ceremony." Immediately Brahma, the Lord of the World, came to him and requested that the ceremony be reinstated. The sun was encircled by a rainbow, which increased until it pervaded the whole of the sky. Lord Jigten Sumgön said, "In like manner will my teaching pervade."

He wished to meditate in a solitary place, but this would have taken him away from the monks. Yet, since the place was a kingdom, it would not attract many monks anyhow, so he determined to return to Drikung. Meanwhile, the Elder Lodrö Zhonnu, Geshe Yorpo, and others requested that he come to the Phagdru seat. Thus, at their urging he returned and stayed in Drikung for two years, gathering many monks, including Khenpo Nagshö.

Numbers of monks saw Lord Jigten Sumgön manifest in many different forms. The contents of one large clay butter lamp lasted for the duration of an entire winter, neither increasing nor decreasing. Even the contents of the small butter lamps lasted five or six days. Some saw every corner of the Lama's retreat cave filled with barley. Gyalwa Gomchen saw the entire plain of Drikung filled with many manifestations of the Lama. When some went to visit him, they could not see him. As for Lord Jigten Sumgön himself, he had visions of Lord Gampopa, Marpa, Milarepa, the glorious Ga Lotsawa, and all the lineage Lamas, and engaged in many discussions with them over the profound teachings. The local guardian Barlha and many other non-humans came to him to receive the teachings, promising him that in the future they would protect the Dharma and practitioners. Once, Khenpo Koltiwa was giving ordinations to the monks without having cultivated Bodhicitta. Lord Jigten Sumgön was displeased, and asked that he give up this activity, but again Brahma requested that Lord Jigten Sumgön permit the ordination. Henceforth, he performed it himself.

Geshe Samyepa, Lama Tsariwa and other great beings requested that the Lama come to the Phagdru seat. When he arrived, he subjugated eighty evil planetary spirits and offered one thousand loads of barley to the grassy hut that had been used by Lord Phagmodrupa. In addition, he offered a golden parasol to Phagmodrupa's stupa. Many practitioners were meditating in huts there at this time.

In the autumn he returned to Drikung. Lama Nenang (Dusum Khyenpa) made offerings to him and showed him much respect. As well, sixty scholars skilled in four special branches of knowledge received him and daily made many offerings, such as eight sets of the vast *Prajnaparamita* text written in gold, horses, butter, and limitless other things. At this time one thousand monks were gathered in one place. Lord Jigten Sumgön sent the glorious Gomshe, On Gom, Ton Jung, Lopon Gyalwa, Lopon Ngephuwa, Jetsün Lhepa and many others into retreat. At this time he was forty-nine years old.

The Lama went to Tsa-ouk and there revealed many holy places and caves where he left hand and foot prints. Later, it became a retreat place for many practitioners. He then summoned Palchen from Tsari and, renouncing everything including his own hut, appointed him to take control of that area. Then he went to Ngam Shö to reconcile warring factions. Although he could not accomplish this easily, his blessing caused the fighting to cease for eighteen years. By his gift of wealth to Samye, the monastery was able to be restored.

Lord Jigten Sumgön next wished to go to India, and on the way stopped at Dagla Gampo Monastery where all the monks and people of the area received teachings. They made great offerings of riches, as well as of the monastery seat. In Sang Dum cave he entered into retreat for three months, during which a radiant light emerged from the forehead of an image of Gampopa. All the Nöjins [wealth deities] brought necessities and wealth so that his hut was filled with offerings.

When the Lama set out for India all the officials of the place vowed that if he left they would in turn go to Phagdru and fight. Feeling that they would carry out their threat, he returned to Phagdru. That summer the chief leaders such as Geshe Jamseng, Palchen, Thagana, Geshe Gongkarwa, Lama Kalden and others gathered there, as well as the mountain dwellers. They built an enormous throne and made offerings of three hundred bolts of silk brocade. Lord Jigten Sumgön bestowed many profound teachings. One morning a line of Dakinis came toward him stretching from Oddiyana to his seat. He did a special meditation and manifested such auspicious signs that instead of taking him away with them, they requested that he remain at Phagdru.

People from Rongpo, Truk-Tsa, and Chaktsam came to the monastery and strongly requested that the Lama return to Drikung, which he agreed to do. There, in the presence of seven thousand monks, he gave many teachings. After a year he went to Thagey where he resolved the concerns of the people and established a discipline for their future guidance.

As summer approached, the three plains of Drikung, Yagru and Bamthang were filled with disciples to whom he gave teachings. During that time he experienced certain negative signs, and Taklung Tangpa predicted, "Obstacles may soon arise." In order to dispel these, the Lama announced that he would go into retreat for twelve years. He remained strictly secluded for five months during which Lama Nyakse went to Phagmodrupa and built a golden shrine. When he returned to Drikung he settled at Ta Chag Teng-ga (Place of the Galloping Horses),[1] and announced, "After seven days Lord Jigten Sumgön will emerge from his retreat." One week later Lord Jigten Sumgön said, "All the negative signs have been reversed." For this reason he decided to emerge and appear in the assembly. The monks celebrated the joyous

[1] Later, this became a famous cemetery.

occasion, and Lama Nyakse requested that he take his seat on the Dharma throne and give teachings. Toward this end he offered the *Gya Bum* text written in letters of gold, and paid him great respect.

After a year, the Lama contemplated going to Tsari. When he sat on the Dharma throne at this time, some disciples saw him as Maha-Bodhi (Buddha Shakyamuni). When all were gathered together, he told them, "Either you make a retreat in the mountains or I will." All the monks agreed to go on retreat. Those who had received the major teachings were sent to different caves and mountains, while eighty novice monks were entrusted to the care of Vajra Master Tisewa, who proceeded with them to Kyishö. That year Lord Jigten Sumgön reached the age of fifty-six years and gathered many more disciples. He was invited to various monasteries where the people made myriad offerings. Returning to Drikung, he looked after an assembly of thirteen thousand disciples. At this time he said, "I have a special, profound teaching, so those of you who wish to receive it should prepare for a retreat." When eight hundred of the senior disciples gathered, he began the teachings which he offered for four months in preparation for their three-year retreat. He himself received teachings from celestial beings.

When the Lama reached sixty years of age, many negative signs occurred, such as the crumbling of important holy places and the collapse of a dam. At the same time Lord Jigten Sumgön became ill with an imbalance of the water element in the body, and it appeared that he would die within three days. All the holy objects in the monastery were brought together and consecrated, and he did a special yogic exercise of the winds and channels. That night he was freed of all illness.

Once, with the monk's bowl in hand and trident staff on his shoulder, he walked away from the monastery, paying homage to it all the while and saying, "If I leave in this manner, the King of Garlog will honor me as his Lama, and will offer me even Bodh'gaya if I ask it." At that time he manifested in India as as white-complexioned monk bearing a bowl and trident staff. When someone asked, "Who are you?" he replied, "I am from Drikung." When they asked where he was going, he said, "I am going to subdue the heretic army of Garlog." And when they asked how he intended to accomplish this, he said, "I will subdue it with the samadhi of great loving kindness. Through that meditation the place will be spontaneously subdued." And it came to pass as he predicted.

Another time, when he was staying at Khangbu Meru, the Lama visited Dewachen in a dream, and was told by the Buddha Amitayus that he was the highest Bodhisattva, Yeshe Wangpo, the chief of the gathering. All those in the vicinity of Khangbu Meru recognized him as the reincarnation of King Tri Ralpachen [the eighth-century King of Tibet who translated many of the Buddha's teachings into Tibetan, built monasteries, and obtained the support of seven families for each monk]. Lord Jigten Sumgön's patrons were similar, his attendants resembled the king's ministers, and his disciples were like the king's subjects. All his activities had the power of a king's activities, though they emanated from the spiritual domain. When he was asked if he were indeed the reincarnation of the King, he did not deny it.

Once, when Jetsun Lhapa (Nyö Gyalwa Lhanangpa) made numerous offerings to all the monks during the giving of the special teachings, thirty thousand disciples gathered. At this time Pandita Shakyashri was in Tibet, and though Lord Jigten Sumgön did not meet him, he honored him and they had much communication. By now the Lama was sixty-six years of age. He offered Dharma texts to Dagla Gampo Monastery from Phagmodru because he knew that this was Lord Phagmodrupa's wish.

As the true seat of the Lama is the two Bodhicittas, where there is Bodhicitta there is the seat of Phagmodrupa. So Lord Jigten Sumgön taught all his disciples to hold and cherish the two Bodhicittas, which is the greatest service one can perform for the Lama. Indeed, it is greater than the twelve hardships endured by Naropa. For this reason Lord Jigten Sumgön personally cared for all the monks—even the young novices sleeping in the dust—as if they were his own heart, seeing them as inseparable from Phagmodrupa.

One day, Heruka appeared in the sky, holding a bow and arrow, which he shot at Lord Jigten Sumgön's heart. At that moment the full meaning of the secret mantra was completely revealed to him.

Besides the retreat practitioners assembled on the plain, Lord Jigten Sumgön gathered fifty-five thousand, five hundred twenty-five disciples. And this is only a superficial account. In detail I cannot tell the full extent of even one day of the Lama's activities. He gave teachings for forty years during which many of his disciples became monks. In the first six months twenty-five disciples became monks, and with the passing of each year the number grew at the rate of one thousand, ten thousand, and one hundred thousand. As offerings Lord Jigten Sumgön received one hundred thousand volumes of texts written in gold, along with horses, yaks, dzos, tea, silk, gold, silver, barley and jewels—in all, hundreds of thousands of articles.

When the Lama was in his seventies, one hundred eighty thousand disciples gathered in Drikung. Many were sent into retreat on Mount Kailash, Lachi Snow Mountain, Tsari, and other holy places. In brief, the entire earth was pervaded with his human and non-human disciples.

The life story of the Dharma Lord
Cannot be expressed,
Because the Buddha's activities
Are without end.
The limited mind cannot perceive it.
But even ignorant beings can see
That this was an extraordinary life story.
Even minor virtuous and non-virtuous thoughts
Are transformed into the four seals,

While the disciplines of morality
Were cherished like his own life.
"Do not use meat and alcohol
Even in the ganachakra feast.
Constantly collect the two accumulations.
Keep nothing of all you are given
Except the three Dharma robes.
Never waste even the smallest objects."
All activities were unified with Bodhicitta,
Dedication, and Mahamudra.
The Lama gave the teaching on cause and effect,
Related to the Buddha's words
On interdependent arising.
He never used psychic power,
Nor fought the seat.
He compassionately asked advice from his enemies.
All the offerings
Of material goods and so forth
He used for the support of the practitioners
Rather than for monasteries, temples, and images.
The more activities he engaged in
The more effective he became in the Dharma.
He showed pleasure in even small good qualities
Shown by his disciples.
He nurtures all, never perceiving any
As improper vessels.
Shedding the skin of clairvoyance,
Rituals, words and conventions,
He concentrated on the essential,
Ripening and liberating beings
Through the precious moral ethics
And the two kinds of Bodhicitta.
These things were recounted by the Precious Lama.[1]

Thus, he completed all his activities when he was seventy-five years of age. The Khenpo, Vajra Master and Director fell heir

[1] the author's Lama, Palden Shawari.

to his precious seat. He intended to pass away on the twenty-fifth day of the second month in the Fire Ox year [1217 A.D.], but by the Precious Lama's request he extended his life by two days. Thus, on the twenty-seventh day at dusk the holy Lama, seated in the meditation posture and gazing upward, entered into Mahaparinirvana, and manifesting many different forms, fully pacified all humans and non-humans. All the great meditation practitioners experienced many different signs. In the four directions disciples performed special ceremonies to collect the great accumulations. From the sky there emerged many rains of flowers and the appearance of rainbows. He dissolved to the Dharmakaya of the Buddha, the ultimate state of beyond-the-holy-purity, beyond-the-holy-pristine-wisdom, beyond-the-holy-bliss, and beyond-the-holy-self, and remained there until the end of samsara.

The Life Story Called "Meaningful To Behold"

by Chen-nga Sherab Jungne

OM SVASTI

I bow at the feet of the lord who is meaningful to behold.

All you who are gathered here, gods and men,
Please listen to these important words with full attention
And without being distracted
By wandering thoughts.

In the northern snow land of Tibet,
In the heart-center of the southern continent of Jambudvipa,
Is the abode of the lord who embodies the Buddha,
The palace of a million Arhats,
The forest of glorious Sho Drikung,
Which is renowned as Magadha.

The precious lama who resides there
Was enlightened from beginningless time.
Although he manifests in inconceivable forms,
Still, in order to benefit mother sentient beings, equal in number to the limits of space,

He was born at the great place Tso-Ngu in Lung
Drigyel,
An area enriched by the holy Dharma.

When he was eight years old,
He clearly saw glorious Vajrabhairava.
When he resided at Tsib Lungmoche,
He perceived all of samsara and nirvana as
reflections in a mirror.
When he arrived at glorious Phagmodru,
(His guru said) "Now, my retinue is complete."
When he practiced at the Echung Cave in the west,
He directly understood the interdependence of outer
and inner phenomena.
When he stayed at Lakmo in Namra in the north,
He was received by Nyenchen Thanglha.
When vultures flew in the sky,
He instructed them in meditation.
When he stayed at glorious Bodh'gaya,
He turned back the Duruka army.[1]
When he thought to give profound teachings,
The gods requested him (to turn the Wheel).
When a steed galloped by,
He spoke one word, and the horse understood.
When, from a distance, the king of Minyak heard of
his fame,
(That king) made offerings to him.

In the three times, such a precious lama
Has not come in the past, will not come in the
future,
And cannot now be found anywhere in this world,
including the realm of the gods.
He is like the glorious udumwara flower.

---

[1] This was a miracle in which Lord Jigten Sumgön, while staying at Drikung, sent an emanation of himself to Bodh'gaya, the site of the Buddha's enlightenment in India. There he turned back an invading army by the power of his meditation on loving-kindness.

Noble Ones, it is difficult to see the face of such a precious lama.
Noble Ones, it is difficult to hear his speech.
Noble Ones, he is very kind.
Noble Ones, there is no way to forget him.
For myself and the sentient beings of the six realms,
There is no other refuge than the Lord of Beings.
The fame of this precious lama
Pervades the southern continent of Jambudvipa.
Generally, he influenced all of Tibet.
Notables of India, China, Hor, Tibet, and other places
Came under his spiritual protection
And offered him much material wealth.
At one time, 70,000 disciples gathered near him.
(Of them), many of the superior ones gained enlightenment in this life.
Those of medium ability achieved various bhumis
And fully realized the nature of their mind.
Beyond that, there were countless others,
Chief among them the great Nyö;[1]
Gyalse Dombuwa of Chegung Pung;
The Great Abbot of Limitless Activities;[2]
The well-known Palchen, the ornament of the world;
The great Se Nyewang Gyalpo;
The administrator Dorje Senghe;
The sole holder of the vajra, Gyalpo;
The four glorious great men;
The unquestionable siddha, Chödingpa;
The lion of speech, Chen-ngawa;

[1] Nyö Gyalwa Lhanangpa, a former incarnation of Jamgön Kongtrul the Great. Nyö later traveled to Bhutan, where he founded the tradition of the Lhapa Kagyu.

[2] This may refer to Gurawa Tsultrim Dorje, the first successor to Lord Jigten Sumgön.

He whose mind is fully accomplished in the Clear Light, Gönkarwa;
The ocean of virtue, Rechen;
The great being called The Mongol;
He whose wisdom is as vast as space, Ngephuwa;
The two who are emanations of Manjushri;
The one of noble family, Serwa Drak Thokpa.

Of these countless siddhas and others,
I have mentioned just a few.
Generally, his disciples are like stars in the sky.
Their abode is the holy palace, glorious Drikung in Upper Sho,
Which is foremost in the ocean of Buddhafields.
The Lord, the Buddha-King, abides there.
There one can find the Dharma, the holy refuge.
There one can find the noble Sangha, the guide.
There one can make offerings to the Triple Gem.
There one can find the bliss and happiness of samsara and nirvana.
There is the place where one can gather the Two Accumulations.
There one can offer whatever one has.
There one can get whatever one needs.
There one can find all enjoyments.
There one can see marvelous things.

Those of lesser virtue and understanding,
Worldly men without the eye (of wisdom),
May doubt when one describes the virtues of that place.
Those who have not seen that place may doubt.
(But) you should not hesitate.
Again, there are wonderful things that one can see:
When, with one voice, the assembly of gods and men requests (teachings),
The Lord, the King of all Buddhas, sits on the Lion Throne

In the center of an ocean of the Sangha,
And his body radiates light;
The great earth quakes, rainbows appear,
And the smell of incense arises (by itself).
Gods offer flowers, like rain falling from the sky,
Along with parasols, victory banners, streamers, canopies,
And the beautiful sounds of various musical instruments.
These are not the riches of a deluded man.
He is the Lord, the embodiment of the Five Buddhas.
Generally, he has the power to bestow attainments and dispel obstacles.
The Lord of Beings promised that those who set foot or stay on that mountain (Drikung), even ants or other insects,
Will not fall into the three lower realms.
Because he always said, "Whoever has devotion from far away, even in India or China, will never be parted from me,"
Generally, if one keeps one's connection,
One will certainly be born in the Buddhafield of Dewachen immediately after death.
This is not the fantasy of a deluded man.
He teaches according to the four kinds of proof:
First, the instructions of the holy lord lamas;
Second, the teachings of Sutra and Tantra of the Sugatas;
Third, the experience of you yogins;
Fourth, the history of the dharma of interdependence.[1]

The precious lord lama said,
"Generally, whoever hears my name will be freed from the three lower realms.
In particular, those who see my face or hear my teachings will be liberated.

[1] General accounts.

Whoever dies at Drikung Thil will not be born in the three lower realms."
Confidently, he undertook this great promise.
Also, in the precious commentary, *The Glorious King, Flying in Space,* it says:
"You Sangha, listen to these words.
If you trust, why should you not attain samadhi?
If I deceive you, I will come to harm."
This is his second confident promise.

Also: "You Sangha who have come from all directions,
Spread your hands over your chest and think again and again from the depths of your heart,
'Why have I come here?'
You came here thinking of me.
Without the attachment or aggression of family, group, or homeland,
(Grow) in devotion to the holy lama
And apply yourselves to the holy Dharma.
Don't be attached to relatives:
Father, mother, uncle, aunt, or others.
You will accomplish the great purpose.
Finally, not only for you but for your parents and others,
When their lives come to an end,
They will remember you through the force of their affection.
Because of that, they will remember me,
And based on this connection their consciousness will transfer to the lama.
Surely, it is my duty to keep them from the three lower realms."
This is his third confident promise.
Generally, even though the suffering of samsara is endless,
Those who aspire and follow that lord
Will arrive in front of the Lord of Beings
Immediately after passing from this life.

Previously, countless kalpas in the past,
The Father, the Lord of the World, the Drikungpa,
The Lord, the King of all Buddhas,
Was born as the Dharma King, the Ruler of a Thousand Universes,
Whose name was Tsibkyi Mukhyu.
He was the father of a thousand and one princes.
While practicing one night,
He achieved Buddhahood, the heart of enlightenment,
And became the Lord, the King of all Buddhas,
Whose name was Lurik Drönma.

After that, he saw that it was time to tame (those princes).[1] To the entire gathering of his sons he gave extensive teachings on death, impermanence, the cause and effect of karma, and the faults of samsara according to the Four Noble Truths. A thousand of those sons gradually became monks, and they perfectly kept the morality of renunciation. Soon after, some attained Arhatship, some achieved the confidence of the Unborn Dharma, some attained the pure vision of the Dharma Eye, and some attained the fruit of full liberation. They then benefitted all the sentient beings of the immeasurable, boundless, endless, limitless realms of the universe. The youngest prince, because he was attached to the kingdom and his queen, could not become a monk. Although he had gone a little against his father's wishes, because of his nobility and in order to confess his faults he made a thousand and one great and marvelous parasols of the finest gold from the Dzambu River, with pleats of the finest vaidurya, adorned with various jewels, and with handles of precious ruby. In this way, he made a thousand and one parasols and offered them to his father and brothers and made the following prayer: "In the future, may I become the equal of you—my father and brothers—in your gathering of retinues, in your

[1] Here, the author changes from verse to prose.

longevity, in your attainment of Buddhafields, in your taming of beings, and in all of your activities." Thus, he made this aspiration.

(Lord Jigten Sumgön said:) "I am the one who was then the Tathagata Lurik Drönma. You, Jetsün (Gar) Chöding, are the one who was the youngest son. (The parasols he made) were the cause of the many golden parasols we have now." (Gar Chöding then asked:) "Of those thousand sons, how many are now present at your feet?" (Lord Jigten Sumgön answered:) "None of them are here. They are benefitting beings in all the limitless realms of the universe."

Again, the precious lama said:
"The body of the previous noble Acharya
(Nagarjuna) is not my body now,
But the Dharma that he taught is present in my
mind."
Because he said this, he is definitely also the noble,
great Acharya.
(Lord Jigten Sumgön said:)
"The nature of virtue and nonvirtue is that they
cannot be exchanged."
The noble, great Acharya said:
"If one acts with attachment, aggression, or
ignorance,
That is nonvirtue."
("If one acts with nonattachment, nonaggression,
and an unobscured mind,
That is virtue.")[1]
This shows that they have the same thought.
Although these words are easy to say,
Their meaning is difficult to understand.
These (virtue and nonvirtue) are the root of samsara
and nirvana.

---

[1] This quotation from Nagarjuna's *Precious Garland* was added by the translators.

They form the line between what is to be taken up and what is to be abandoned.
This is where scholars become confused.
This is where faults and good qualities become concealed.
This is where the clever become bewildered.
This is where warriors stumble.
There are many ways to explain this.

If one does not understand the deeper meaning of this teaching,
No matter how hard one practices the 84,000 collections of Dharma,
One will be walking in the day as if at night.
It would be as though, without understanding who is fighting whom,
One were to say, "I also threw a stone."
For example, one may wish to travel east,
(But) if he faces west, he will never get there.
The farther he travels, the farther away he will get.
Therefore, if one doesn't know how to practice,
Though he may boast that he has practiced the holy Dharma,
He will be near the edge of a great, unseen precipice.
Therefore, it is important to choose and cherish
The door to the unmistaken path.

Again, the noble, great Acharya said:
"Because of the arising of propensities,
The seeds of (further) propensities are sown.
From the gathering of the causes of propensity,
The sprouts of samsara are grown."
The precious lama said:
"Although many traditions say that the body or the mind wanders in samsara,
I don't have a special view.
(But I would say that) causes and conditions give rise to conceptual thought,

And because of this, propensity wanders in the body."
These two teachings have the same meaning.
This is a brief example from the past.
There are countless others like it.

The Mirror-Like Wisdom of the Lama's Mind,
In which blossoms the mandala of the objects of knowledge of the three times,
Neither increases nor decreases.
Since even the Buddhas of the Ten Directions and the Three Times
Could never fully relate the life of the Father, the
Lord of the World,
Even if they were to describe it for kalpas,
How could it ever be expressed by the Bodhisattvas of the Ten Bhumis, like Lord Manjushri,
To say nothing of others?
Whether or not disciples have faith,
It can be proved—by following the prophecies and reasoning of the profound Sutras and Tantras—
That he is a Buddha.
Of this there is no doubt.
That Lion, the Supreme Man,
Said in the mandala of the entire assembly:
"There are no lamas other than me.[1]
The Buddhas of the Three Times are also me."
Therefore, relying on his vajra speech,
We can trust the stories of the lives
Of the precious Lord of the World.
I can't comprehend the Father's life,
But to increase the devotion of followers in the future,
What I have said will be activity (for that time).
He is the leader of all the primordial Buddhas of the Ten Directions

---

[1] This means that his nature is that of Vajradhara, the source of the manifestations of enlightenment.

In the past, present, and future.

With authentic presence, that glorious, great Vajradhara
Overpowers and conquers the supreme enjoyments, genuineness, and quality of life
Of samsara and nirvana.[1]
He extracts the essence of the Tripitaka
And reveals the vitality of the Four Classes of Tantra.
Although he clearly perceives the qualities of samsara and nirvana,
He continues to investigate their nature.
He possesses full understanding of all dependent arisings: outer, inner, and secret;
Of the causes of birth; of the ground of abiding;
And of the causes of destruction.
Under the Tree of the Essence of Enlightenment,
He confidently subdues millions upon millions of the armies (of Mara)
With his fearless vajra wisdom.
As the Wish-Fulfilling Wisdom Rain falls from the Ocean of Effortless Wisdom,
Limitless objects of enjoyment
Flow from his unrestrained generosity.
(Not satisfied with his attainments),
That Lord of the Five Perfections[2] continually develops
The ocean of limitless qualities
Of all the Buddhas of the Three Times.
Happily, he is very easy to please.
That lord does not care to be honored.
His (wisdom) reaches that of all the Buddhas,
And his (understanding) reaches the minds of all sentient beings.

---

[1] This means that even these are within the sphere of his manifestation.
[2] Perfection of teacher, teaching, time, disciples, and place.

He manifests in both samsara and nirvana.
He is not affected by conditions.
He is the Universal Vajra King
Who manifests in limitless forms.

That holy lama departed from this life at dusk and must certainly have arrived before the lord, Phagmodrupa, in the immaculate Eastern Buddhafield at dawn, since, as it is said, this is the activity of all Buddhas. Although he is a teacher to Lord Maitreya in Tushita, he appears as one of his retinue and—together with Lord Atisha—receives the teaching of the Sutra of the Great Drum. And this was said by Gampopa's disciple Dingpa, a spiritual master, scholar, and mahasiddha who possessed great clairvoyance and who could speak directly with the Wisdom Dakini Kalwa Sangmo: "The Wisdom Dakini said it like this: 'Those who attended the lama for only a short time or who did not see his face should not lament. That lama will accept and bless those who have devotion.' I don't know if this is true, but that is what she said."

Even now, in what is called the Eastern Great All-Pervading Buddhafield, the ground is made entirely of pure gold. (In the center is) a great Lion Throne adorned with various jewels, including the essence of ruby and other precious stones. On that sits the unequalled, supreme Vajra Body, the Self-Arisen Bhikshu, pure in form, possessing radiant dignity and smiling warmly, showing that he is blessing all of us. He is surrounded by a retinue of many hundreds of thousands of monks, and he teaches the various vehicles of Dharma. Occasionally he says to the gathered assembly: "Now, when my followers in Jambudvipa pass away, they think of me, and they arrive before me in the time that it takes a strong man to throw a punch." Thus he speaks, and immediately he places his right hand—gold in color, marked by hundreds of virtues, radiating the light of dignity, blazing with glory—on the crown of the head (of such a one) and says, "Welcome, my son!" Thus he speaks, greatly pleased.

Therefore, for all of us,
If there are no obstacles to our devotion to the holy lama,
It is certain that we will instantly arrive
At the feet of the precious Lord of Beings after death,
Without entering the Bardo.
This is a journey of the mental form.
Like the Bhikshu Dharmakara,[1]
He holds with compassion (those in that realm)
By the power of his aspiration.
As is said in the *Manjushrinamasangiti:*
"Swift as the minds of all sentient beings."
This refers to cases like this.
For this same reason,
All the great Bodhisattvas
Knowingly reincarnate in samsara.

Even though I, an ignorant man,
Cannot perceive the limitless future manifestations
Of the precious Lord of the World,
I have been able to joyfully relate a small part of them.
You great beings—scholars and realized ones—
Who have the eye of wisdom,
Forgive me if I have made any mistakes.

Whoever sees or hears this "Meaningful To Behold,"
The life story of the Father, the Lord of the World, the Drikungpa,
Will not be separated from that lord.
By all the virtue of samsara and nirvana,
Including that of this work,
May all the confused mother sentient beings of the six realms
Be freed from all temporary bondage,

---

[1] This is the monk who, through the strength of his practice and aspiration, became the Buddha Amitabha and created the Buddhafield of Dewachen. Depending on one's connection, it is said to be easier to be reborn in Dewachen than in any other Buddhafield.

And may they attain the wisdom of the Ultimate
Meaning.

This extraordinary life story of the Precious Lord, the Drikungpa, called "Meaningful To Behold," was composed by the Shakya Bhikshu Sherab Jungne.[1]

By the merit of reading this life story,
May all sentient beings, including our parents,
Fully abandon the darkness of ignorance
And develop the Five Wisdom Bodies.
May they actualize the lama's life story (for
themselves).
May they attain the state of the Dharma Lord.
I supplicate the Lord of the Three Worlds,
Who was the supreme Arya Licchavi (Vimalakirti)
at the time of the Buddha,
Who was Lord Nagarjuna at the Glorious Mountain,
And who is the unequaled Drikungpa in this Land of
Snows.

May his teachings remain for a hundred kalpas.
May the lives and activities of those who hold his
teachings increase.
May the assemblies (of practitioners) increase,
And may they make effort in the Dharma activities
of the Three Vows.
May all beings enjoy the glory of peace and
happiness.

This was written by the insignificant Drikung Bhande, Tendzin Pemai Gyaltsen,[2] at the request of the throne-holder Tripa Döndrub Chöwang.

(Translated from the Tibetan by the Ven. Khenpo Könchog Gyaltsen with the assistance of Rick Finney.)

---

[1] Chen-nga Sherab Jungne (1187-1241), an emanation of Saraha, was one of the two chief disciples of Lord Jigten Sumgön and was the compiler of his teachings.

[2] The Fourth Drikung Kyabgön, Chetsang Rinpoche (1770-1826).

The Continuous Stream of the Blessing Lineage of the Precious Drikung Kagyu

Dorjechang (Vajradhara)—The Celestial Buddha

Siddha Tilopa	988–1069	
Siddha Naropa	1016–1100	
Marpa	1012–1097	
Milarepa	1052–1135	
Gampopa	1079–1153	

(Four Major Kagyu)

Phagdru Karma Tselpa Bahram

Phagmodrupa	1110–1170	

(Eight Great Kagyu)

Drikung Taklung Trophu Drukpa Yamzang Shukseb Martsang Yerpa

		(Dates of holding the Lineage)
Lord Jigten Sumgön	1143–1217	1179–1217
Khenchen Gurawa Tsultrim Dorje	1154–1221	1217–1221
On Rinpoche Sonam Drakpa	1187–1234	1221–1234
Chen-nga Rinpoche Drakpa Jungne	1175–1255	1234–1255
Telo Dorje Drakpa	1210–1278	1255–1278
Thog-khawa Rinchen Senge	1226–1284	1278–1284
Chen-nga Tsamchedpa Drakpa Sonam	1238–1286	1284–1286
Dorje Yeshe	1223–1293	1286–1293
Chu-nyipa Dorje Rinchen	1278–1314	1293–1314
Nyer-gyepa Dorje Gyalpo	1283–1350	1314–1350
Nyernyipa Chökyi Gyalpo	1335–1407	1350–1395
Shenyen Dondrup Gyalpo	1369–1427	1395–1427
Dakpo Wang[1]	1395	1427–1428
Chogyal Rinchen Pal Zangpo	1421–1469	1428–1469
Rinchen Chökyi Gyaltsen	1449–1484	1469–1484
Gyalwang Kunga Rinchen	1475–1527	1484–1527
Gyalwang Rinchen Phuntsok	1509–1557	1527–1534
Rinchen Namgyal Chodak Gyaltsen	1527–1570	1565–1570
Chokyi Namgyal	1557–1579	1570–1579
Tsungme Chogyal Phuntsok	1547–1602	1579–1602
Naro Nyipa Tashi Phuntsok	1574–1628	1602–1615
Jetsün Könchog Rinchen (lst Chetsang)[2]	1590–1654	1615–1626
Kunkhyen Chökyi Dragpa (lst Chungtsang)	1595–1659	1626–1659
Könchog Trinley Sangpo (Chetsang)	1656–1718	1659–1718
Trinley Dondrub Chogyal (Chungtsang)	1704–1754	1704–1754
Könchog Tenzin Drodul (Chetsang)	1724–1766	1724–1766
Könchog Tenzin Chökyi Nyima (Chuntsang)	1755–1792	1755–1792
Tenzin Padme Gyaltsen (Chetsang)	1770–1826	1770–1826
Tenzin Chöwang Lodrö (Regent)		1826–1827
Jetsün Chonyi Norbu (Chungtsang)	1827–1865	1827–1865
Könchog Thukje Nyima (Chetsang)	1828–1881	1828–1881
Könchog Tenzin Chökyi Lodrö (Chungtsang)	1868–1906	1868–1906
Könchog Tenzin Zhiwe Lodrö (Chetsang)	1886–1943	1886–1943
Tenzin Chökyi Jungne (Chungtsang)	1909–1940	1909–1940
Tenzin Thubten Wangpo (Regent)		1940–1942
Tenzin Chökyi Nangwa (Chungtsang)	1942–	1942–
Könchog Tenzin Kunzang Thinley Lhundrub (Chetsang)	1946–	1946–

[1] He went to the Five Peaked Mountain in China and achieved the state of immortality.

[2] Chetsang Rinpoche is the emanation of Chenrezig. Chungtsang Rinpoche is the heart emanation of Padmasambhava and Manjushri. From the first Chungtsang Rinpoche there have been a continuous line of reincarnations that have been the Drikung Kyabgöns, the throne holder of Lord Jigten Sumgön.

In order to maintain this pure blessing lineage, His Holiness the Drikung Kyabgön Chetsang Rinpoche is establishing a monastic institute in Dehra Dun which offers courses in Buddhist philosophy, metaphysics and other related subjects to young monks as well as interested Westerners. Anyone wishing further information may address inquiries to:

Jangchub Ling
P.O. Box 48
Dehra Dun 248001
(U.P.) India

Printed in the United States
by Baker & Taylor Publisher Services